REVERENCE

REVERENCE

Renewing a Forgotten Virtue

SECOND EDITION

Paul Woodruff

Foreword by Betty Sue Flowers

OXFORD
UNIVERSITY PRESS

Oxford University Press is a department of the
University of Oxford. It furthers the University's objective
of excellence in research, scholarship, and education
by publishing worldwide.

Oxford   New York
Auckland   Cape Town   Dar es Salaam   Hong Kong   Karachi
Kuala Lumpur   Madrid   Melbourne   Mexico City   Nairobi
New Delhi   Shanghai   Taipei   Toronto

With offices in
Argentina   Austria   Brazil   Chile   Czech Republic   France   Greece
Guatemala   Hungary   Italy   Japan   Poland   Portugal   Singapore
South Korea   Switzerland   Thailand   Turkey   Ukraine   Vietnam

Oxford is a registered trade mark of Oxford University Press
in the UK and certain other countries.

Published in the United States of America by
Oxford University Press
198 Madison Avenue, New York, NY 10016

Library of Congress Cataloging-in-Publication Data
Woodruff, Paul, 1943–
    Reverence : renewing a forgotten virtue / Paul Woodruff. —Second Edition.
        pages   cm
    Includes bibliographical references and index.
    ISBN 978–0–19–935080–3 (pbk. : alk. paper)
1. Honor.   2. Respect.   I. Title.
    BJ1533.H8W66 2014
    179'.9—dc23   2013035307

For Lucia,
with whom I am learning these things
and many more

Remember this, when you
Lay waste the land of Troy: Be reverent to the gods.
Nothing matters more, as Zeus the father knows.
Reverence is not subject to the deaths of men;
They live, they die, but reverence shall not perish.

> —Heracles, speaking to leaders of the Greeks,
> in Sophocles' *Philoctetes* (lines 1439–44)

CONTENTS

FOREWORD

Reverence is a topic we don't discuss or even think about. And yet this book makes us care deeply about the subject, leading us to examine assumptions and become utterly convinced of what, in retrospect, are astonishing, bold conclusions—for example, that "Leaders are responsible for the compassion of the groups that follow them."

While the practices of reverence differ from culture to culture, Woodruff shows that reverence itself is a virtue that can be detached from particular beliefs and rituals. One of the many ways he demonstrates this is by exploring reverence in two very different cultures: China and ancient Greece. From the Greeks we learn that the opposite of reverence is not irreverence but hubris—forgetting, in the pride of power or glory, that you, too, are human, with human limitations, and must respect the humanity of others. Reverence, says Woodruff, is the *source* of the capacity for respect. But it lies deeper than respect, because it is not simply a behavior; it is aligned with truth. *Reverence* is the "capacity to have feelings of awe, respect, and shame when these are the right feelings to have."

This rare thoughtfulness about feelings—and a profound respect for them—is a signature feature of the book, highlighted most vividly in an exploration of the experience of playing in a string quartet, even without mastery, when one becomes connected to something larger, something that can elicit awe. We think of awe and respect in relation to the sacred, but in one of his many fine distinctions,

Woodruff says that while we owe *respect* to all sacred things, even those of other cultures or religions, we do not owe *reverence* to anything that is merely sacred. In a closely argued explanation, Woodruff shows that reverence is incompatible with relativism.

This argument raises the issue of the ethics courses so often taught in professional schools, which students almost uniformly find a waste of time. Figuring out what the rules are and being able to follow them in a difficult situation is a slender bulwark when compared to the development of the capacity "cultivated by experience and training, to have emotions that make you feel like doing good things." The capacity for "awe, respect, and shame" would have been far more likely than training in ethics to have prevented the abuses at Abu Ghraib, as Woodruff convincingly shows us.

Like the Abu Ghraib discussion, some of the most telling explorations of reverence in this very illuminating book are based on military examples, where reverence can literally save lives. Woodruff shows, for example, that the idea that mutual respect flows from good opinions people have of each other is exactly backwards. The ceremony and ritual of the military is, in part, designed to support the giving of respect before the opportunity for opinion can even arise. "Respect is given, not earned, and to think otherwise would tear any hierarchy apart."

Far more powerful than mere civility, reverence is necessary for community. An ancient Greek story tells how Prometheus stole fire from the gods, in the hope that this superior technology would help the human species survive. But the highest god saw that "technology alone, without virtue, is no defense against mutual destruction"— and so humans were given reverence and justice "as means for their survival, which depended on their ability to live in society." When we look at our own society, we often speak of justice—or the lack of it. *Reverence* provides the other half of a very necessary conversation.

Betty Sue Flowers

PREFACE TO THE SECOND EDITION

In 1999, I wrote that reverence is our best defense against hubris. Without reverence, I wrote, religions can show their nasty side and plunge their believers into religious wars. And without reverence, hubris will lead powerful people to make terrible mistakes. They will protect their ignorance from criticism and try to punish those who know better. Then they will fall, and they will take many of us with them. Without reverence, I wrote, a great power will stumble. All that was in the first edition of the book you now have in your hands. I had learned most of it from reading ancient Greek plays and history, but I am sorry to say I have had to learn it again from current events.

The first edition of *Reverence* was released in September 2001—during the very week of 9/11. I had composed the manuscript well before the events of that day shook the United States into war. Since then I have had the sad experience of seeing my predictions come true. Without reverence, religiosity has indeed fed the flames of war. And without reverence, a great power—the United States—has stumbled badly. The nation's leaders have blundered into two wars, both long and ineffective. The decision-makers chose to go to war in a state of ignorance, which they protected with a wall of boasts, while they did their best to stifle disagreement. The result has been great loss of life, and little progress in the countries where they brought war. Further bad decisions shattered the United States' reputation for justice, as the world learned how this nation—founded on the premise of human rights—threw rights to the winds in its new prisons.

To make matters worse, a string of poor decisions drained the country's economy, while a ruthless political storm is pushing our people further behind on almost every measure of success for a modern, developed nation. Today, the United States may vie for first place in rates of incarceration, homicide, and teenage pregnancy, while it is behind or lost in the pack on voting rates, literacy, health care, and social mobility. All these show failures of reverence. A great power stumbled soon after I wrote the book, and even now, still with reverence largely in abeyance, it continues to stumble.

These stories are well known, and I have nothing to add to them. The makers of bad decisions need no more blame from me than they have reaped already; they succumbed, in the ordinary way, to the confidence that grows from power, which so easily grows into over-confidence. I have felt this in my own careers as soldier and teacher and dean; I have had power, and I have sometimes overreached. "You are part of what you criticize, or you don't know enough about it to criticize," says poet William Stafford.

I write for the future, however, not the past. I mention our stumbles only to show how reverence could have made the difference between life and death for countless people. That is why we need to educate future decision-makers. They need to know how dangerous it is to hold power, how power leads to hubris, and hubris to disaster. And they need to see how reverence can serve as a shield in the soul against hubris.

I would not belabor *Reverence* with a second edition if I did not believe that reverence saves lives. I won't say that my book will save lives—that would be hubris—but I firmly believe that reverence has saved lives and will save lives if only it has its proper place in the souls of people who wield great power. At the end of my epilogue I give a few examples to seal the point.

In this second edition I have made small corrections and additions to the original chapters, in order to clarify some of the fuzzier points. I have also provided three new chapters:

I have added a chapter called "Sacred Things" (chapter ten). Reverence has an uneasy relationship with sacred things, but reverence does entail that we respect whatever people hold sacred, if we can do so while still respecting all the people concerned. Americans abroad have stumbled by failing to respect sacred things.

A second new chapter, "Compassion and Responsibility," discusses compassion as a consequence of reverence (chapter twelve). Without compassion, we declare open season on the helpless, and without ethical leadership, we are all too often without compassion. Compassion is easily drowned out by a rush of events, by fear, or by anger. Reverent leaders take responsibility for compassion in their neighborhoods. I now believe that the most important message of this book is this:

Leaders are responsible for the compassion of those who follow them.

In writing about reverence, which is timeless, I have generally avoided the controversies of our time, but not on this topic. Failures of compassion touch us too closely. The section in chapter twelve called "A Failure of Leadership" is based on the case of Abu Ghraib, which illustrates in shocking detail how irresponsible it is to give power to very young people without training and oversight by leaders who have values.

Because I have often been asked how individuals may renew reverence in their lives, I have provided an epilogue on the subject (chapter 15): "Renewing Reverence." I end with examples to illustrate the urgency of this project: Reverence saves lives.

ACKNOWLEDGMENTS

I owe thanks to many: to audiences at the U.S. Air Force Academy and at Boston University who heard drafts in which I developed these ideas and pushed me to carry them further with their questions; to Peter Ohlin and various anonymous readers for Oxford University Press; to T. K. Seung for many conversations on Greek and Chinese philosophy; to John Silber for pointed and friendly criticism and to David Roochnik at Boston University for an e-mail discussion of the moral range of reverence as a virtue; to Betty Sue Flowers for much editing, for reminding me to write about ceremony, and for suggesting that I quote Yeats; to Xiusheng Liu, for teaching me Chinese philosophy, which he gave me as a gift, along with the insight that *Li* is a virtue; to Roshan Ouseph and Paul Domjan, who asked the right questions; to my colleague Reuben McDaniel, who understood much of this book better than I did; to David Reeve, Harvey Hix, William Gibson, and Charlotte Rhodes for helpful comments; to Bill Moyers, Ursula Goodenough, and Harry Wilmer for helping me to understand the book after it was published; to Katherine Woodruff and James Collins for editorial help with the first edition; to Betty Sue Flowers a second time for a careful reading of the new material in the second edition; to Chiu-Mi Lai for last-minute help with translation; and to the late A. E. Raubitschek, who taught me Greek in an unforgettable example of a reverent classroom at Princeton University in 1961. And to Lucia Norton Woodruff, for questions and encouragement, and for more than I can say.

TEXT CREDITS

INTRODUCING
REVERENCE

Reverence is an ancient virtue that survives among us in half-forgotten patterns of civility, in moments of inarticulate awe, and in nostalgia for the lost ways of traditional cultures. We have the word "reverence" in our language, but we scarcely know how to use it. Right now it has no place in secular discussions of ethics or political theory. Even more surprisingly, reverence is missing from modern discussions of the ancient cultures that prized it.

Reverence begins in a deep understanding of human limitations; from this grows the capacity to be in awe of whatever we believe lies outside our control—God, truth, justice, nature, even death. The capacity for awe, as it grows, brings with it the capacity for respecting fellow human beings, flaws and all. This in turn fosters the ability to be ashamed when we show moral flaws exceeding the normal human allotment. The Greeks before Plato saw reverence as one of the bulwarks of society, and the immediate followers of Confucius in China thought much the same. Both groups wanted to see reverence in their leaders, because reverence is the virtue that keeps leaders from trying to take tight control of other people's lives. Simply put, reverence is the virtue that keeps human beings from trying to act like gods.

To forget that you are only human, to think you can act like a god—this is the opposite of reverence. Ancient Greeks thought that tyranny was the height of irreverence, and they gave the famous name of *hubris* to the crimes of tyrants. An irreverent soul is arrogant and shameless, unable to feel awe in the face of things higher than itself. As a result, an irreverent soul is unable to feel respect for people it sees as lower than itself—ordinary people, prisoners, children. The two failures go together, in both Greek and Chinese traditions. If an emperor has a sense of awe, this will remind him that Heaven is his superior—that he is, as they said in ancient China, the Son of Heaven. And any of us is better for remembering that there is someone, or Someone, to whom we are children; in this frame of mind we are more likely to treat all children with respect. And vice versa: If you cannot bring yourself to respect children, you are probably deficient in the ability to feel that anyone or anything is higher than you.

Reverence has more to do with politics than with religion. We can easily imagine religion without reverence; we see it, for example, wherever religion leads people into aggressive war or violence. But power without reverence—that is a catastrophe for all concerned. Power without reverence is aflame with arrogance, while service without reverence is smoldering toward rebellion. Politics without reverence is blind to the general good and deaf to advice from people who are powerless. And life without reverence? Entirely without reverence? That would be brutish and selfish, and it had best be lived alone.

It is a natural mistake to think that reverence belongs to religion. It belongs, rather, to community. Wherever people try to act together, they hedge themselves around with some form of ceremony or good manners, and the observance of this can be an act of reverence. Reverence lies behind civility and all of the graces that make life in society bearable and pleasant. But in our time we hear more praise of irreverence than we do of reverence, especially in the media. That is because we naturally delight in mockery and we love making fun of solemn things. It is not because, in our heart of hearts, we despise reverence. In my view, the media are using the word "irreverent" for qualities that are not *ir*reverent at all. A better way to say what they have in mind would be "bold, boisterous, unrefined, unimpressed by pretension"—all good things. Reverence is compatible with these and with almost every form of mockery. The one great western philosopher who praises anything like reverence is Nietzsche, who is also the most given to mockery. Reverence and a keen eye for the ridiculous are allies: both keep people from being pompous or stuck up. So don't think that this book is an attack on laughter. Far from it.

Another easy mistake to make about reverence is to confuse it with respect. Respect is sometimes good and sometimes bad, sometimes wise and sometimes silly. It is silly to respect the pratings of a pompous fool; it is wise to respect the intelligence of any student. Reverence calls for respect only when respect is really the right attitude. To pay respect to a tyrant would not be reverent; it would be weak and cowardly. The most reverent response to a tyrant is to mock him. All of this is because reverence is a kind of virtue. A virtue is a capacity to do what is right, and what is right in a given case—say, respect or mockery for an authority figure—depends on many things.

Reverence is one of the strengths in any good person's character. Such strengths are called "virtues," and the study of virtues forms an important branch of ethics. Virtue ethics makes a strong assumption: that some people are better than others because they have greater strengths of character—stronger virtues, in other words. Virtues are sources of good behavior. Moral rules and laws set standards for doing right, but there is nothing about a rule that makes you feel like following it. In fact, there is something about many rules that makes many of us feel like breaking them. According to virtue ethics, a good person is one who feels like doing what is right. People who do good are aware of moral rules, but so are people who do bad. The difference is virtue. Virtue is the source of the feelings that prompt us to behave well. Virtue ethics takes feelings seriously because feelings affect our lives more deeply than beliefs do.

Virtue ethics holds that you learn a virtue as your capacity for feelings is attuned over years of experience. You may learn rules intellectually, and therefore you may learn or forget them very quickly. But virtues are habits of feeling, and these are much harder to learn or to forget. A fine violin that has not been played for many years will not stay in tune, and when it is first played it will have an ugly sound. A superior instrument must be played well, year after year, for it to sound beautiful. So it is with moral character. You may have as good equipment as anyone, but if your feelings have not been well played upon over the years, you will not stay in tune, and you will not respond well to life's challenges.

Virtues grow in us through being used, and they are used mainly by people living or working together. A family develops common virtues by the way its members live together, a team by the way its members play together, and so on. If you are surrounded by vice, you will find it hard to stay in tune with virtue. By the same token, a team or family will find it hard to cultivate virtues unless every member helps. Virtue ethics, then, deals with strengths that people develop in communities. Communities, in turn, depend on the strengths of their members.

I am interested in the virtues we should be cultivating today, as I write. But I begin my work from two classic models—one ancient Greek, the other ancient Chinese—because of their clarity, their beauty, and their apparent difference from each other. These two ancient civilizations were set too far apart to have had any communication (unlike India, which had early communication with both). If we find a common thread in Greek and Chinese ideals, we should take it seriously. It may well turn out to be a kind of thread that any society needs if it is to sew itself into an enduring shape. If so, reverence is a cardinal virtue, like justice or courage, and not the particular property of this culture or that. I don't think we should imitate ancient Greek or Chinese culture, but I believe we are better off for studying them. Both peoples cared deeply and thought long about the meaning of ceremonies in the texture of their religious and political lives, and in this meaning they saw the deeper value of reverence.

We have ceremonies in our own time too, but we try not to think about what they mean. In fact, I believe reverence gives meaning to much that we do, yet the word has almost passed out of our vocabulary. Because we do not understand reverence, we don't really know what we are doing in much of our lives, and therefore we are in no position to think about how to do it better.

Defining Reverence

Reverence compels me to confess that I do not know exactly what reverence is. I can't do any better for justice or courage or wisdom, though I have a pretty good idea in each case. Take courage. I would say that courage is a well-developed capacity for feeling confidence and fear in the right places, at the right times, and in the right degrees of intensity; that is, courage lies somewhere between fearlessness (which often looks like courage) and timidity (which no one would mistake for courage). This account of courage has a grand history—it comes from Aristotle—but is hardly a complete definition. I would call it a definition-schema—something like a form full of blanks that we need to fill in as best we can, after life experience and critical reflection. The schema for courage tells us that we can't go wrong by being courageous, but it does not tell us how to be courageous. It points to a distinction between courage and fearlessness, but it does not spell out the difference between them—aside from the obvious point that one is always good while the other can go too far. Before filling in the blanks in the schema we would need to know the difference between right and wrong. That looks easy enough in some cases, but it seems to call for divine wisdom in others.

I cannot claim divine wisdom, and so I cannot offer a full account of any of the virtues, least of all reverence. My schema for reverence looks like this: Reverence is the well-developed capacity to have the feelings of awe, respect, and shame when these are the right feelings to have. This says that reverence is a good thing, but not much more, except by pointing to further questions. Sometimes it is right to be respectful and sometimes wrong; that's obvious. Sometimes our feelings should rise to the level of awe, but not always. So when should we be respectful, and how deep should our respect be in each case? Of what should we be in awe? No capsule definition will tell you. Nor can any human wisdom give you a complete and final answer. The best answer I can give is this book.

Some writers use the words "reverence" and "respect" as synonyms, but these words are not synonyms in this book. I need one word for an ideal, "reverence," and other words for the feelings—respect, awe, and shame—that may or may not serve that ideal. You can never follow an ideal too closely, but you can have too much—or too little—of the feelings to which it gives rise. You are too lavish with awe, for example, if you are in awe of your own wisdom and treat it as sacred. That's arrogant, and it's not much better if you feel that way about the accumulated wisdom of your own tradition, for both are human products. On the other hand, you are too sparing of awe if you never feel awe for a great whale, a majestic redwood, or a range of tall mountains. You need not enjoy these things—awe can be frightening, after all—and you need not be moved by them every time you encounter them. But if you do not have the capacity to be awestruck at the sight of the majesties of nature you are missing part of the usual human endowment.

Why This Book

The topic surprised me. I never expected to write a book about reverence, but I came to this as I explored material for a footnote to a chapter I was writing in a still unfinished tome on ancient Greek humanism. But I soon came to think that this abandoned topic deserves to have a new life.

My footnote was on Thucydides, the most thoughtful of the ancient Greek historians. Writing in the fifth and fourth centuries BCE, Thucydides adopted the humanist position that gods do not intervene in human affairs. He believed that purely human currents in history would bring about most of the results that traditional thinkers expected from the gods: If a tyrant rises too far and too fast, or if he exercises his power with too much arrogance, other people will fear him and hate him, and they—not the gods—will unite to bring him down. But if the gods never punish human beings, why bother with reverence? I used to think that it was only fear of the gods that made the ancient Greeks reverent. Thucydides does not seem to fear the gods, but he fears human arrogance, and therefore he cares a great deal about reverence, which he treats as a cardinal virtue. Some scholars argue, in spite of appearances, that he does believe the gods punish human beings when they violate reverence. But then why doesn't he say so? That was the puzzle I took on in my footnote.

The footnote exploded as I went deeper and deeper into the concept of reverence. I had been content in former years to accept Plato's view that reverence is not a primary virtue at all. Plato taught that all you need do for reverence is to practice the other virtues that the gods favor, principally justice. Plato was afraid that the Greeks of his day were trying to use reverence to win over the gods, in the hope that the gods would forgive any kind of wickedness on the part of people who gave abundant sacrifices. That is why Plato treated reverence as a part of justice, so that no one would think you could be reverent without also being just. But if reverence is part of justice, then you will have it all if you cultivate justice as a whole—as you should—and you need not spend another moment's thought on reverence.

After Plato, I turned to the ancient poets and became disenchanted with Plato's simple theory. From Homer through Euripides, the poets treat reverence as a substantial virtue, and I began to see their point. More surprising, I began to suspect that reverence has more to do with power than with religion. I was struck by the fact that Thucydides prizes reverence while condemning credulity in people who persist in seeing a divine plan behind the natural consequences of their own mistakes. If Thucydides believes that reverence is good but that credulity is foolish, he is plainly thinking of reverence as a moral virtue that is detachable from traditional beliefs about the gods. Could this be possible? Could reverence be detached from belief? The answer turned out to be complicated. Reverence depends to some extent on belief, but not at all on formal creeds. And so I realized with shock and delight that reverence could—in theory, at least—be shared across religions. In fact, what religious people today admire in other religions cannot be faith (since they reject most of the content of other faiths), but reverence. So they know about reverence, though they don't know to call it by that name.

I began to feel that something has been lost in modern times. This virtue, so important to the ancients, has fallen beneath the horizons of our intellectual vision. And yet reverence is all around us, even in the most ordinary ceremonies of our lives. It is as if we have forgotten one of the cylinders that has been chugging along in the vehicle of human society since its beginning. And now, because we do not know the cylinder is there, we have no idea how to tune it up, or even how we might gum it up completely by inattention. The more I pondered this, the more I wanted to know what reverence is, not just to the ancient Greeks, but for us—for all of us trying to live good human lives. If reverence is a cardinal virtue, it belongs to the family of justice and courage and wisdom, and those are ideals that bear study in their own right, not merely as they occur within the boundaries of this or that culture.

My quest for universal reverence took me out of ancient Greece and across to ancient China, then back to the European tradition and to writers of our own time. I soon found that I had been reading the wrong books. Most modern philosophers have forgotten about reverence. But poets are aware of it, as they have always been. I might have expected that Yeats would turn out to be a poet of reverence. And Tennyson. But Philip Larkin? This has all been a delightful surprise.

In studying reverence I have come to a new view about how ethics should be discussed and about how a book like this should be written. A writer who is serious about virtue can't stay behind the boundaries of a single academic discipline; the subject brings together poetry and philosophy and the history of ideas and puts them all to work on a huge live-wire of a question—how we should live our lives. Also, a writer about virtue must not expect to deliver the sharp-edged definitions or the clear criteria that some philosophers crave. Aristotle urges us—with virtue in mind—not to ask the same precision of ethics that we would of mathematics. Poets often understand virtues better than philosophers, so that the wisdom of poets over time is essential to this subject. Also essential to the study of virtue is the experience that you, the reader, bring to the subject. Virtues are about emotions, and you can't learn much about emotions from a book. I could write a volume ten times the length of this one, and it would still leave many questions for you to work out on your own. Reverent students of ethics will understand that this is a project not for a book but a lifetime.

Why Reverence?

Why write about reverence? Because we have forgotten what it means. Because reverence fosters leadership and education. Most important, because reverence kindles warmth in friendship and family life. And because without reverence, things fall apart. People do not know how to respect each other and themselves. An army cannot tell the difference between what it is and a gang of bandits. Without reverence, we cannot explain why we should treat the natural world with respect. Without reverence, a house is not a home, a boss is not a leader, an instructor is not a teacher. Without reverence, we would not even know how to learn reverence. To teach reverence, you must find the seeds of reverence in each person and help them grow.

Religious wars are endemic in our time, which is a time with little care for reverence. Perhaps these wars are cooling down in some places, but they are heating up in others, as they were when as I wrote this book in 1999, and even now as I update it in 2013. If a religious group thinks it speaks and acts as God commands in all things, this is a failure of reverence. A group like that may turn violent and feel they are doing so in good faith. Nothing is more dangerous than that feeling.

War is nothing new, and neither are killer strains of religion, pathogens that take hold of a people and send them into paroxysms of violence. War and religion will always be with us; we can't expect to shake them off. But we can ask what it is in religion that might keep the dogs of war on leash, and what it is that whips them into a frenzy and lets them loose. It is reverence that moderates war in all times and cultures, irreverence that urges it on to brutality. The voices that call in the name of God for aggressive war have lost sight of human limitations. They have lost reverence, even when they serve a religious vision. So it is when a people believe that their god commands them to take land from others, or insists that they force others into their way of thinking. Even when the goal of war is something as noble as freedom or peace, it may be irreverent to think we can impose these goals by violence.

When Agamemnon waited on the beach with his ships and chariots and with the men who hungered to capture Troy, the winds remained hostile, and he asked a diviner what he should do. He had faith in his diviner, and the diviner had faith in his power to speak for the gods. He said he knew what the gods desired—the life of the king's daughter. And so Iphigenia came, summoned to her wedding in all the veiled finery of a bride. At the altar stood her father with the priest. But there was no young husband, only the great sharp knife poised to end her life.

The poet Lucretius tells this tale, as I have done, to be the introduction for his work of philosophy. He ends with the strong line, *tantum religio potuit suadere malorum* (1.101)—"so great is the power of religion to lead us to evil." He gives us Iphigenia to stand for all the huge unholy cost of war when it is driven by men who believe they know what the gods want. But he does not mean to condemn everything that falls under religion. Lucretius may be hostile to some kinds of faith, but he begins his work with an invocation to the goddess who stands for Nature. He too is a poet of reverence.

Reverence runs across religions and even outside them through the fabric of any community, however secular. We may be divided from one another by our beliefs, but never by reverence. If you desire peace in the world, do not pray that everyone share your beliefs. Pray instead that all may be reverent.

We know where light is coming from by looking at the shadows. These stories are about shadowy places where reverence does not reach; they are mostly my own invention, but they may strike a familiar chord.

2 | WITHOUT REVERENCE

God Votes in a City Election

The signs say, "God voted against Proposition Two." They are everywhere in this city of many churches—painted on billboards, scrawled on wooden signs, assembled from movable letters on rented panels that are wheeled out from churches to the sidewalks. No one in the city could miss the message. The issue is benefits. Should the city offer the same package to same-sex partners as it did to the husbands and wives of its employees? The council has approved a plan to do so, but opponents have brought on this referendum—in which, if the signs are true, God has long since cast His vote.

Here the difference between faith and reverence is glaring. The people behind the signs are showing faith, and plenty of it. But they are acting against reverence. They are human beings, and yet they suppose they know the mind of God so clearly that they can declare His vote on a civic matter. Reverence requires us to maintain a modest sense of the difference between human and divine. If you wish to be reverent, never claim the awful majesty of God in support of your political views.

You cannot speak on such matters with the authority of God. It is an especially vicious and harmful falsehood to say that you do—vicious

13

because it is irreverent, harmful because it is like pouring fuel on smoldering disagreements. By every new follower you have, and by everyone you persuade that God is on your side, you make a tough situation harder to resolve. Your followers will never listen to the other side, never enter into discussion, never consider a compromise. In fact, by claiming that God votes with you, you have effectively opted out of political process altogether. When we Americans of European background read the most extreme claims of religious leaders from the Middle East, we have no trouble seeing that those claims are ruinous to political life. So it is easy for us to see how ruin springs from irreverence, at least in countries other than our own. But we may all too easily say, "What does this have to do with us? In distant countries, in religions not well represented in the United States, such things happen. But not among us, not among Christians or Jews." Think again. All too often, believers in any religion set themselves against reverence. We often see a powerful religion, without a scrap of reverence, stamping out its more modest rivals in one crusade after another. But we never see a working political process without reverence.

Don't misunderstand me: I do not mean that reverence must never speak up for what is right. Of course you must speak up for what you believe to be right. Silence is just as dangerous as dogma, equally destructive of the conversations that sustain community. There are reverent ways—often poetic—of trying to lend a human voice to God's will. Great prophets and teachers have used them from time immemorial; they take reverent care that their words cannot easily be mistaken for a literal representation of the mind of God.

Feeding Time

Now is the time when phones are ringing around town with calls from telemarketers. Someone somewhere is sitting down to dinner with a family, but not here, not in this house. Dad stopped off on the way home for his workout and ran into some friends; Mom brought Sarah home after soccer but had to turn right around for a meeting. David is over at a friend's house.

Now Sarah is on the phone with a friend—her cell phone, not the one that's ringing off the hook. She has the TV on in her room, algebra homework spread out on her bed, and a bag of chips open beside her. She's very responsible, and she remembered to feed the dog before she went into her room and closed the door. The dog is not hungry yet, but when she is, she will go over to her dish and eat as much of it as she feels like, as a dog does when it is alone.

Food may eventually appear on the table in this house, but it is very unlikely that as many as two members of the family will be eating at once. This family will not eat together, hold hands or pray together before a meal, or talk about the day's events. Chances are they'll go to their respective dishes to feed, like the dog, when they feel like it. Something is missing from these people, something that makes the difference between feeding time and meal time, between a home and a kennel. If you ask them why, they will answer, "Who has time for family dinner? It's only an empty ritual after all." True. Without reverence, rituals are empty.

No One Votes at All

Janice has never voted and she tells me vehemently that she never will. "Tweedledum and Tweedledee," she says, speaking of the candidates. "They are as like as two peas in a pod. What difference does it make?" She is in middle age, and I think she ought to know better.

She has been engaged for many years in the debate about abortion and choice; the next election is for president, the winner will appoint people to the federal bench, and those judges will make decisions about abortion, decisions that will affect her life. "But aren't you passionate about the abortion issue?" I ask. "Of course the election will make a difference."

She looks at me with the pity in her eyes that she reserves for foolish children and philosophy professors. "My vote? My vote makes a difference?" She is convinced that the outcome will be the same whether she votes or not; the polls have already announced the winner. "And anyway," she goes on, "even if the other guy wins, special interests won't let him do anything different."

Well, I lost the argument, and she kept her record unblemished. No votes. Forty years living as an adult in a democracy, and she has never voted. She is not alone. What could I say to change her mind? Not much.

Janice is right about her vote. It won't make a difference. The odds that one vote could turn an election—even a very close one, such as occurred in November 2000—are so small they vanish for all practical purposes. She has made her decision unconsciously on the basis of what philosophers call "rational choice theory." There is no way—none, ever—to show that she would be making the best choice *for herself* and acting in her own best interest, by going to the polls and casting her ballot. She has nothing to gain from this, and at least an hour of her valuable time to lose. Voting is irrational.

If everyone made that calculation, no one would vote. I tried out that line on her, and she gave me the same pitying look. "Ask me something real," she says. "Don't waste my time with 'if'." She's right again: She has no reason to worry about hypothetical questions. What happens in a scenario with a wild "if" clause will never really happen—never cost her a penny or cause her to lose a minute's sleep.

So why should Janice vote? I tell her to see this as a matter of pure ethics, since my appeals to Janice's personal advantage and even to her political interests have failed. "Ethics!" she snorts. "Where does it say, 'Thou shalt vote?' You know me. I don't lie or cheat or steal. I give to charity and volunteer at the hospital. Are you telling me I'm a bad person because I do not vote?" I am foiled again. As we generally understand ethics these days, Janice has got it covered. She lives a good life *without* voting. In the end, I have no argument for Janice.

Voting in a democracy is a ceremony, and the peoples who turn out in large numbers to vote, unlike Americans, have a strong feeling for the value of ceremony. That feeling comes from reverence, but there is no argument for a feeling. Or for any other virtue as the source of feelings. You must grow up with a virtue in order to appreciate it. Janice has grown up with very little ceremony in her life and no appreciation for reverence. I can see that she has a vacuum in her mind where some people have a fountain of strong feelings. But she can't see that now, and no philosophical argument will change her into the sort of person who would see it.

Voting is a ceremony. It is an expression of reverence—not for our government or our laws, not for anything man-made, but for the very idea that ordinary people are more important than the juggernauts that seem to rule them. If we do not understand why we should vote in this country, that is because we have forgotten the meaning of ceremony. And the meaning of ceremony is reverence.

Trees Are Merely Cash and Sawdust

The great trees in the hills behind town are awe-inspiring—at least to the occasional tourist who has taken a wrong turn on the way to the national park, where the trees are even grander. To the people of the town, who have been lobbying for years, along with a timber company, for permission to cut the trees, the trees are jobs and cash and sawdust—and much more. They are a promise that the town's way of life will be preserved for another generation. In an open meeting to debate the issue, a tiny group of environmentalists bring out argument after argument on behalf of the trees, with no success.

Seeing the well-kept churches, they decide to appeal to the Bible. Citing Genesis 2:15, they say God put us here to "till the garden and keep it"; but they find that the majority of townspeople believe the opposite. To them, Scripture is unambiguous: we are appointed to make use of the things of this earth, not to preserve them, they say, citing Genesis 1:26–28. Perhaps there is scriptural authority on both sides.

The defenders of trees have been unwise to bring up religion, because then their opponents accuse the environmentalists of idolatry. "Are you telling us we should worship trees like the old pagans? Shame on you. We are all Christians in this town."

Trying a secular tack, the defenders reply: "All right, this is not about religion. It's about your long-term interest. If you cut them down, the trees will be gone forever. But if you leave them standing, they will be a steady source of income over the years. Tourists will come to enjoy them along with the wildlife that flourishes around them."

But the town knows better. It will never be a tourist mecca. There are parks enough and they are easier for tourists to visit. The trees are more famous in the parks and their natural beauty is stunning. "The only thing our trees will ever do for us, if we leave them standing, is fall down and rot," says a retired logger, and the town agrees. The environmentalists talk about erosion and the loss of habitat, but the logger has answers for them. "Look where the company has logged and replanted," he says, and shows slides of contented wildlife in young-growth forest. The environmentalists talk about preserving species of trees, small plants, and animals, but the town knows there is nothing unique in their hills. And besides, why worry about species? Scientists may find ways to use the DNA of lost species, at some point in the future, but we do not need to keep things alive in order to preserve their DNA.

In the end the environmentalists realize they have no good argument for preserving the trees. They are astonished that the townspeople do not feel about the trees the way they do, but they know that arguments do not compel feelings. And they have to confess to themselves that they do not quite know why they want to save the trees or why they shudder at the thought of their being destroyed.

The great trees have been alive on these hills for centuries. They rise on strong bases to great heights, they are homes to many creatures, they bear clouds of greenery above and provide dense shade below. Like everything that calls for reverence, these trees are beyond our understanding. We do not know what will happen when they are cut, and we cannot expect to be able to control all of the consequences of cutting them. No farmers can cultivate such trees; even if humans could live long enough, they could not duplicate the conditions under which this forest came to be. But these trees will be felled and then peeled, sliced, or chipped into the materials for homes that will probably be demolished in less than a human lifetime to make way for new construction. And why not? Trees must be cut and will be cut. Why not these?

It is very hard to show why not, and perhaps in the end the trees might as well be cut. But as things are, the environmentalists believe that the townspeople do not feel that anything is at stake besides money. They are blinded by their own concerns to the townspeople's devotion to preserving their past. Something is missing on both sides, something without which there can be no contest in the meeting. What is missing is a sense of awe, a sense that depends on reverence. What can the environmentalists do to make the townspeople feel differently at the sight of their tree-covered hills? And how can the townspeople make the environmentalists see what it is they wish to preserve?

A remarkable feature of virtues is that you cannot argue people into having them when they do not. Imagine trying to persuade a squad of cowards to take courage and stand their ground. Aristotle's chapter on courage would be wasted. You'd do better to open a bottle of strong liquor, as leaders of troops have known for centuries. Better than either argument or liquor would be to instill courage over time in a community of people who will support each other in doing what is right. Virtues are cultivated over time, and they have the greatest lasting power in close-knit communities.

So it may be too late for this town. But the town is reverent about something, and so are the environmentalists, and reverence has a way of breaking out of narrow channels. No virtue can grow large in an atmosphere that stifles any part of it. You cannot bring up your children to be principled or brave and also expect them to cave in to your authority. In matters of character, strength leads to strength, and one lapse leads to another (unless the force of community works strongly the other way). That is the idea behind Socrates' famous belief that every lapse in virtue damages the soul.

The challenge for both sides, then, is not to find better arguments. It is to change this community, not radically, but by building on what is already there. Anyone who tried to transplant altogether new virtues into the town would see them rejected by the town's immune system. Perhaps there are townspeople who are already in awe of some aspects of nature, but they are so familiar with the trees in their hills that they need to see them with new eyes. Perhaps the arts will help. Art speaks the language of reverence better than philosophy does, and so art can speak to the reverence that is already in the town. Paintings and photography, hymns and songs may widen the sphere of majesties for which people can feel a sense of awe. Once reverence is awakened, a little argument won't hurt: People who are losing the capacity to feel awe are in danger of losing a great deal more. Both groups do care about reverence, but now suppose they also realize that reverence is not to be divided. Then the environmentalists should begin to feel the value of what their adversaries are trying to preserve. And the townspeople should conclude that they will be better people if they start finding in themselves, before it withers away entirely, the power to walk reverently in the enormous shadow of the trees.

Why Go to a Meeting?

The meeting finally peters out. Attendance was poor to begin with, and the discussion has outlasted the patience of most of those who came. For nearly an hour now we have not had a quorum. The coffee pot is dry, residue caking on the bottom until someone thinks to switch off the machine. One of our long-winded colleagues, who has been hectoring us for some time, has run out of wind—or perhaps realized that no one was listening. "I guess we're done," says the chair, and we survivors push back our chairs in disgust, muttering about how much time we waste in meetings. Waste, because we have accomplished nothing that we are aware of.

We did manage to have one vote, and it came out roughly as we all knew it would. We have heard each other say what we expected each other to say (most of us could have written the script). Powerful arguments have been deployed, but none of them has changed anyone's mind. The outsiders feel more outside than ever, while the insiders are fed up with the outsiders for not recognizing that the majority position is truly the position of the department. We drift apart into caucuses, each one complaining of the intransigence of the others and the weakness of the chair in not putting down the people we disagreed with. A young colleague asks plaintively, "Why can't we ever get anything done in a meeting?"

Why indeed? What is there, after all, to be "got done" in a meeting? Much as we believe in the power of argument (we are academics, after all), we have learned that we simply do not have the arguments that will change each other's minds. The majority has already discussed the issues in corridors and on e-mail, and they know they have the votes to win. So why do we bother to meet at all? Do we forget, momentarily, the many failures of the past? Or have we forgotten, more generally, the purposes of a meeting?

Without reverence we think that it is irrational to spend time on any project that does not get results, and we understand results narrowly in terms of tangible benefits. But meetings are rituals, and the benefits of ritual are rarely tangible. If you do not realize that a meeting is a ritual because you hate ritual, and so you pass over its ritual aspects, then your meeting will yield no benefit at all. A good meeting does not drift on without a quorum, speakers do not continue till they are out of gas, and the coffee pot does not run dry (even if no one wants coffee). The chair is formal in opening the meeting, closing it, and directing discussion. All right, says my critic, suppose we do repackage our meeting as a more elegant ritual. In the end, won't we still leave in disgust, with the major issues unresolved and neither side able to claim total victory?

Of course. Meetings are not about resolving issues or awarding total victories. Differences always remain in any human organization. Meetings are about how to go on in view of our differences, how to keep our differences from stopping us in our tracks or from breaking us up into two units. Most important, good meetings keep us from giving up on the department altogether and trying to accomplish our ends through other means, such as running to the dean or the president or a major donor. On very rare occasions, a meeting will yield workable strategies or compromises that all members can applaud. More often, though, a meeting will leave people on both sides dissatisfied—at least about the issues.

We *can* disagree and still not be dissatisfied with each other or with the existence of the unit itself. The ritual of a meeting should remind us that we are a group, and that we ought to be a group that works together, in spite of differences, to accomplish common goals through mutual respect. In a brilliant book entitled *Ritual, Politics, and Power,* David I. Kertzer shows how the ambiguity of ritual enables it to support the fellow feeling of groups in which there are deep divisions. Call this an irrational effect, if you will, but it is an effect we must try to bring off, or we face the collapse of our group.

Consider the ritual, every four years, of the party convention in the United States. Rarely is anything accomplished at these summer extravaganzas. The candidate and platform are already known in most cases, and the party has nothing to do but listen to its leaders tell it what a majority of its members already believe, and then to make a show of unity that includes all factions of the party. Irrational? An echo of dying traditions, as useless as a cavalry charge? John Kenneth Galbraith thought so. But any politician knows that a successful convention is an essential step in moving towards national elections. It is a ceremonial event of great power for bringing people together, but it is a political disaster if it goes awry.

All right, you say, meetings are rituals, voting is a ritual. But what does this have to do with reverence? Is there such a thing as reverence for the platforms of the GOP or the Democratic Party? No. Those are made by human beings, and true reverence, we'll see, cannot be for anything that we humans make or control. In these cases, I think the object of reverence is the ideal of unity, because that transcends politics altogether. Unity is an ideal; it is what it is no matter what we think of it or what means we take to achieve it. Our ideas of unity may be more or less adequate to reverence, depending on how broad a view we take. At the narrow end, defying reverence altogether, would be the mere unity within one warring faction in my department; at the wide end, setting us up for reverence, would be the unity we build around goals of research and education we share with scholars and teachers everywhere. Ultimately, ritual in academic settings expresses reverence for truth. Truth, like unity, is not of our making, even though we have devised our own means for seeking it and expressing what we find.

Blame the bad meeting, then, not on factionalism or stubbornness, not on poor arguments, not on the cussedness of human nature. Blame it on a failure of virtue, a shared failure in the group and its leadership.

Dad Slugs the Umpire

He was only doing his job. On his last day at the diamond, his job required him to call a series of balls against a pitcher in a children's league. The child was in tears, humiliation and defeat staring her in the face. The father was in a mounting rage.

The umpire's sudden injury was a hit with the newscasters, who played it for all it was worth: interviews with stunned children, sports officials, representatives of the umpire's professional association, and a psychologist. The doctor of the mind chosen for this occasion had a simple message for the parents of child athletes: "Learn to control your emotions." Anger, he implied, even rage, is normal in such circumstances. Just keep it down to a safe level.

"Control your emotions"—that makes a virtue-ethicist pay attention. Virtue, after all, is supposed to be the capacity to have the right emotions from the start. If you have emotions that need to be controlled, you are already in trouble. Dad should have been living his life all along in ways that strengthened his capacity for feeling anger just when he should feel anger and just to the degree he ought to feel it. Of course a father should be angry when his child is in danger, and he should be prepared to kill someone who threatens his child—in certain circumstances. In those circumstances, self-control would be a disaster. Even when self-control is called for, it is painful and prone to failure because it runs against our grain. But reverence runs with the grain—or, rather, as you cultivate reverence, you are changing the way your grain runs.

Christians believe that it is not good enough merely to contain your anger and not commit murder: "anyone who nurses anger against his brother [without good cause] must be brought to judgment" (Matthew 5:22). The father would have been a better person if he had not been angry at the umpire in the first place. Plato and Aristotle both understood self-control through metaphors of mastery by violence or force. As such it is a painful second best to virtue. The emotions should be our allies, not our enemies or our slaves. The need for self-control is a sign of undeveloped virtue.

In the case of the cold-cocked umpire, it is partly right to say that the father should have been able to control his anger. Anyone who is prone to anger at the wrong times had better learn to control it, or else prepare for a life in jail. But this way of thinking is misleading, because it suggests that the father's major failing was in self-control. The father's real weakness was in reverence.

The sanctity of the umpire is fundamental in any game or in any system of conflict resolution. The divinity that in old days was supposed to hedge a king was due, I think, to the king's role as judge or umpire over disputes in his realm. This role also requires reverence on the part of the judge or the umpire, who must make every effort to be impartial, and not use the position to obtain victory for one side or the other. The reverent sports parent, like any other reverent sports fan, feels respect for the umpire, however foolish or unjust the umpire's decisions seem to be, as long as the umpire stays in that role.

That feeling of respect is enough to balance the anger that parents should feel on seeing their children unjustly treated. If you even feel that you could slug an umpire, you have failed in reverence.

Sports are the ritual events that are most widely known in modern life; they are therefore the best arena for us to observe our common habits of reverence and to contemplate the horror that follows from a breakdown of this virtue. It used to be said that sports build character, and it should be said more often and more loudly. The increasing number of assaults on umpires is just one piece in a large pile of evidence that modern society all around the world is forgetting the virtues that ought to grow on playing fields. Sports are becoming like war.

War is the ultimate game. This too has its rituals (in almost every culture that practices war), and these too can build or destroy character. In war there remain openings for reverence, in leaders especially, but also in the ranks.

We Know the Enemy Loves to Die

The team leader—our commander—has a hangover, but he pulls himself together long enough to address the troops. Three things the old man wants us to remember. "Always wear appropriate headgear, especially when you may be seen by the Vietnamese; you need to have the respect of all of them, allies and enemies both. Second, keep your hair short [this is 1969]; if you receive a head wound it will be easier to treat. And, third, don't worry too much about killing the Vietnamese. Their religion is different from ours, and they don't mind dying the way we do. They think that when they die they go up and join the great god Buddha in heaven."

Some of us know a little about Buddhism; almost all of us in this group have witnessed a Vietnamese funeral. We know the old man is full of shit, but then we have known that for a long time. Still, the audacity of this particular lie is breathtaking: these people do not mind dying? We know better.

Professional soldiers usually know that they are trained to fight people very much like themselves (at least when the parties belong to similar cultures). But amateur armies, gathered from levies of civilians, are a different matter. They do not have much training, and they do not think of themselves first and foremost as soldiers. Studies have found that such armies are reluctant to shed their civilian ethics; they are, in brief, loath to kill. Our old man is doing his best to counteract our civilian ethics in an especially tough situation. Unlike most American units, we have had prolonged contact with Vietnamese people in the role known as "advisers." We know they are people like us, with passions and fears we can recognize, with virtues of loyalty we can admire, and with tendencies to go wrong not unlike our own. But the old man wants us to forget our common humanity. Looking back, I now think he wanted us to abandon reverence.

I believe that wars can be fought by reverent people. This may be the most controversial suggestion I make here, but it has foundations as deep as Homer's *Iliad*. If it were not so, then we could not pick out, as Homer does, failures of reverence in the opposing armies. Reverent soldiers do not go on a rampage, desecrating enemy bodies or killing enemy soldiers who have become harmless. Reverent soldiers take no joy in killing, and they never forget that the human beings on the other side are just that—human. This is a hard thing to remember, even at the best of times. But reverence is not easy.

Well, says my imaginary critic, suppose there are a few reverent soldiers. They are the ones I would like to know after the war is over, in civilian life. But in combat, give me a platoon of brutes who have no thought for the humanity of anyone who is not in the unit.

This seems plausible, but it is wrong. First, in almost any combat zone there are people who are not in your unit but whose respect you need. This was crucial in Vietnam, where the war was being fought, as we said, "for the hearts and minds of the Vietnamese people." Training troops to be brutal to anyone who was not American would backfire. Second, you should consider how your actions will affect the other side. If you want them to take and exchange prisoners (rather than lining them up to be shot), then you must be willing to spare prisoners yourself.

Third, and this is the most important reason, you cannot simply disengage a virtue like disengaging the clutch of a car with a standard transmission. A virtue, if you have it, is not under your conscious control, and if you give it up, no act of will can bring it back to you. (That is one of the lessons of posttraumatic stress.) Even if it were true (which it is not) that brutal soldiers are better soldiers, we would still have to count the enormous moral and psychological cost of turning so many people into brutes. Perhaps that would deter us from war altogether; I think it should. If you are not a pacifist, therefore, you should hope to work out a way for war to be waged without a great sacrifice of virtue.

A World Power Will Stumble

As I wrote this book, in 1999–2001, the United States was in the supreme moment of its power. For what the United States has done since 2001, see my preface. But in 2001 the nation was not far from where England stood in 1897, when Kipling wrote "Recessional" as a reminder that power leads to arrogance, and arrogance to a fall.

> The tumult and the shouting dies;
> The captains and the kings depart:
> Still stands Thine ancient sacrifice,
> An humble and a contrite heart.
>
> ...

If, drunk with sight of power, we loose
Wild tongues that have not Thee in awe,

…

Lord God of Hosts, be with us yet,
Lest we forget—lest we forget!

Indeed, it would be less than twenty years before England began bleeding away its young men in Flanders, and the long, slow, irreversible march began to the loss of empire. Even in this poem, in lines I did not quote, Kipling betrays some of the symptoms of arrogance—racism above all (when he speaks of "lesser breeds without the Law")—that would eat away at the empire and its economy.

History has never doted on a world power. A great power may frighten the rest of the world into gearing up and joining hands to destroy it for their own defense (as happened to Athens). It may grow into a rich plum for pillage by outsiders, as happened to Rome and China. It may grow so complacent that its people forget to pay the price of power, or, with no external threat to unify them, they may fall to wrangling and so take themselves apart. Most likely, however, they will rely on whatever they have done in the past to protect them, and at some point technology or world affairs will have passed them by.

"Lest we forget," writes Kipling, drumming the refrain into our heads through the recessional. Lest we forget what? The ancient Greeks would have answered, "That we are mortal, that we are born and die, and that in between these events each of us has time to make a fatal mistake."

There Is No Reverence

You don't learn a virtue from outside. You cannot even appreciate a virtue from outside. You won't see why you should be reverent unless you already are at least a little bit reverent, and you'll never learn reverence unless you already practice it. You learn it by finding the virtuous things that you do and doing more of them, so that they become a habit. Aristotle understood that. So did Mencius: if virtues must be imposed from outside, they will always run across our grain. Luckily, reverence is all around us, so there are plenty of starting points for anyone who wishes to cultivate reverence.

Look at the many things we do with reverence every day: They are all the things that go wrong without it. Ritual and reverence in common life are so familiar that we scarcely notice them until they are gone. In sports, entertainment, the law court, the voting booth, the boardroom, there are ritual and reverence. We see them in the church whose members live in genuine awe of God, the community that votes, the department that meets well, the sports events that run with due ceremony. Most importantly, we see reverence in good leadership, in education, and in a home that is more than a place for eating, sleeping, watching television, and playing games. Home above all is the place where small rituals bring a family together into a family, where the respect they share is so common and familiar that they hardly recognize it as flowing from reverence.

All of these things are changing, however. Old ceremonies die away, and the new ones may not look at all like ceremonies to us. What place does ceremony have in the routines that emerge in e-mail and on the web, or in the living arrangements of unmarried couples, or in ways of sharing children between remarried parents in blended families? How in this new world of ours do we show respect? And why, amid so many changes, should we show respect for each other at all? Isn't ceremony a waste of time? And so we seem to be losing sight of respect and our ceremonial ways of showing it.

Reverence is even harder to defend than ceremony. Listen to the news or read the papers and you will find that "irreverent" has become a word for something good. Anything bold or innovative may be called irreverent because it is not held back by old-fashioned tradition, and so is anything that pokes fun at pomposity. Artists and thinkers have good reasons to break with tradition, of course, and in doing so they seem to break with reverence as well.

They *seem* to break with reverence; we *seem* to be losing sight of respect and ceremony. In reality, I argue in this book, reverence, ceremony and respect do not disappear—they cannot disappear from a functioning society. It is only that we fail to recognize them. So I am not saying that ancient societies functioned better than modern ones do. Far from it. I am saying that the ancients had a better understanding than we do of the virtues on which any society depends. What we are losing is not reverence, but the idea of reverence. We go on unconsciously doing reverent things, and this is fortunate, because the complete loss of reverence would be too grievous to bear.

Perfect Reverence

This is how a great poet imagines the loss of reverence:

> Turning and turning in the widening gyre
> The falcon cannot hear the falconer;
> Things fall apart; the center cannot hold;
> Mere anarchy is loosed upon the world;
> The blood-dimmed tide is loosed, and everywhere
> The ceremony of innocence is drowned;
> The best lack all conviction, while the worst
> Are full of passionate intensity.
> (W. B. Yeats, "The Second Coming")

"The ceremony of innocence is drowned"—not dead by drowning, not floating belly up in a tide of blood, but drowned *out* by a cacophony of irreverent voices, which prevent the falcon from hearing the falconer. In a totally reverent society, the center would hold, the falcon would hear the falconer, ceremony would rise to the surface. Passions would settle, through audible ceremony, into harmony. A world like that is the poet's dream, free of conflict between innocence and intensity, harmonizing the best and the most passionate. The reverence of that dream is an ideal, a perfection never achieved in human history. We have never been God's trained falcons.

So where do we live in relation to reverence? Somewhere between the gyres of the trained falcon and the anarchy of the blood-dimmed tide. We have neither lost reverence altogether nor achieved it; we are, as we have always been, in between. An in-between state is always hard to describe; we must avoid the temptation to go to extremes. True, we lack the reverence of a traditional Confucian village, but that does not mean we lack reverence altogether. Nor does it mean that the Confucian village was ideal; it may have had an authoritarian structure that fed the arrogance of its leaders and starved their reverence. Again, perhaps our lives on the Internet are guided by subtle rituals that allow us to work together with respect for each other's rights and goals, but that does not mean that the society of the internet is a reverent one.

What we have lost is not reverence but the idea. We do not know well enough what it is, or why we need it, or how we should cultivate it. I am not proposing that we reestablish old dress codes or rigidly maintain forms of courtesy that are vanishing. No one has the power to do those things, least of all a philosopher. What I am proposing is that we restore the idea of reverence to its proper place in ethical and political thought. We will be better off, I think, if we know what it is and why it matters. Only then can we consciously preserve and cultivate it as we run down the rapidly accelerating current of cultural change. Otherwise we may be like passengers clinging to the gunwales of a craft tossed by white water, unaware of the steering paddles at their feet.

Losing the Idea of Reverence

Perhaps it is best forgotten. Ceremony and reverence fell out of favor among intellectuals ages ago. Plato started the trend when he repudiated old ideas of reverence along with traditional myths about gods at war with each other, competing in violence and duplicity. Reverence is tied to aspects of traditional religion that intellectuals of all periods have wanted to criticize or reform. Critics have good reason to put old ideas behind them, either for the sake of intellectual freedom or in the hope of moral progress. And, indeed, we ought to forget some forms for expressing reverence, along with old myths, but there are other forms, and there is an underlying idea to remember.

"Reverence is for prigs!"

"I have a great reason to hate reverence," says one of my friendly critics. "It almost ruined my life. When I was a child, older people kept trying to shut down my mind by throwing a blanket of reverence over it. It was as if they were fighting a fire. Reverence is for prigs. If you invite them to bring reverence storming back into our lives, won't it throttle laughter, subdue humor, make irony straight? Besides, reverence is like patriotism. Scoundrels appeal to it—people who use the language of virtue to talk others into submission. And then there's all that about how you dress. Philosophers ever since Socrates have dressed comfortably, thank you. They don't show respect by wearing starched shirts and shoes that hurt their feet. Fashions can be really cruel, especially to women."

It is true that bad things have been done in the name of reverence or with reverence as an ally. Any virtue can be distorted and abused; no doubt Hitler would have been less successful if his people had been less courageous or, for that matter, less reverent. But courage did not belong to the Nazis any more than reverence belongs to the extreme right of the present day. No one owns reverence. It is not cruel or repressive in itself. It does not put down mockery or protect pompous fools. And most important, it cherishes freedom of inquiry. Reverence sets a higher value on the truth than on any human product that is supposed to have captured the truth.

"Who needs reverence, anyway?"

"All right, maybe I should try to stop hating reverence. But I can't see why we need it. It's superfluous. If there is any moral content to reverence, that is covered equally well by other virtues, such as justice and wisdom." This objection goes back to Plato, who declared reverence to be a mere part of justice and then left it off his lists of virtues in later works. Suppose, as many believed, that reverence is service to the gods. But then what service do the gods want or need? If the gods have the sort of wicked goals we read about in ancient myth, then serving those goals could hardly be a virtue. But suppose the goal of the gods is justice; in that case, serving the gods would be a good thing to do, but the moral content of that service is entirely due to justice. Reverence on this theory would be like patriotism again. Patriotism is a virtue when your country follows justice, otherwise not. And if it is good, that's because it belongs to justice, not because it belongs to your country. We shall see, however, that justice does not suffice for a healthy society. Justice can be arrogant, rough, and heedless; without reverence justice can tear people apart.

"But rituals are meaningless!"

"I agree that justice is not enough. But why bring back reverence, of all things? You yourself admit that reverence is mainly expressed in rituals or ceremonies, and those things are always perfunctory. People just go through the motions. Sure, those rituals may mean something to the folks who perform them, but really they're just a spectacle for tourists. If reverence is tied to ceremony, it can't have any value that could run across cultures. So let's keep talking about justice. It may not be all we need, but at least we have some hope of finding universal principles of justice. Leave reverence to those people who are still bogged down in tradition."

My critic thinks that rituals belong only to primitive societies or in the more primitive churches that he avoids—though he would never use the word "primitive" in cultivated society. He's not aware that his own society is riddled with rituals. Just as we scarcely know, from breath to breath, that it is air we are breathing, so we are unaware of the ceremony that attends our common lives. Ceremony does not need to be perfunctory; reverent ceremony in any culture is performed with feeling. And the feelings are often universal: there is grief and reverence in the face of death wherever there is a funeral, and there are funerals wherever there are human beings.

Modern antipathy to ceremony has prevented our coming to a full understanding of the classical Chinese tradition. Wherever ceremony is practiced, there will be people who go through the motions, and some will say that going through the motions is all that is required. But that is not the burden of classical Confucianism, though you might miss the point from most translations. In translations of the *Analects,* reverence comes across as something like "ritual," which is not recognizably a virtue at all. Consider this famous passage from the *Analects* of Confucius:

> The Master said, "Without *Li,* respectfulness becomes a laborious bustle; without *Li,* carefulness becomes timidity; without *Li,* courage becomes insubordination; without *Li,* frankness becomes rudeness." (*Analects* 8.2.1)

Going through the motions of empty rituals could not make the difference between tiresome courtesy and the real thing. To translate *Li* as "rituals," in view of the way most moderns understand the word, would be like translating a sewing manual as instructing its readers to run thread through the eye of a garden hoe. *Li* does involve ritual, but Confucius insists again and again that there is more to it. What has been lost in all the standard translations is the reverence that has to be in the minds of those who practice *Li.* Reverence lends ceremony the feelings that make ceremony worthwhile.

"Reverence is only about feelings"

"Feelings!" exclaims my critic. "Feelings are too messy to define. If reverence is about feelings, there's no way you can talk about it with the precision that philosophy demands. And besides, feelings are too hard to control. Feelings just come over us, but ethical theory is supposed to deal with choices we can make. Philosophers should take justice and integrity as standard virtues, because these can be understood in terms of rules. Reverence defies conversion into rule-based ethics; there is no rule about the feeling that should go with courteous behavior, or how much one should grieve at a funeral, or how genuine must be the respect one shows to a superior. Why don't you leave this subject to psychology?"

Yes, I agree, feelings are hard to write about, and yet they are what move us best: We hardly ever do something well if we do not feel like doing it. That is one reason why reverence is important. Unlike rules, virtues put our feelings in tune, and well-tuned feelings give us strength to live well and avoid bad choices. Reverence, for example, gives us the ability to shudder at going wrong. When it fails, as it does all too often, people in power forget how to be ashamed. A world leader may feel himself invulnerable and so desecrate his office with a tawdry affair. A captain of industry may feel herself outside the law and so seek to destroy competition by any means that come to hand. The head of a nation may feel that he is right to destroy a people in his territory who lack the strength to save themselves. The leader of a religious sect may claim that she speaks with the full authority of the one true God. These people do not shudder at doing what they do or at claiming what they claim. But if reverence were at work in them, they could not bear to be as they are.

And so, for all these reasons and more, reverence has been fading out of our conscious lives. We have not lost our capacity for reverence. The capacity for virtue belongs to all of us as human beings. What we are losing is a language of behavior—a self-conscious sort of ceremony—that best expresses reverence in daily life; and, along with self-conscious ceremony, we are losing many of the occasions on which people used to find ways to be reverent. Still, all is not lost. We are aware of reverence in our daily lives more often than we know how to put a name to it. The falcon hears the falconer for a moment, glides round on steady wings, and does not know what it has heard.

His interests were entirely academic;
He wouldn't ever use a word he didn't need,
And what he said was reverent and precise,
Brief, to the point, and high-toned.
Moral virtue reverberated in his speech,
And gladly would he learn and gladly teach.

Chaucer's description of an Oxford
scholar, Prologue to the *Canterbury
Tales (Woodruff translation)*

3 | MUSIC AND A FUNERAL

Finding Reverence

Chaucer's scholar is a prig. He has set himself against the world of work and play; all he wants to do is study and lecture to others on virtues. Is he reverent? Perhaps. But he is not the model of reverence for us. You do not have to be a prig to be reverent. Reverence and sex are not enemies.

In "High Windows," the poet Philip Larkin writes of a young couple recently liberated by the sexual revolution of the sixties. He asks whether they have found a paradise, and starts to show that this is a paradise in imagination only. But then, suddenly, in place of the expected irony, the poet sends us "the thought of high windows"—a moment of inarticulate awe. Whatever does the poet mean? What has Larkin seen or thought that inspires awe? Perhaps he is impressed by the repetition of desire and frustration that is the lot of human beings. Or perhaps he remembers that although we are all destined to large dreams of endless happiness, we are all doomed to die. And this remembrance would be sharpened by the thought of God He who is, or perhaps is not, endlessly beyond those high windows. These windows—do they light up a church? We don't know. There is no thought of color in the windows, no stained-glass images of God or prophet. The poet's thought is without faith, without memory of cross or altar. More to the point, the thought bears no reference to himself. In the face of the infinite whatever beyond the windows, his own thinking personhood drops away. Faithless, alone, at the boundary where his dream of happiness clashes with an immense reality or an immense nothing, he feels awe, and for this moment he knows reverence.

Is it strange to find reverence in a poem about sexual revolution? Not really. Every aspect of human life gives occasion for reverence. The obvious place to look for reverence is organized worship, but the argument of this book is that worship is not central to reverence. Members of a modern society do not all worship together, and some do not worship at all, so we need to look for reverence in surprising places. Otherwise we may truly lose the ability to bind ourselves together as a society through common virtues. Family life, education, sports, music, military training, even sex and marriage can, in the right form, be occasions for reverence.

Worship is a confusing place to look for reverence. To begin with, worship is not always reverent; even the best forms of worship may be practiced without feeling (and therefore without reverence), and some forms of worship seem downright vicious. Besides, some forms of worship put great emphasis on faith, which is quite different from reverence, and this too may confuse a seeker for reverence. Reverence is not faith, because the faithful may hold their faith with arrogance and self-satisfaction, and because the reverent may not know what to believe.

That is why this chapter looks for reverence in odd places, outside religion. If your form of worship or your faith is reverent, so much the better. You know one place to look for reverence. But you should look further, so that you can see how you might share reverence with people who do not worship with you or share your faith. You can construct your own examples of reverence, once you have a glimmer of what I am talking about. Here is mine. I have deliberately chosen an example that has nothing to do with religion. I will come back to religion at the end of the chapter.

The String Quartet

The four amateur musicians in a pool of light have reached the last note of Mozart's "Dissonant" quartet, and they have done so more or less at the same time. They find contact with each other's eyes, all looking to the first violin to see how long to draw out the note. Then they fall silent for a moment, subdued by a sense of awe none of them could fully explain. They are not impressed by their own playing; all are conscious of measures counted incorrectly, of pitches missed. They know the piece, however, and they have been aware of harmonies they have not played or heard: from one perfectly resolved dissonance they can extrapolate the perfections of the piece.

Their egos as musicians were out of the picture. They have no audience to make them self-conscious; each has for a time lost the sense of being an individual with goals and values that might be at variance with those of the others. They have followed the lead of the first violin without feeling themselves to be followers, and she has led without feeling herself to be a leader. She has not been annoyed at slowing down for the barely competent cello during a hard passage, and the cello has outdone himself, drawn by her musicianship to play better than usual.

There was ceremony at the start—the chairs and music stands arranged in a certain way, respectful discussion of what to play, decision deferred to the first violin, no audible complaints about the viola's first note, and so on. There is also, plainly, a hierarchy at work. The first violin is the first violin and by happy coincidence the best musician of the four. All know roughly where they stand in this pecking order, but all are happy to be where they are, and they play without envy. And tonight, for once, no one has apologized for missing a note; no one has been conscious enough to take personal responsibility. And that is good in the context of this group effort, in which every apology breaks the spell.

What spell? They have felt awe. But at what? Not at Mozart; they have not been thinking of him either. Not at the elegant counterpoint Mozart has used; though conscious of the demands it makes on them, and the beauty that emerges from it, they are not analyzing this music as they play it. They would say, if asked, something like, "That Mozart!" or "What a lovely piece!" But those remarks, which will soon break the silence, also break the spell. They do not quite catch the mood or explain it. There really is no saying what wonderful thing it is that they feel has brushed them in their imperfect performance.

Reverence has been at work in this scene; this sort of music-making does provide an occasion for realizing the musicians' capacity for reverence. We can see in the scene as I have described it many of the features of this virtue that will occupy me in this book: (1) The musicians have been engaged, more or less harmoniously, in a project as a group; (2) their project involved ceremony; (3) they have felt themselves largely without ego; (4) they have felt themselves to be part of a clearly defined hierarchy that was painless for all of them; and (5) they have achieved in the end a shared feeling of inarticulate awe. One activity, four kinds of feelings—all become possible for these musicians at the same time and at least partly because of each other. A sense of impending awe, for example, allows the ego to slide back in the order of awareness, and that makes the hierarchy painless, so the four people become able to play as a group.

They have not played as one. Truth to tell, they have not been playing very well at all together. But they feel as if they have played as one, even though they are fully aware of their deficiencies. Had they actually played as one, I might have said that was due mainly to musicianship—to their skill as musicians—but that is not the case here, and my goal is to explain feelings, not technique. Even professionals must have the right feelings if they are to advance beyond a boring perfection of technique. To say that musicians should have certain feelings implies that they have the capacities for those feelings. Reverence, as a virtue, is primarily a capacity for having certain feelings at the right time and in the right way. In the case of the music, the root feeling was awe, and this made the rest possible. That is why I think it right to say that the virtue that was realized on this evening of quartets was reverence.

Notice a certain striking absence. I have told this story without mentioning God or faith. The first violin believes that nature itself is divine, the second violin is a Lutheran, the viola is a Jew, and the cellist is an agnostic. Yet they have been united in reverence. For this they must have something in common; in their case it is the culture of amateur chamber music, and this supports the small elements of ceremony that were essential to their evening—the unspoken rule against apologies, for example. Ceremony is like a language: You cannot simply invent it and you cannot do it all by yourself; it must be part of the texture of a shared culture. You need not believe in God to be reverent, but to develop an occasion for reverence you must share a culture with others, and this must support a degree of ceremony.

Sex could be an example; reverence ennobles sex as, I believe, every well-joined couple intuitively knows. The act of sex may reflect a hierarchy and hierarchies may be brutal: there may be one who takes and one who is taken. Even in a bed of love we may feel like animals. But nothing is brutish in a bed of reverence. There is a sense of awe that follows reverent love, and where awe is felt, the acts of love are human.

The Funeral

In the presence of death we expect ourselves and others to be reverent; the expectation feels natural, and yet the ceremonies through which we express reverence at such times take very different forms in different cultures. We have such a mix of cultures in the United States today that we face a special challenge: Death calls us to be reverent together, but we often find ourselves in groups that do not know how to do this.

The young men and women sit in clumps around the church. It is a strange place for many of them, and they are wearing strange clothes, the young men in suits bought by their parents for a wedding or a funeral or a job interview. They do not know the family of their friend from college who has died; they do not think their friend liked her family very much, and so they keep to themselves. They are from a variety of backgrounds—Christian, Jewish, Confucian, Jain, Muslim—and many of them are questioning the religious beliefs or practices of their ancestors. They do not think their friend was religious. For some of them, this is their first funeral. They take part in hymns, prayers, and a few formal silences. They hear a sermon about faith and salvation, applied meticulously to the case at hand. When all is over, they will remember this most clearly: The one personal thing anyone said about their friend was about her faith, and it was not true.

Reverence should leave no gap between generations, but there is no reverence among these students on this adult occasion—only sorrow and the sense of alienation they think they shared with their friend before she died. This ceremony has been empty for them; rather than bringing them together with the other mourners, it has been a barrier. A few days later, they will mount their own ceremony in their own place on the campus. They will talk about their friend, they will tell the truth as they remember it, they will share sorrow and silences, and this will be for them an occasion of reverence. Together, they will be conscious of the fragility of their own lives, and perhaps they will feel a sense of awe, like Philip Larkin's, at the immensity of a reality that does not conform to human wishes, the reality of death.

Why could they not be reverent when faith was in the air? And how can they now be reverent without faith? Is their reverence an illusion? Or is it a symptom of a submerged faith they are not prepared to admit? If there is true reverence here, it must be reverence without faith. These students belong to their era; they are Americans of many backgrounds and there is no faith that they share. They do not even have a set of different faiths in the sense that Christians have faith. They have religious traditions, some of which involve faith, and some of which do not. Many of them are questioning their traditions; others come from parents who turned away from ancestral religion, and some of these young people are trying to find their way back.

Yet they have, on the memorial occasion they put together for themselves, been reverent together. How can they have done this?

Reverence Across Cultures

My reverent students have few religious beliefs in common. They do not all believe in God; some believe in more than one divinity, and some believe in divine powers that are not all benevolent by human standards. But some shadow of belief appears to be universal among those who practice reverence; it is the idea that human beings are weak and fragile by comparison with whatever ideals they have of power or longevity or moral perfection. Philip Larkin, in the poem discussed at the start of the chapter, leaves open the question of God; what he does not leave in question is the puniness of human beings: his dream of happiness, like that of the young people whose freedom he envies, clashes with something immense and resistant to human will. Whether it is an immense reality or an immense nothing makes no difference. Either way, it is the largest context the poet can imagine, and it inspires in him awe and the sense that he belongs to a race that is puny, vulnerable, and easily self-deceived.

You might reply that there could be no true reverence without belief in the Christian God; you would, in effect, be declaring that there was no true reverence in pagan Greece or ancient China—only something deceptively like reverence. If you are right, then reverence is not a cardinal virtue. No one would insist that a cardinal virtue like courage is to be found only among Christian believers; why should reverence be a different case? Much hangs on the definition of reverence. Suppose reverence is primarily a matter of belief. If so, when we use the word "true" of reverence, we would be transferring it from the associated beliefs, and reverence would be true if and only if its defining beliefs are true. Then we would have to insist, for example, that Unitarians and Presbyterians cannot both be reverent. Their two beliefs about the nature of God are contrary—that is, they cannot both be true—and it follows that one of the two religions is false and cannot be reverent—if, that is, the truth of reverence is tied to the truth of belief. But both groups claim to be reverent. How can we adjudicate their claims? If reverence required specific beliefs, then only God—who should know whether or not He is a Trinity—would be able to make a final judgment as to who is reverent and who is not.

Suppose, on the other hand, that reverence is to be defined as a capacity for certain feelings—the central hypothesis of this book. When we say that reverence is true or false, I think we mean that the feelings that flow from reverence may be sincere or faked. Perhaps you wanted to object when I drew the inference in the preceding paragraph that Unitarians and Presbyterians are not both reverent. If you did, that shows you probably do accept the view that reverence is about feelings; you may have known believers in both camps who are sincere in their reverence, and though you cannot agree with both doctrines—because they cannot both be true—you do not wish to deny the claims of both to have genuine and deeply felt religious feelings.

I may call your reverence true even when I am sure that your beliefs are false. By means of this distinction between belief and feeling we can avoid the trap of relativism and still appreciate a sort of truth in many clashing religious traditions—the truth of genuine feeling. Christian and non-Christian beliefs cannot be equally true, but the associated feelings of reverence may be equally sincere. This result is fortunate for my grieving students. If I ask them whether they agree that Christian belief is true, they will break out into disagreement. But they all want the ceremony to express feelings that are true—that are sincere, deeply felt, and really belong to them—unlike the feelings they thought the official funeral was asking them to fake.

At this moment of grief, the students want to share something with each other. Do they want to share each other's beliefs? Certainly not. They want to share real feelings, their affection for their lost friend, their grief at her loss, their gratitude for having known her. And they want to do this in a way that will allow them to begin the next day without these feelings hanging over them. I would say that they want the closure that only ceremony provides. Their ceremony is stripped to the bare essentials: They speak in turn, they include everyone, they take food together, no more. But it is enough. Their ceremony has the kind of meaning for them that can come only from reverence.

How can we conceive of reverence as a virtue this group may practice together? What may become of reverence in a society that cannot share a faith? These students are at a pivotal point in the history of reverence—indeed, in the history of cultures—but their experience is not entirely unique. Something like this has happened before. Religions have faded, religions have been displaced by violence, religions have fractured; but ceremony and reverence live on. Ceremony is older than any surviving religion, and wherever there has been ceremony, there has been a way of taking ceremony seriously, and that requires reverence.

There was reverence before the birth of the great modern religions that divide my students from each other and from their elders. What was that early form of reverence? "What it always has been," I would like to say. If reverence is a cardinal virtue, we should be able to define it—as I believe we can define courage—apart from its many expressions in human culture. Can reverence be defined in this way? Is there such a thing as "bare reverence" that can be detached in theory from particular beliefs and practices? That is one of the central questions of this book.

Whenever they gathered into groups, [early human beings] would do wrong to each other, because they did not yet have the knowledge of how to form society. As a result they would scatter again and perish. And so Zeus, fearing that our whole species would be wiped out, sent Hermes to bring Reverence and Justice to human beings, in order that these two would adorn society and bind people together in friendship.

—*Protagoras in Plato's* Protagoras *322c*

4 | BARE REVERENCE

The center will not hold unless virtue is among us. The ancient Greeks knew that very well. They disagreed among themselves, however, over where virtue comes from. Is it learned or inherited? Is it natural—is it, in mythological terms, a gift of the gods? Does it belong to the aristocracy alone or the people in general? Can anyone acquire virtue? And if so, how? A broad consensus in ancient Greece (as in ancient China) held that all humans have a natural capacity for virtue, but that this capacity must be developed by teaching and may therefore be developed differently in different people. According to Plato, Protagoras held such a view.

Protagoras invented a myth in which the highest god gave reverence and justice to human beings as means for their survival, which depended on their ability to live in society. Reverence and justice supplement an earlier gift of fire and technology, which Prometheus stole for us from the gods, hoping that they would keep our species alive. But Zeus saw that technology alone, without virtue, is no defense against mutual destruction.

The gift of technology is divided among specialists: Some are doctors, some are shoemakers, some are housebuilders, and so on. Would it make sense to give reverence and justice to a handful of specialists—priests and judges, perhaps—and let everyone else practice their trades of law or medicine or farming without those virtues? Surely not. Zeus instructs Hermes to give reverence and justice to everyone.

The story comes as a surprise from Protagoras, because we know that he said he was an agnostic. Why should he, of all people, tell a story about Zeus? We shall see that he is not alone among humanists who support reverence. But why should Protagoras of all people say that reverence is part of the package Zeus gives to us? Later philosophers thought that justice was the foundation of society. Why add reverence? Why insist that the foundation of society is justice *and* reverence?

Protagoras understands what poets have been teaching since Homer: That justice is not enough. In the *Iliad*, Agamemnon has the right to take Achilles' prize away from him—no violation of justice there. But when Agamemnon insults Achilles by taking the prize, he divides his army, with disastrous results. His failure is a failure of reverence.

Protagoras seems an odd source for this story for another reason: He is a teacher who believes that he and a few others are able to teach reverence and justice. But if these virtues are a gift of Zeus, why go to a teacher for them? If Zeus gives us reverence, then reverence should be ours by our god-given nature. But if it is ours by nature, why should we need a teacher? Culture is one thing, and nature is another; culture is invented and taught and learned by human beings, while nature is inherited at birth—or so we would like to think.

Protagoras' myth will not allow so simple a distinction. In fact, the development of cultures is natural for human beings. Invention, teaching, and learning are our natural tools of survival; they are as natural and as important to the survival of our species as claws are to a lion or fertility is to a rabbit. There is this striking difference, however: All lions have pretty much the same sorts of claws whether they like them or not, and rabbits cannot help having the same remarkable fertility. Human beings, by contrast, invent different ways of surviving and different kinds of ceremonies to foster their sense of community. Technology looks different in different cultures, and so does virtue—especially reverence.

Protagoras says, however, that Zeus sends the same reverence to all people, and as a Greek of his time he must understand this to imply that Zeus gave the same reverence to all cultures. Some individuals, he admits, will have more reverence than others, and the same should go for societies. But all societies must have some reverence or be hopelessly vulnerable to becoming unraveled. Protagoras knows that foreigners have different customs than Greeks do regarding the dead, but he cannot overlook the fact that both groups have funeral customs and care about them deeply. He must mean that all human beings have a natural capacity for reverence, and that they must develop this capacity in their own cultures by invention and teaching. Of course this means that different people will invent different ways of being reverent. But then how could there be one thing that is reverence? How, in other words, could this book—the one I am writing now—have a coherent subject?

My subject is what Protagoras meant by the gift of Zeus to all human beings—reverence as an ideal that rises above cultural difference. My job is to show that we can talk usefully about bare reverence—not reverence as it has been practiced in this or that traditional society, but reverence as dreamers anywhere could try to foster it in hopes of improving the quality of their lives. Yes, this is an abstract idea, and it will be difficult to discuss—but no more difficult in principle than justice or courage or integrity, and we frequently try to consider those values outside any one cultural context.

The justice that philosophers seek to describe as a goal, for themselves or for the world, is not the justice provided in ancient Athens, or in T'ang Dynasty China, or in eighteenth-century Philadelphia. When modern philosophers seek to understand justice, they are doing the same thing that seekers were doing in those times and those places—seeking to translate a bare ideal into practice, which is pretty much the same ideal in each culture. So it is with reverence.

As a philosopher, then, I will try to present a sketch of reverence laid bare, the single core of the many conceptions of reverence that are found in the human world. I will illustrate this sketch from actual cultures, however, both ancient and modern, making special use of ancient Greece and ancient China. Because Greece and China were distant from each other, so distant as to be totally out of communication in ancient times, we would not expect their cultures to have much in common. But on the topic of reverence they show considerable overlap. This should not be surprising. Both cultures celebrate reverence in the belief that it is reverence above all that maintains social order and harmony, both cultures have a horror of civil war, and both are contending against the same human enemies of harmony—ambition, greed, fear, pride, and bad judgment. The ancient Greeks and the ancient Chinese were, in effect, trying to solve the same human equation. No wonder they arrived at similar solutions. If today, in the pride of modern thinking, we arrive at solutions that are quite different from theirs, we should ask ourselves how we know that our solutions are better. And if we cannot answer that question, we should take thought: we may have something to learn from the ancients.

Before I turn to the history of ideas, however, I need to sketch carefully the limits of the idea I am tracing back to its sources. How, in the abstract, do I understand the bare gift of Zeus? To answer this, I will work from a general theory of virtue that derives partly from the Greek thinker Aristotle and partly from ancient China. Most of what I say here is parallel to what should be said of any other virtue—courage, for example. My aim in this sketch is to provide answers to basic questions about how I am defining my subject. This is a preliminary sketch, an answer to the question, "What sort of thing is reverence?" Once we are clear on that, we can proceed to ask what it truly requires of us.

A Philosopher's Questions

Can I give a complete account of reverence?

No. A virtue helps you feel like doing what is right. To give a complete description of a virtue such as reverence, I would have to figure out everything that is right that might fall into the province of reverence. I cannot do that. Suppose I give an account of reverence and then discover that some horrible things would be reverent according to my account. Then, because a virtue can't lead you astray and still be a virtue, I would have to go back and revise that account. Nothing I say will be the last word on reverence. A philosopher would say that definitions of virtue remain defeasible.

What is a virtue?

The person you love is beautiful in your eyes. Of course. Now imagine that age or disease has taken away every trace of physical beauty—the strength, the symmetry, the delicate coloration of the skin—but you are still in love. Then ask this question: What beauty remains? Personality, a sense of humor, and above all, character—these can be beautiful. Beauty of character is what the ancient philosophers meant by virtue.

Plato presents a scene in which Socrates is introduced to a youth who has a body of breathtaking beauty, which would be fully apparent if he would shed his clothes. Socrates impishly suggests that if the boy could only shed his body they would know whether or not he is truly beautiful. Socrates then sounds the boy's character by asking his famous questions.

A virtue is the capacity to have certain feelings and emotions when this capacity has been cultivated through training and experience in such a way that it inclines those who have it to doing the right thing. Emotions affect action; they are motivators. Fear makes you feel like running away, anger makes you feel like lashing out, grief makes you feel like crying. A virtue is a capacity, cultivated by experience and training, to have emotions that make you feel like doing good things. Take courage, for example: insofar as you have courage, you are able to feel the right sorts of confidence and fear—the sorts of emotion that move you to do whatever is courageous.

Does a virtue provide moral rules?

Not exactly. The more virtue we have, the less we will need to think about rules. This is helpful, because we sometimes find it hard to feel like following a rule, but it always feels natural to act in accordance with a virtue—if we truly have that virtue. Virtue-talk has been revived in recent years, but it runs against the grain of modern ethics, which is mostly about doing what is right whether you feel like it or not. By contrast, virtue is about cultivating feelings that will lead you in the right way whether you know the rule in a given case or not. Rules are hard to apply and hard to follow. Feelings, on the other hand, are easy to follow and hard to resist. That's why, from the standpoint of moral education, virtue is best.

Laying down rules may give good results in many cases, but we cannot be sure that people who follow rules are doing so for the right reason. If they are not, then we cannot be sure they will do so in future. That is why we should not praise a person's character merely for following rules. What is the right reason for following a rule? Some thinkers (following Kant) would say that this depends on knowing the rules in a certain way; others (following Aristotle and Plato) would say that it depends on being a certain kind of person—in other words, it depends on having virtue.

Do virtues replace rules?

No. A complete ethical theory will talk about rules and rights and duties. This book, however, concerns virtue, and one virtue in particular. But rules cannot replace virtues, because virtues are self-motivating, and rules are not.

What sort of virtue is reverence?

As I said in the beginning, reverence is the capacity for a range of feelings and emotions that are linked; it is a sense that there is something larger than a human being, accompanied by capacities for awe, respect, and shame; it is often expressed in, and reinforced by, ceremony.

Why is reverence a capacity for three types of feelings rather than one?

These three are associated with reverence in both ancient Greek and ancient Chinese traditions, and they all belong to the affective side of what we might call "knowing your place" as a human being. We feel awe for what we believe is above us all as human beings, and this feeling helps us to avoid treating other human beings with contempt (chapters five and six). Shame is more complicated. Without reverence, we may feel shame as the pain of being exposed to other people for having violated community standards—and this is not a virtuous response, because it may have nothing to do with right and wrong. But when reverence is in play, we feel shame when exposed in our own minds to shortcomings vis-à-vis the ideals toward which we stand in awe, and this reaction does belong to virtue (see chapter eleven, "The Reverent Leader").

Could reverence replace other virtues?

No. Reverence is not enough by itself for a completely good character. You will need to develop other capacities in order to live a morally good life. But you may find that reverence is necessary—as is courage—to the regular exercise of all other virtues. Obviously, it can take courage to stand up for justice. Does it take reverence to be courageous? I think so. One of the differences between courage and fearlessness is that courageous people would be ashamed and therefore afraid of doing wrong because of the respect they feel for moral ideals. Their capacities for shame and respect grow from reverence.

What is the difference between reverence and ceremony?

When ceremony is empty of reverence, it loses its point and becomes mere ritual; but reverence never loses its point. Most cultures that reflect on their own ceremonies recognize the danger of performing ceremony with the wrong attitude or with no attitude at all. Reverence helps supply the right attitude for ceremony. Ceremony supplies one way of expressing reverence. There are others, such as Larkin's poem.

What is the difference between reverence and faith?

Faith is not a virtue; it is either a specific creed or a specific relationship between a believer and God. Reverence has little to do with belief except insofar as belief is entailed by the emotions of awe, respect, and shame. I will enlarge on this issue in chapter seven.

Is reverence supposed to take the place of faith or belief?

Not at all. Anyone who shows reverence will have beliefs associated with reverence, and some of these beliefs will be religious. Nietzsche says that European Christian culture shows its greatest nobility in reverence for the Bible. But people may have different beliefs and still be reverent. I am detaching reverence from belief because I am in search of an account of reverence that is as neutral with respect to cultural differences.

Take away belief, and what is there for anyone to be reverent to?

Reverence is the capacity for a related set of feelings and emotions. Each has a different object: respect is for other people, shame is over one's own shortcomings, and awe is usually felt toward something transcendent. Respect and shame are clear cases of emotions, according to the theory I am using here, and they are associated with beliefs about distinct objects—respect for your child follows beliefs you have about her (that she is human, for example); shame over a lie would follow your belief that you told a miserable whopper yesterday. Awe is a little different, because its objects are usually transcendent, and we do not know them as well as we know our children or our misdemeanors. You may feel awe in the face of the power of nature, without having clear ideas about what that is. I classify awe as a feeling rather than an emotion, because it tends to have objects that are not distinct and may occur in the absence of articulate belief. When we experience awe, we usually do not know how to say what we are in awe of. (The Larkin poem discussed in chapter three expresses awe without being reverent toward anything in particular.)

The principal object of reverence is Something that reminds us of human limitations. We speak of reverence to God, to nature, and to ideals such as justice and truth. Reverence toward objects like these yields primarily what I have called awe and it is usually inarticulate. A scientist who is reverent toward the truth is reverent in seeking the truth. Her very reverence makes her cautious; it prevents her from saying that she knows exactly what the truth is and keeps her mind open to evidence that should make her adjust her theory. To say that I am reverent toward X does not imply that I think X is spooky (the truth is not spooky to a scientist); but a claim of reverence does imply that I recognize that X is not entirely under my control, that I think X is what it is no matter what I do or believe, and that I accept a degree of mystery about X which I am trying to penetrate (see chapter seven, "Reverence Without a Creed," on the object of reverence).

Will reverence go equally well with any religion?

No. Reverence is not neutral with respect to religion, nor is any other virtue. If there is a religion that neglects or downgrades justice, then worshippers who learn to promote justice must fall away from that religion or else try to reform it. I will say the same of reverence. Some religions place a high value on reverence, and some do not. Because reverence is not the same thing as faith, faith-centered religion may place a low value on reverence, exactly as some faith-centered religion places a relatively low value on justice.

What is the difference between reverence and respect?

The main difference between reverence and respect is this: You can have too much respect, and you can have respect for the wrong things.

It is wrong to respect false judgments or vicious people. But if reverence is a virtue, it can never require of you anything that is wrong. So reverence does not require respect for just anything, and reverent people will feel contempt for whatever deserves contempt. Reverence includes the power to feel the right degree of respect in each case. Go back to the example of courage. What is the difference between courage and confidence? You can have too much confidence, but you can never have too much courage, because courage is, among other things, the power to feel confidence when you should and not when you should not (for more on respect, see chapter eleven, "The Reverent Leader").

One more difference: reverence entails a capacity for respect (among other things). Respect is something you feel. Reverence (as I am using the word) is the capacity to have feelings. It is not simply a feeling in itself.

What is the difference between reverence and humility?

Reverence is not humility. The opposite of reverence is hubris—which is always a bad thing—but the opposite of humility is pride, and pride can be a good thing. The reverent soul has much to be proud of, and should be proud. Leaders should be proud of their teams and of their missions. Humility smacks of obedience to authority, sometimes even of obsequiousness. But a reverent soul can stand up to authority and is never obsequious. Humility in a person with authority is usually a fraud, and the reverent soul does not stoop to fraud.

Does reverence carry compassion?

Yes. Reverence means keeping in mind that we share human weakness and vulnerability with other people. Compassion grows from a sense of common weakness. Reverent people, seeing someone suffer, are aware that they could suffer in the same way. Compassion understood in this way is compatible with justice. (See chapter twelve, "Compassion.")

Does reverence belong to religion?

No. If you have reverence, you may exercise it in religion, but you may also exercise it in politics, in the classroom, on the battlefield, or wherever you have moral choices to make. You may be fair-minded or courageous without being religious, and you may be religious without being fair-minded or courageous. It is the same with reverence: Reverence and religiousness overlap, but they do not entail one another. Even an atheist or a non-theist may be reverent.

But don't Christians and Jews, for example, have different kinds of reverence?

Not if reverence is a virtue such as courage. If courage is what we think it is, then Jewish courage is no different in kind from Christian or Buddhist courage; indeed, we would be silly to call it by such names. Courage is courage, regardless of the religion of those who display it. Reverence is the same; it straddles boundaries between religions and bridges the gap between religious and secular life.

Religions may come into conflict over points in theology, forms of worship, or specific ethical rules. They may disagree over the relative importance of justice and faith, and they may quarrel over exactly what justice requires or how it should be administered. Still, religious people should be able to recognize that the justice they are trying to foster in their own minds is the same sort of thing as the justice they recognize (or find missing) in people who belong to religions other than their own. They should find the same true of reverence, if reverence is a virtue.

My claim that virtues straddle cultures and religions should be controversial; many philosophers and social scientists will reject it. Most elements of the controversy are not germane to this small book. My argument for the claim is simple—it is the book itself. If the book can give its readers a fairly clear sense of what reverence is without bowing to the demands of this or that religion, then it will have made a case for my thesis.

Reverence has to be toward something. Does it make a difference what people are reverent toward?

Yes, but not as much as you might expect. Reverence in polytheism is still recognizably reverence, even if it is directed at gods who are thought to be evil. The chief limitation on reverence as a virtue is this: it must have an object that is not a slave to human interests, and that is not held to be a mere product of culture. Why? This is a complicated matter. (See chapter seven, "Reverence Without a Creed".)

Can there be reverence for evil?

Several modern religions, along with many ancient ones, practice reverence toward gods who are capable of evil—or so it is believed. If the divine is not capable of evil, these believers would ask, where does evil come from into our world? That is a hard question. One common answer—and a very reverent one—is that we human beings do not know enough to judge whether the actions of divine beings are good or evil. In any case, we would be wrong to withhold reverence from what we feel to be divine simply because we do not find that it measures up to our human standards of goodness.

In any case, reverence in religion supplies a strong sense of distance between human and divine, and reverent people think it foolish to try to take on divine attributes. For this reason, reverence toward evil gods does not put people into danger of becoming evil. Religion that is centered on reverence is not afraid to face the idea that the divine may seem evil in human terms.

Can reverence be abused?

Any virtue can be abused. Tyrants can exploit the courage and reverence and even the justice of their peoples. We have seen this in our own time; vicious rulers in both European and Confucian cultures have taken advantage of their people's habits of respect—habits bred in reverence. Savage commanders exploit the courage of their troops. Honesty among friends is prohibitively dangerous when the friends are likely to be reporting to the secret police. To say that virtues are always good, then, is overly simple. They are never bad in themselves, but they can lead to trouble in a bad context. People pay a high price for clinging to virtue when they find themselves in a vicious system, and so one of the classical goals of statecraft is to build a system in which virtue may safely flourish—so that one may call for virtue without demanding enormous sacrifices. Also, most people's virtues are not complete, and partial virtues may be very bad indeed. Soldiers may follow a vicious leader into danger and be party to a terrible crime. In doing this they may show some measure of courage. But soldiers who had a full measure of courage would not be party to a crime; they would instead join the resistance against the vicious leader.

Is reverence good all the time? What about reverence for tradition?

The virtue of reverence is good in itself, if it is a virtue, but since we do not always know what it is to be reverent, we are liable to use the word "reverence" for something that is bad, such as rigid adherence to tradition (see chapter nine, "Relativism"). Virtues are notoriously hard to define, and we are often taken in by what I call "imposter virtues"—ideas that can make us feel good about doing bad things. Clinging to tradition is not reverence; it is an especially harmful imposter, masquerading as reverence.

Many people think that clinging to tradition is simply what reverence is, but virtue ethics does not ask what it is that many people think. It asks how we may best live our lives. People's opinions are helpful in this inquiry, but they cannot be the final arbiter. How could they be, when opinions vary so widely? If reverence meant following tradition no matter what, then it would be no better than the tradition in question, good on some points and bad on others. So clinging to tradition cannot be a virtue, and if it cannot be a virtue, it cannot be reverence. It is an imposter. There is a reverent way of respecting tradition, even after it has been abandoned, and that is to treat it as one might a glorious building from antiquity. The Parthenon in Athens is worth preserving as a monument to the past, but no one should live in it, and it would seem irreverent to renovate it in ways that could make it habitable. There is also a reverent way of respecting a tradition while it is still alive. If we are going to live in a tradition and not abandon it, we must respect it enough to maintain it through renovation and not preserve it as a monument. And this does not transgress the line between human and divine, as clinging to tradition does, if it mistakes human customs for the will of God.

How can we tell virtues from imposters?

It's not easy. Ethics is not an easy subject. The short answer is that virtuous people will steer away from imposter virtues, whether they can fully account for their choices or not. The long answer is that we would be wise to consider the imposter virtues that are easily identified; if we do so, then we can aim to avoid whatever closely resembles them. The catch is that imposter virtues resemble real ones fairly closely. That is why they are so tempting.

Courage looks a lot like the ability to take great risks without hesitation, but an addict who pumps heroin from an unknown source into her veins is taking a great risk without hesitation, and she is not courageous. She is oblivious to risk, owing to her addiction, but if she feels a moment's satisfaction at the thought of her own courage, she is being taken in by an imposter virtue—and so are her more timid friends if they admire her. False courage may come from a bottle or a vial or a box of pills, but real courage is not blind to danger. Real courage has a clear mind; it makes distinctions between one sort of danger and another. Imposter virtues generally cloud the mind; that is why they are dangerous.

Narrow adherence to tradition is like narrow patriotism ("my country right or wrong"), which is good if your country is well led, bad if your country is poorly led. The analogy is helpful, because narrow patriotism is plainly an imposter; in the previous century, we have often seen that narrow patriotism allows people to think well of themselves while committing the greatest atrocities. Patriotism on behalf of the Third Reich was no virtue. But true patriotism was possible even then; it led to brave acts of resistance to policies that were a disgrace to Germany. Narrow adherence to tradition and narrow patriotism go wrong in the same way, by offering us what appear to be morally valid excuses for suspending our own moral judgment or closing the lid on our own moral compasses. And false courage does the same: if you are drunk or addicted you cannot think or feel as you otherwise would.

So good advice for avoiding imposter virtues is this: Never accept as a virtue any condition that clouds the mind.

If true reverence is not for tradition, must it be secular or humanist?

No. Tradition is not God. Reverence flourishes in religions that understand the difference.

Does reverence stand in the way of humor and mockery?

No. Mockery serves reverence in two ways: by reminding stuffed shirts about their imperfections, and by awakening a sense of shame in people who have allowed theirs to lie dormant.

Can there be shame without reverence?

No. You cannot feel shame without feeling respect for something larger than yourself—family, society, or moral ideals. And reverence is the source of your capacity to feel that there is something like this that you should respect.

What good is shame?

Shame is not a bad feeling. Like most emotions, shame can be good or bad depending on the circumstances; shame in particular can move us powerfully to make sacrifices. (Only love, I think, rivals the power that shame has over us for good or ill.) Athletes may win out over pain in order to escape the shame of defeat, soldiers may risk their lives to escape the shame of leaving a comrade to the mercy of their enemy, a lonely hero may tell a hard truth so that she can avoid the shame of facing her conscience with a lie. Most of this is good, but, like respect, shame can go terribly wrong: in the *Iliad*, Homer tells how Hector lost his life, and the war, because he was ashamed to face his troops after a minor defeat.

Virtues are capacities for having feelings in good ways. Insofar as you have courage, you will feel confidence only when that is a good way to feel. In the same way, you will feel the good sort of shame insofar as you are reverent.

Shame is different from guilt. Perhaps we would be better off if we could live without feelings of guilt; but feelings of shame, and the fear of shame, push us to live better and be better people. Life without shame would be a disaster.

How can I become reverent?

By doing reverent things, just as you become courageous by doing courageous things, or fair-minded by doing what is fair. But, then, how to start? It seems you must *be* reverent in order to start *becoming* reverent. But that would be impossible.

There is a similar chicken-and-egg problem for any virtue. The ancient Chinese took the issue very seriously. The prevailing trend in Confucian philosophy, developed by Mencius, was to suppose that every human being is endowed with the seeds of virtue. I think that is what Protagoras had in mind when he said that Zeus gave us justice and reverence. On both views we are born with capacities that we may or may not develop in good ways.

So a better question to ask would be, "How can I become *more* reverent?" And the answer is, "By looking to see what you are already doing that is reverent, and doing more things that are like that."

How can I tell whether an action is reverent?

By the feelings from which it springs. This is not easy. You can do things that look brave without actually being brave. Suppose you fight hard merely because you want your friends to think that you are brave. That is not bravery. In the same way, if you act respectfully in order to make a good impression on your boss, you are doing something that looks respectful. But an action is truly respectful only if it proceeds from a feeling of respect.

Even if you know that you are moved by feelings of respect, however, you still do not know that this feeling springs from the virtue of reverence. For this you need to look at a wide pattern of your feelings: Do you feel and show respect for your underlings as well as for your boss? If not, your respect has nothing to do with reverence. This makes the chicken-egg problem all the harder. You need to know where your actions and emotions are coming from before you can know yourself well enough to cultivate a virtue. This is one reason why the ancient Greeks cared so much about the command they believed came from Apollo—"Know thyself."

Why should I be reverent?

If you ask this question and really think you need to know the answer, you are a hopeless case. You are like a cellist who sets out to play the Bach suites, stops suddenly, and asks, "Why should I try to play the right notes?" Or a mathematician who pauses in the middle of a proof to ask why he shouldn't slip in a few fallacies. You are a living human being, and you are living through a complex set of social practices; you cannot ask whether you should take those practices seriously without stepping outside of them. But you can't step outside a practice while you are engaged in it.

There is a tough problem for philosophers here. Most modern ethicists are looking for a theory that will provide a grounding or a foundation for ethics or morality—a rational answer to the why-be-good question. But hardly anyone who takes virtue ethics seriously, whether ancient or modern, thinks it worthwhile to wait for external foundations to be secure before setting to work on virtue.

Does reverence belong to ethics or to morals?

Not a helpful distinction: the English words derive from Greek and Latin for exactly the same thing. Some modern thinkers apply "morals" to timeless ideals and "ethics" to norms that are embedded in social practices, but they rarely say what to do if these seem to conflict. Virtue ethics generally resists the distinction, and reverence plainly cuts across it, since reverence serves timeless ideals through social practices.

Can a reverent person do evil?

Sadly, yes. A virtue may have more or less purchase on the mind, and it may be competing at times with other internal forces too powerful for it to overcome. Brave people may act in cowardly ways; fair-minded people may commit injustices. And even those who have developed the virtue of reverence to an uncommon extent may not act always in accordance with it.

Can an evil person be reverent?

Perhaps. Is there justice among thieves? Is there reverence among people who are cruel, foolish, or vengeful? This is a hard question, and not unique to reverence. Philosophers call this the problem of the unity of virtue: Can you have just one virtue and leave the rest aside? Or does the cultivation of one virtue bring other virtues along with it? We have already agreed that no virtue is a guarantee against wrongdoing. You can have a virtue and still do wrong things. But can you have a virtue along with a set of vices? I think not. Cowardice will undermine reverence or any other virtue, especially when danger threatens; cruelty and injustice are flat-out incompatible with reverence.

On the other hand, no vice is complete. Protagoras had a point: Any human being capable of working with others must have basic virtues at some level. That is why there is some justice, and even some reverence, among thieves. A perfectly vicious man would have to operate entirely on his own.

Can I show reverence in an irreverent society?

Not easily, at least not in action. "Virtue has neighbors," says Confucius (*Analects* 4.25), and virtue never works as it is supposed to work in a vacuum or in a hostile human environment. If you are a soldier, and if you are the only one in your unit who has courage, then you will not be able to give full expression to your courage in action. In fact, you may have to act in as cowardly a way as the others unless you can miraculously communicate your courage to them.

Suppose you decide to show the others what courage is, and you leap out of your foxhole alone into a firestorm. Even if you live, you will not have shown courage. Courage is not that stupid; it cannot require you to throw away your life hopelessly in an action you take by yourself.

The social factor is even more important for reverence, which typically affects the shared behavior and shared feelings of people in a group (as in my example of the musicians). It is virtually impossible to act alone in the exercise of reverence. That is because reverence uses ceremony as a kind of language of behavior, and you cannot use a language all by yourself. You must be around other language users both in order to learn a language and to use it. That is why people who seek reverence don't merely try to improve themselves—they try to involve family or church or community in the language of reverence—in shared events, in ceremony, even, perhaps, in poetry.

Writing poetry is one way you can show reverence in an irreverent society. In "High Windows," Larkin sees no reverence around him, and yet his poem finds language for reverence.

Can I act reverently toward someone who is irreverent?

Of course. I can speak correct English to someone who does not. If English is spoken in my group, there is a good chance that my ungrammatical friend will understand me, and there is a faint chance that he will follow my good example. In the same way, if there is some behavior that expresses reverence in my group, I can act reverently toward people who are irreverent—and I ought to do so. They may understand me, and they may follow my example. But our experience of bad grammar is not encouraging. Bad grammar is contagious. People admire those who are tough enough to break the rules of grammar. And they tend to admire those who break with reverence or undermine ceremony. All the more important, then, is leadership.

Why should leaders be any stronger in reverence than the rest of us?

Because even in democracy, virtue—or vice—trickles down. All virtues belong to leadership, but reverence is particularly a virtue of leaders. Both Greek and Chinese traditions bring out reverence in discussions of leadership. If leaders do not show reverence, then their followers will need to act crudely in order to be heard. A boss who is arrogant will come to a bad end, because he will not hear the opinions of other people, and so he will have no check on his natural human tendency to err—unless someone breaks through his barriers of contempt. Breaking barriers leads to habits that are fatal to reverence. But around a reverent leader there are no thick walls to crash through, and habits of mutual respect can flourish.

Is irreverence ever a virtue?

No, but many of our contemporaries would say yes. In an irreverent society, crude behavior may be highly successful. Crudeness then looks like irreverence, with the result that irreverence looks like a virtue. Not so. Both of these appearances are misleading. Protesting bad leadership is never irreverent. Irreverence is the violation of reverence, but in the neighborhood of bad leaders there is little reverence to violate.

When people praise a film or a song or a book for its irreverence, I think they almost are always using the wrong word. They mean to give praise for boldness, independence, honesty, and a boisterous contempt for anything pretentious or arrogant. All this is compatible with reverence. For extreme, but reverent, protest, think of Antigone. In Sophocles' drama, Antigone protests against her uncle, the king, who has denied burial to her brother. The unburied brother may have been wicked, but after his death he belongs to the gods, and it is gross irreverence to deprive the gods of what is their due. The Chorus in the play seems to think that Antigone's protest has gone too far; they think her enthusiasm for reverence is dangerous, and perhaps also unjust, but they recognize that she has exhibited true reverence, and they admire her for this (853–56, 872–75).

But with this example, I have passed beyond *bare* reverence. No actual example of reverence or its violation is bare in my sense, because reverence always occurs within a culture. Antigone speaks for the ancient Greek way of being reverent—one way, out of many, for remembering what it is to be human, and by that memory to play a truly human part in life's drama.

Wisdom? It's not wise
To lift our thoughts too high;
We are human and our time is short.
        —The Chorus in Euripides'
                Bacchae *395–97*

5 | ANCIENT GREECE
THE WAY OF BEING HUMAN

Remember that you are human: this is the central message of ancient Greek reverence. "How could I forget?" you ask. Very easily, especially if you are so rich, so powerful, or so successful that you push every thought of failure away from your mind—every thought of human error, madness, or death. But you will err, if you are human; you will do crazy things, no matter how hard you cling to the notion that your mind is sound; and you will die. Between now and death you will have many opportunities to crash down from whatever height you have reached, and you will fall harder if you forget that the human path is strewn with stumbling blocks.

The greatest wealth and power in the neighborhood of ancient Greece belonged to Croesus, king of Lydia. Croesus forgot. He thought he was the happiest and most fortunate of all human beings, living or dead, and he asked a visiting Greek wise man to confirm this opinion of himself. The sage was an Athenian named Solon, who was already legendary for wisdom. Solon knew the question was irreverent, because no human being could be the best in any contest for very long. He was not willing to answer the question as asked; instead, he replied with a sentence that became one of the most famous expressions of Greek wisdom: "Call no man happy until his life is over." By this he meant that a human life is too uncertain to be judged on the basis of any part of it: no one can safely claim to be living a totally successful life. The future holds surprises.

Soon after his conversation with Solon, Croesus provoked war with his mighty neighbor Persia; he was defeated and slated for execution by fire. As he perched on the great pile of wood that the Persians had set alight, Croesus remembered Solon. He gave a huge groan, and cried out Solon's name. The Persian king heard him and asked his interpreters what Croesus was saying:

> So Croesus related the story [about Solon]. And the fire, which had now been lit, was licking around the edges. When Cyrus [the Persian king] heard from his interpreters what Croesus had said, he had second thoughts and it came into his mind that he—himself a human being—was about to put another human being into the fire alive—a person who had once been no less fortunate than he had himself. Then Cyrus was afraid of having to pay for this, and he reckoned that nothing is safe in human affairs, and so he ordered the fire extinguished as quickly as possible... (Herodotus, *History* 1.86)

But the fire was already out of control. Croesus began to pray, and according to legend the god Apollo heard the prayer, sending rain to put out the fire. So Croesus was saved, and in the experience he recovered an understanding of his own humanity. So did the Persian king, who came to admire both Croesus and Solon for their wisdom.

The story teaches us a curious fact about the ancient Greek notion of reverence: that it is supposed to be universal, to transcend cultural boundaries. This surprises modern readers, especially if they know how clearly the Greeks understood the differences among human customs. Reverence is expressed in ceremony, but there are no universal human ceremonies (just as there are no universal human languages). So how could reverence be universal?

Herodotus, who tells the story of Croesus, is well aware of cultural difference, and in commenting on the variety of funeral customs, he quotes Pindar's famous line "Custom is king." Still, when he comes to the fate of Croesus, he does not ascribe it to Persian custom. Instead, he reports that the Persian king wanted to save Croesus because he was struck by the thought of their common humanity. In all the Greek stories of reverence lost and regained, humanity is at issue. You can forget your humanity in either of two ways: by taking on the airs of a god, or by acting like a beast of prey. Either way, you come back to reverence when you recover a sense of your humanity in common with others. And the others in these stories are usually people you were tempted to regard as inferior—foreigners whom you happen to have conquered, children who (in your judgment) do not know as much as you do, or just plain citizens who (you think) ought to accept your leadership without a fuss.

A reverent soul listens to other people even when they are inferior; that is a large part of remembering that you are human together with them. The king of Persia showed his reverence by listening to Croesus; Croesus showed his lack of reverence by not listening to Solon. In both episodes, reverence requires a king to listen to an inferior, and in both cases the person who is inferior is also foreign. The story I have told involves a Greek, a Lydian, and a Persian. Herodotus is not forgetting that these three have different languages and customs, because he tells us that it was a *translation* of Croesus' story that reminded Cyrus of their common humanity.

Reverence does not stop at any of the boundaries that human beings make among themselves; reverence overlooks differences of culture, social class, age, and even gender. Reverence is more democratic than Greek democracy, which was limited by age and birth and gender. Reverence calls us to be conscious of bare humanity, the humanity of our species. The ancient Greeks were very clear about this: reverence is about just being human, and *not* about a distinctly Greek or Persian way of being human.

Reverence does require adherence to custom and ceremony, but not to every ceremony (for Greek customs of reverence, see the notes to this chapter). Greek city-states had ceremonies that were peculiarly theirs, designed to celebrate citizenship in one city as opposed to another. But those are not *the* ceremonies of reverence; reverence is about being human, not about being Greek or Athenian, or about belonging to just this family.

The most important practices of reverence—burial and sacrifice—have to do with death and eating. Wild beasts feed too, and die, but (it seemed to the Greeks) without ceremony, and many ancient Greeks had a terror of falling into the ways of wild animals. Still, custom and ceremony are of small importance compared to attitudes of reverence. The ancients appear not to have cared too much about minor violations of ceremony; hardly anyone was punished for these. And if they did prosecute someone for violations of reverence, they did not accept the defense that the accused had been faithful to the rituals. Rituals, they knew well, could be empty. The great cases of irreverence—the famous cautionary tales of ancient Greece—are about feelings and thoughts gone wrong. They are, in other words, about failures of virtue—and failures of knowledge. Great heroes and leaders have a way of forgetting their human limitations, with disastrous results.

Heroic Failures of Reverence

Greek poetry thrums with great heroes who pay a price for forgetting their humanity. Common people, apparently, are less prone to failures of reverence. This should be no surprise; ordinary lives pass within the fabric of family and city, a fabric held together by constant small acts of reverence. Reverence is most obvious when it is missing, and it is missing most often in people who are—or who think they are—exceptional. Irreverent heroes put themselves above the human level sometimes, and sometimes below; they can go wrong either way. The most famous examples from poetry are in Homer's *Iliad*.

Hector wins too often

Hector is the defender of Troy, the city, the family, and civilized life in general—all of which are supposed to be preserved by reverence. But Hector wins too many battles; success goes to his head. After defeating Achilles' beloved friend Patroclus, Hector is flush with a string of victories. He rips the armor of Achilles from the dead Patroclus, who had borrowed it for the day, and clothes himself in it. But Achilles is the son of a goddess, and the greatest warrior of them all. Zeus is shocked:

> Unhappy man, you have no thought of death,
> Yet death is close. You are putting on
> The immortal armor of a man who makes you
> And others tremble. You killed his comrade,
> Gentle and strong, and you violated the order of things
> When you took the armor from his shoulders and head.
> (*Iliad* 17.201—205 [Trans. Lombardo, 199–204])

Violating the order of things is the proud heart of irreverence. Hector parades back into battle wearing Achilles' armor, although the man he has slain is not Achilles. Even Zeus respects the order

Hector violated—*kosmos*, in Greek. The same brash irreverence will soon prevent Hector from listening to good advice from a comrade, Polydamas, who urges Hector to take the army behind the walls of Troy. But Hector, because of his string of successes, is confident that Zeus is on his side. He ignores the advice and insists that the army follow his example:

> Not a Trojan here will listen. I won't let them.
> (*Iliad* 18.296 [Trans. Lombardo, 317])

And because of Hector's failure to listen, which is a failure of good judgment, he will lead his army to defeat, and he will feel such great shame over this that he will decline to follow his defeated army to safety, because there he would have to face the man whose advice he has not taken (22.99ff.; Lombardo 115ff.). And so Hector will face his death alone, while his parents watch in horror from the walls of Troy.

Achilles plays the beast

Achilles is a man of rage. In his furious grief for Patroclus, he begins to see himself as a violent beast of prey—a lion or a wolf. When he closes in on Hector for the final battle between them, Hector begs him to agree that whoever wins will honor the body of the other by turning it over to relatives for proper burial rites. Achilles' response is calculated, inhuman:

> Don't try to cut any deals with me, Hector.
> Do lions make peace treaties with men?
> Do wolves and lambs agree to get along?
> (*Iliad* 22.261–63 ([Trans. Lombardo, 287–89])

In this Achilles violates reverence three times—once by promising to neglect ceremony due to the dead, once by denying a suppliant, and once by taking the part of an animal. Beasts of prey have no respect for the remains of their victims, and neither does Achilles in his inhuman rage.

Later, Hector makes his dying request to Achilles, and Achilles wishes he could be even more inhuman than he is. Hector cries out:

> "I beg you, Achilles, by your own soul
> And by your parents, do not
> Allow the dogs to mutilate my body…"
> And Achilles, fixing him with a stare,
> "Don't whine to me about my parents,
> You dog! I wish my stomach would let me
> Cut off your flesh in strips and eat it raw
> For what you've done to me. There is no one
> And no way to keep the dogs off your head…"
> (*Iliad,* 22.338–48 [Trans. Lombardo, 375–87])

Achilles will remain in this bestial frame of mind until Hector's father, Priam, visits him in his shelter by the shore. Then, simply by being who he is, old and stricken with grief, Priam reminds Achilles of his own father. Achilles remembers his father, and in that moment he remembers himself, remembers his humanity.

Remembering your humanity is not like remembering the date of your birth or how much money you borrowed from your neighbor. It is not about simple facts. The reverent soul remembers how to feel what it ought to feel about itself and about other people—a remembrance that is moral from the start. The most violent sociopath may, in some sense, remember that he is human—indeed, he may remember that he is a sociopathic human at the very time he commits the most odious crime. Achilles does remember the fact that he will die at the height of his killing rage. The moment comes when Achilles has at his mercy a young prince of Troy, Lycaon. The boy clasps Achilles' knees in the classic gesture of supplication and begs for his life, but Achilles reminds him of their common mortality:

> You die too, friend. Don't take it hard.
> Patroclus died, and he was far better than you.
> Take a look at me. Do you see how huge I am,
> How beautiful? I have a noble father,
> My mother was a goddess, but I too
> Am in death's shadow.
> (*Iliad* 21.106–10 [Trans. Lombardo, 112–17])

And with that he kills the boy, though reverence would require that he spare him as a suppliant. Achilles has remembered only that all men die, but this is not enough for reverence. The Persian king in Herodotus' story gets it right. When he remembers his mortality, he acknowledges his fear of the future. With that comes something like sympathy for a fellow human being in trouble, and he is moved to do the right thing.

Most modern philosophers are not satisfied with this sort of account. How could it make you a better person to remember your mortality? They tend to draw a clear line between facts and values, and they have called it a fallacy to derive an "ought" from an "is"—a value from a fact. And yet the *Iliad* seems to blame Achilles and Hector for failing to draw just that sort of inference. Achilles remembers he is mortal, but he forgets that, as a mortal, he should behave in a certain way. So what? There's no mistake in that.

Yet much of ancient Greek thought, from poets to philosophers, builds on the idea that virtue depends on knowing what it is to be human. (This sort of idea is called ethical naturalism.) I won't take on the colossus of modern philosophy here, except to give one example that brings light on the old Greek idea. If you know what a knife is, you know that it is supposed to cut, and that it must therefore be sharp. Bad knives don't cut. If you were a knife, and you knew what you were, you'd know that you should be sharp and, unless you forgot, you'd try to stay that way. By analogy, if you know what a human being is, you know that human beings are supposed to live in society (otherwise, being dependent, they die off), and that human beings must therefore have the virtues that enable them to function in society. Bad human beings don't function in society; good ones maintain the edge that allows them to be useful parts of a community. Most ancient Greek thinking about ethics starts with this inference from the "is" of vulnerable human nature to the "ought" of virtue.

Tyrannical Failures of Reverence

Not all rulers are as wise as the Persian king in the story Herodotus tells us about Solon and Croesus. Athens became especially skittish about tyrannical kings as the city grew attached to its new-fledged democracy. In Homer's world, all great people were supposed to have had great opportunities to go wrong. But Athenian poets of the fifth century BCE trained their spotlight on the egregious failures that follow one-man rule. They were writing for an audience that feared tyranny above all. Tyrants (to judge from their representations on stage) are monarchs who have achieved power on their own, by their own strength or cunning, and who live in the fear that others will follow their example. If you seized power from someone weaker than you, you would have every reason to expect that someone else will try to find the strength needed to overthrow you.

Tyrants are suspicious, overly dependent on their own judgment, and stubbornly reluctant to hear anyone's advice. Above all, they are prone to failures of reverence, and with their failures of reverence come failures of judgment. Human judgment has a way of going wrong, especially in isolation from competing points of view. We need to think together, if we are to take due notice of all the things we could do wrong. Tyrants isolate themselves through a combination of fear and overconfidence. They do not listen, not to the common people, not to women, not to children, and not even to prophets who claim to speak for a god. Too sure of themselves to take counsel, they set themselves high and fall hard.

Oedipus

In his most famous play, *Oedipus Tyrannus,* Sophocles has his chorus sing a hymn to reverence "Be with me always, Destiny." The second stanza of that hymn begins with these lines:

> Hubris grows from tyranny,
> hubris overflowing
> with a monstrous waste
> of all that has no use, no profit:
> it climbs high,
> it rushes to a precipice jutting out—
> the end, no foothold saves it now.
> (Chorus, *Oedipus Tyrannus*, 873–79)

This is a Greek way of articulating the evergreen idea that power corrupts. Hubris is best understood simply as the opposite of reverence, in action or attitude. But why mention hubris in connection with Oedipus? His famous sins against father and mother were committed when he was a powerless young man. The road rage that killed his father began in his father, and the fantastic marriage to his mother was the natural outcome of his leadership in Thebes. But those famous Oedipal actions are merely the backdrop to this play, which concerns Oedipus' last hours as tyrant in Thebes. Oedipus' irreverence belongs mainly to the way he rules his people: he rejects advice from the people of the chorus, from his wife, and from a prophet. He flies into a rage at his brother-in-law (and uncle) before hearing the man out.

As a young man he has solved, by his own wits, the riddle of the Sphinx; this success made him master of Thebes and husband of the queen. Now a mature man, he is confident that he can find out what has caused the plague with a little help from his fellow citizens. He presents himself to his people as equal to a god, and he evidently thinks himself superior to Tiresias, prophet of Apollo. Tiresias failed to solve the Sphinx's riddle at that time, while he, famous Oedipus, unraveled it without divine assistance. Now, when Tiresias seems to speak against him, Oedipus quickly jumps to the conclusion that the prophet is part of a conspiracy. Deafened by his own suspicions and his fear of a coup, Oedipus lashes out, even at his wife-mother. There is more to his irreverence, but this would be enough for Sophocles' audience to know that Oedipus is in for a great fall.

Creon

In the *Antigone* of Sophocles, Creon travels the clear, easy road from failure of reverence to failure of judgment. Again, the story is familiar: Oedipus' two sons quarrel over whose turn it is to rule in Thebes; one of them runs for help to an enemy city and brings its troops against his own homeland. Thebes repels the invaders in the famous battle of the seven heroes at the seven gates. At every gate but one, the defender beats his enemy:

> Except for a savage pair, full brothers [i.e., the sons of Oedipus]:
> Their two spears stand upright, conquering,
> Each in the other's dead breast.
> (Chorus in *Antigone,* 144–46)

Creon decrees that the rebel brother's corpse be left unburied for birds to peck at and wild beasts to gnaw. He is flirting with a gross violation of reverence, which requires burial ceremonies for human dead in all normal circumstances. Still, after such a war, ancient custom did allow rulers to set aside burial and display the dead as a warning to others and a supreme punishment. So this decree by itself does not make Creon irreverent. Sophocles' audience probably thought that Antigone goes wrong in her extreme, death-defying argument for burial customs above all else. Still, the audience must have judged Creon outrageous because he proceeds like a tyrant, confident in his judgment, fearful of conspiracy, and unwilling to listen to anyone who disagrees with him. That is his irreverence, and the cause of his downfall. The point is made throughout the play, but most clearly by his son, Haemon:

> Father, the gods give good sense to every human being,
> And that is absolutely the best thing we have. (683–84)

Good sense to *every* human being. This is an explosive idea; we can be fairly sure it was widely held in Athens and helped to detonate the series of upheavals that led to the establishment of democracy, based on the rule that any citizen had the right to be heard in assembly. (Yes, I know that women and slaves and immigrants could not have this privilege, but the idea behind this privilege was truly universal, as you can see from these lines.) Haemon goes on to remind his father to listen to what others say:

> And now, don't always cling to the same anger,
> Don't keep saying that this, and nothing else, is right.
> If a man believes that he alone has a sound mind,
> And no one else can speak or think as well as he does,
> Then, when people study him, they'll find an empty book.
> But a wise man can learn a lot and never be ashamed;
> He knows he does not have to be rigid and close-hauled.
> You've seen trees tossed by a torrent in a flash flood:
> If they bend, they're saved, and every twig survives,
> But if they stiffen up, they're washed out from the roots.
> It's the same in a boat: if a sailor keeps the footline taut,
> If he doesn't give an inch, he'll capsize, and then—
> He'll be sailing home with his benches down
>   and his hull to the sky.
> So ease off, relax, stop being angry, make a change.
> I know I'm younger, but I may still have good ideas;
> And I say that the oldest idea, and the best,
> Is for one man to be born complete, knowing everything.
> Otherwise—and it usually does turn out otherwise—
> It's good to learn from anyone who speaks well. (705–23)

Creon does not respect his son. He fails to listen, makes bad decisions in consequence, and ruins his life. "Beat your megaphones into hearing trumpets," wrote the poet William Stafford. Good advice for anyone, but especially for leaders.

Reverence is the greatest virtue of leaders, because it gives powerful people the strength to listen to those who are weaker than they, and it reminds them that no one, no matter how successful, was "born complete, knowing everything." Gods do know everything (or almost everything), according to the ancient Greek mythology. To present yourself as all-knowing, then, is to forget your humanity and play the part of a god. Both Oedipus and Creon fall into this trap.

Think yourself equal to a god, and you will commit the most dangerous kind of irreverence. Many ancient Greeks believed that the gods will take note if you have such arrogant thoughts, and they will cut you down to size. At the same time, early humanists believed that such stories can be told without the gods. If you set yourself too high, we—the other human beings in this case—will bring you down, because we, no less than gods, will not tolerate divine pretensions in a mortal (see chapter seven).

Pentheus

Playing god is a double outrage, because a man who intends to play god succeeds in playing only the part of a beast or a monster. In Euripides' *Bacchae*, from which I quoted at the opening of this chapter, a young king sets out to do battle against the god Dionysus. He does not know what he is doing, because he does not believe that Dionysus is a god at all. A new cult has come to his city of Thebes, bringing with it the danger that men will lose control of women. The women of Thebes have left their duties at home—their looms and their children—so that they can run in the mountains and worship Dionysus. Pentheus plans to put down unruly behavior—with no thought that he is proposing to fight a god.

Like many tragic heroes, Pentheus has lost his wits. His outrage at the independence of the women deafens him to advice and explanation. He does not hear his grandfather or the prophet Tiresias or the women, or anyone else, and he never doubts the rightness of his decision to eliminate the new cult.

The Chorus of the play worship Dionysus, and they are shocked by the king's irreverence:

> Intelligence gone mad,
> Spirit struck to arrogance, he has appointed
> Himself to suppress the unconquerable by violence.
> (*Bacchae*, 999–1001)

But who dares to fight with gods? In ancient Greek mythology it is not human beings who actually threaten the gods, but monsters and giants. Naturally, then, that is how the Chorus see the young king:

> …a wild-eyed monster
> Without a human face who
> Like a deadly giant wrestles with the gods!
> (*Bacchae*, 542–44)

Even the young king's mother will see him as a beast. Before bringing out his army, Pentheus decides on a personal reconnaissance. When his mother catches him spying on the sacred rituals, she thinks he is a lion. She and the other worshippers hunt him down under this illusion, tear him apart with their bare hands, and bring his head home in triumph, like a hunting trophy.

Pentheus is the most famous mortal in ancient poetry who takes arms against a god. Keep in mind that Dionysus is a new arrival; no one in Greece, till now, has believed in his divinity, and no one has been practicing his rituals. Yet only Pentheus and his family are punished. The sin for which they are accountable, then, is not disbelief, and it is not failure to worship, for they share these failures with everyone in Greece. Their sin, as the Chorus clearly says, is that they have set themselves up as adversaries to the god. This is both an insult to Dionysus and a fatal mistake about what human beings can safely undertake to accomplish.

Normal Reverence

Conspicuous failures of reverence are like shadows in a sundrenched landscape. Reverence is the norm in a smooth-functioning society; as a result it is easily confused with the normal behavior that expresses reverence. Everything that the ancient Greeks considered normal and customary they also considered reverent:

> [Dionysus] hates the man who does not try—
> Each day, each longed-for night—
> To live a flawless life
> And wisely steers away,
> In heart and mind,
> From men who stand out above others.
> What is ordinary,
> What the crowd thinks right,
> Is good enough for me.
> (Chorus, Euripides' *Bacchae*, 424–32)

Speakers in the *Bacchae* link reverence with a number of virtues—all the cardinal virtues, in fact, except for courage: good judgment (386–402, 997–1004), wisdom (395ff.), justice (893ff., 1005ff.), and sound-mindedness (1149). But certain types of custom belong especially to reverence, those by which human beings distinguish themselves most importantly from beasts of prey: treating the dead with due ceremony, observing certain laws of war, protecting suppliants, keeping oaths, offering meat animals to the gods, and respecting sacred places or the secrets of certain rituals.

Most of these customs of reverence are not available in Austin, Texas, in the year 2014; we do not recognize ancient Greek burial rites here, we buy meat from a butcher, and we never heard of suppliants. We do think it a good idea to keep our promises, and we share some of the ancient Greek ideas about war, but on the whole, ancient Greek reverence is denied to us. Or it would be, if the reverence were simply in the customs. Then reverence would be subject to cultural relativity. But reverence is not *in* the customs; reverence is something you bring *to* the customs. Socrates, we are told, "thought that the gods take the greatest joy from honors they receive from the people who are most reverent" (Xenophon, *Memorabilia,* 1.3.3), and this seems to have been the conventional view.

Custom is relative to a culture in a time and place. So is language, but the relativity of language does not carry over to what a sentence means. "Two is the square root of four" will be said differently in different cultures, but what it says is true in all of them. Funeral rites are different in different cultures, and to some extent they have different meanings as well, insofar as they express different beliefs about death, the body, and the possibility of an afterlife. But when Confucius says that funeral rites are empty without grief, anyone can see what he means, and when Achilles realizes that he will be tormented by Patroclus in his mind until he sees to his friend's burial, we understand that too. We feel the same need for closure; it is not for nothing that we spare no expense in searching for the bodies of those who die in war or natural disaster.

The ancient Greeks did not think that deviations from the norm were, in themselves, great failures of reverence. The great failures belong to the heroes and tyrants who go too far, too fast, too thoughtlessly. The examples I have reviewed here are easy to understand from any cultural viewpoint. What the Greeks most cared about, under reverence, is a virtue that can cross cultural boundaries with ease.

Joyful Reverence

If I ended here, you might think that reverence in ancient Greece was only about tragic resignation and the acceptance of mortality. But there is also a reverence of joy that arises in mystery religions. These began in ancient Greece as early as the sixth century before our era and center on initiation ceremonies by which, through symbolic death and rebirth, individuals believe they come into a special relationship with a god. Leaving fear to outsiders, the re-born worshippers revel in newfound joy. They believe that they take on attributes of the god they worship, power, youthfulness, and a blessed afterlife. The religious practices that meant the most to ordinary Athenians by the end of the fifth century BCE were elaborate initiations into the Eleusinian Mysteries. We cannot give a complete account of these because they were secrets which it was a violation of reverence to betray. Whatever they were, they apparently brought their initiates joy and a sense of the presence of the god, and by symbolic death and rebirth they released worshippers from the weight of their mortality.

Joyful reverence therefore shows the way to cross the boundary that was so important in tragic plays—the line between human mortality and the immortality of the gods. Tragic poetry often says, "Do not even dream of being like a god; never forget your human limitations." Joyful reverence answers, "Follow your guide through initiation and you will find the way to be as nearly divine as a human being can be." The two sides of reverence are partly reconciled in Euripides' *Bacchae*. There, the Chorus celebrates the joy of initiation while inveighing against the perils of thinking thoughts too high for mortal human beings. The solution lies in the clear boundaries that set off the experience of joyful reverence. There are well-defined times and places for the initiations and other revels in which human beings are permitted to venture into divine territory. At that special time, and in that special place, with extraordinary rapture, they step across the line. But they must return to the norms of civic life, and they must never tell an outsider what they have done. The secret life of the initiate is suffused with joyful reverence, while the open life of the citizen is governed by its tragic cousin.

Aside from Euripides in the *Bacchae,* the ancient author who tells us the most about joyful reverence is Plato. Plato uses the heightened language and emotion-laden imagery of mystery religion to give his readers a sense of what philosophers would experience as they ascend to full knowledge of reality. Students of philosophy become more godlike as they approach the truth, and their immortal souls become less subject to corruptions of all kinds.

The great myth of Socrates' second speech in Plato's *Phaedrus* is suffused with joyful reverence. Here Plato visualizes a heaven in which the souls of gods and the souls of human beings, both immortal, race upwards in the form of winged chariots to the high rim from which they can see what lies beyond heaven. Both kinds of souls must feed on the sight of a splendid and remote reality that lies there. Gods have the power to see all of this, as they must in order to maintain their divine strength, and so they never fall from heaven. The charioteer of a human soul, however, is distracted by trying to control a mismatched pair of horses, and so never gets a really good view of reality. And when human souls fail to see reality, they are sent down from heaven to be imprisoned in mortal bodies.

The souls that follow the gods most closely in their winged journey will remain most like them, with no tincture of mortality. In this myth the important boundary is between minds and truth, rather than between gods and humans. Both life-forms must see the truth from a distance, over the edge of heaven, and neither group can take home a lasting knowledge of what they have seen. Instead, like worshippers in acts of repeated ritual, they must revisit the boundary of heaven again and again in order to see what is beyond and so to nourish the ability of their souls to take wing.

The reverence that the winged souls feel when they catch sight of reality is something new in the history of ideas. It is not reverence for any of the gods; it is a reverence that is felt in company with the gods, for a reality that is higher even than they, that resides in a space beyond even heaven. In the last analysis, the joyful reverence of Plato is reverence for truth.

Loving him, the mother takes thread in hand;
Leaving her, he'll have this coat on his shoulders.
Now that he's about to go, she mends with fine, fine stitches;
She knows the fear that he'll be gone a long, long time.
Who would say the heart of a tiny blade of grass
Could repay the sun for all the warmth of spring?
—Meng Zhao (751–814 CE, Tang Dynasty)

6 | ANCIENT CHINA
THE WAY OF POWER

The boy is now a man, set to go out into the world. His mother prepares for his departure, mending his coat, possibly for the last time. He feels that he is in her debt as strongly as if he were a blade of grass and she the sun, a debt he can conceive only through images, a debt he can never repay. In the tiny universe of his family he feels he is like the earth looking up at heaven, and he is in awe.

Filial piety expresses reverence within the family. Children learn to be reverent by practicing on their parents; they pay them the respect that propriety demands and in so doing they learn to play their proper parts as adults in the larger hierarchies of society. They are restrained. They come under control. And this is how many westerners think of filial piety in Confucian China—as the basis for a system of powerful restraints that bend individuals to the will of the larger society.

This is wrong—terribly wrong as an expression of Confucian ethics, and quite a bit wrong about China. Genuine filial piety does not bend a child's mind, but provides a structure for the expression of its natural feelings towards its parents. Filial piety must be sincere and reverent, and it expresses feelings that are natural in the sense that they distinguish human beings from animals: "to acknowledge neither father nor king is to be in the state of a beast" (Mencius 3B:9.9).

When Zi-you asked about filial piety, the Master said: "Nowadays filial piety merely means being able to feed one's parents. Even dogs and horses are being fed. Without deference, how can you tell the difference?" (*Analects* 2.7)

All acts of reverence must reflect appropriate feelings, and these must come from within. They cannot be imposed from outside by force or discipline. The metaphors "inside/outside" mark the difference between what is natural and what is forced: Water naturally flows downhill; it would have to be forcefully carried uphill; and left on its own it will resume its downward path. So it is with virtue: It belongs to the character of the person who has it. A good person behaves well without being forced to do so; that is why virtue is of the utmost importance when men are so powerful that they have no one to force them to behave.

Like ancient Greek *hosiotēs,* Confucian *Li* leads human beings to accept their proper niche between the divine and the animal. The ethical consequences are similar; both virtues act as restraints on human power, and both work indirectly to protect the weak. The main difference is obvious: ancient Greek culture harps on the cognitive aspect of the virtue—on *knowing* human limitations— while Confucian practices build an implicit sense of those limitations through the careful observance of ceremony.

Ceremonious Virtue (*Li*)

Ceremony matters to Confucius only when it expresses feelings that belong to one's character—when, in other words, it flows from what I have been calling a virtue. As I said earlier, a virtue is a developed capacity to have the right feelings at the right time. It begins in a natural capacity for those feelings, and is developed by the exercise of that virtue into a fairly reliable condition of one's character. In the *Analects* and in *The Book of Mencius, Li* is primarily the exercise of virtue through ceremony. In some contexts, *Li* is *also* a virtue in its own right, close kin to ancient Greek reverence.

Usually translated as "rites," "rituals," or "ceremony," *Li* refers also to civility or reverence. In Confucius, *Li* is the practice that leads to the primary virtue, Humaneness (*Ren*). In Mencius, *Li* itself is one of the four virtues, along with Humaneness, Justice, and Wisdom, that flow from four natural sets of feelings known as the four beginnings. Taken together, the two Confucian positions place *Li* at the pivot between natural feelings and developed virtue:

> Filial piety and brotherly obedience are perhaps the roots of Humaneness. (*Analects* 1.2, cf. 1.9 and 12.1)

> A human being without the feeling of modesty *(ci)* and deference *(rang)* is not human…the feeling of modesty and deference is the beginning of *Li*. (Mencius 2A: 6.4–5 [Cf. 6A: 6.7 where the feelings of deference and respect, *gong* and *jing*, are said to be the source of *Li*])

Through filial piety, children cultivate a sense of their positions in the scheme of things, along with habits of reverence which they will apply as adults on a larger stage than that of the family. Even if one becomes emperor, he is supposed to remember his habit of deference through the practices of *Li,* and this habit of deference is not mere ceremony, but a developed capacity for moral feelings. Those who have cultivated *Li*—that is to say, not mere ceremony, but ceremony accompanied by the right feelings—have developed their capacity for feeling grief, shame, respect, and reverence when appropriate. They have also developed capacities for virtues other than *Li,* most notably *Ren,* humaneness (about which I have more to say in a moment).

Filial piety is an expression of gratitude from child to parent. Meng Zhao's poem (the one in the epigraph to this chapter) is crafted through an artificial balance of oppositions—loving/leaving, thread/coat, hand/shoulders, fine stitches/long time—but we would be wrong to dismiss it as an exquisite artifact. The feeling it expresses is strong enough to bring tears to the eyes of those who know it in its own culture. Personal as that feeling is in its beginning, however, the poem shows that such feeling grows, by heartfelt analogy, to fill a larger stage: as the boy feels grateful to his mother, he feels himself in harmony with earth in its gratitude to Heaven.

The hierarchy of Heaven over earth lies behind every expression of *Li.* This gives us a clue to the most important fact about it: Although it begins as an exercise for children, *Li* ends as an internal restraint on the most powerful people of all, on kings and emperors. To call the emperor "Son of Heaven" is to remind him that there is something of which even the most powerful human being must stand in awe. After the decline of ancient Chinese polytheism, we would not expect an emperor to be naively afraid that the gods would punish him for wrongdoing, but he should nevertheless be capable of dreading the loss of Heaven's favor. A grown-up son no longer fears the penalties his parents imposed on him as a child, but he still wishes to remain on their right side, because he has taken their values as his own. So it is with *Li.* Weaker people may have no choice but to follow *Li* out of fear, but not the powerful; if they truly follow *Li* they do so because they feel that it is right to do so— because *Li* has become a settled virtue in them. The holders of power, more than anyone, require training in *Li,* because holders of power are restrained only from within, only by means of a virtue. And the virtue of internal restraint *is Li.*

Violations of Li

As with Greek reverence, we bring *Li* most clearly into focus when we plot its boundaries. What, exactly, do you have to do in order to violate *Li*? Except for Book Ten (which may be a fairly late addition), the *Analects* do not give detailed directions for the practice of *Li*. On the contrary, the Master asks advice from others (*Analects* 3.15, 10.21) and gives different people different sorts of advice on the same topic (for example, filial piety, *Analects* 2.5, 2.6). What he says, moreover, is often deliberately vague:

> The Master said: "A gentleman enlarges his learning through literature and restrains himself through ritual; therefore he is not likely to go wrong." (*Analects* 6.27)

And sometimes explicitly allows variations from ancient rules:

> The Master said: "According to ritual, the ceremonial cap should be made of hemp; nowadays it is made of silk, which is more convenient; I follow the general usage." (*Analects* 9.3, in which he proceeds to mention a case in which he keeps up the old way.)

Some rules, however, are sacrosanct in the *Analects*. These mainly turn out to be rules restraining powerful people from usurping the dignities of the Son of Heaven, the Emperor. Confucius has nothing to say about minor violations of *Li* by ordinary people; he addresses himself to rulers, and it is rulers he most plainly seeks to hold in check through the cultivation of *Li*. The hierarchy that is supported by *Li*, I conclude, is mainly a moral hierarchy and not a human one, since it serves mainly to keep in line rulers who have no human superiors.

There was no emperor at the time of Confucius; he considered the rulers he addressed ("princes" in Legge's translation) a substantial step down from the Son of Heaven. This title refers in Confucian teaching not to any historical character but to the supreme human ruler conceived as a moral ideal—rather like one of Plato's philosopher-kings. Philosopher-kings must give up theoretical philosophy when they involve themselves in the daily work of administration; but Confucius' Son of Heaven seems untroubled by administrative duties. He is fully a sage when he is on the throne—a man of such perfection that all the world will follow him by the sheer force of his example.

In other respects, however, Plato and Confucius have similar ideals for rulers: both believe that competition has no place in the lives of those whose primary goal is virtue. Neither author finds there to be an ideal ruler in the corrupt society of his own time, and both are careful to see that no impostors pretend to the power or dignity that goes with perfection. Confucius would set up a guardian in the personal character of every candidate for power—the habit of reverence developed by practicing *Li* for a lifetime with precision. Plato would guard the avenues of power by refutation (he portrays Socrates as one who can refute all unworthy aspirants), but he too thinks of virtue as a kind of vaccine against moral decay. Both recognize that such guardians are not sufficient, that a corrupt society is corrupting, and that no matter how "inner" your virtue may be, you will have a hard time keeping it up by yourself, isolated from the shared practices of a virtuous society.

Li as support for other virtues

The central virtue of Confucian ethics in the *Analects* is Humaneness or benevolence *(Ren)*. Now *Li* is at least instrumental for *Ren*, and

Confucius would agree with Plato that reverence is instrumental to order in society, but both Confucius and Mencius hold, in addition, that *Li* is a cardinal virtue conferring value on other virtues:

> The Master said, "Without *Li*, respectfulness becomes a laborious bustle; without *Li*, carefulness becomes timidity; without *Li*, courage becomes insubordination; without *Li*, frankness becomes rudeness." (*Analects* 8.2.1)

> "When gentlemen treat their kin generously, common people are attracted to Humaneness; when old ties are not neglected, common people are not callous." (8.2.2)

The Greek and Chinese traditions are closely analogous in this. The fate of Pentheus and his family, in Euripides' *Bacchae,* could be an illustration for what Confucius thinks goes wrong without reverence. First, a lack of reverence vitiates what would otherwise be admirable behavior. Kadmos (Pentheus' grandfather) and Tiresias the prophet exhibit respectful behavior to each other and to the new religion, but without reverence they are tiresome, even comical, since their acts of respect border on charade. As for Pentheus, he has a bravery which, without reverence, is quarrelsome; and his frankness to Tiresias and the visitors from abroad is brutal. Second, the same loss of reverence that loosens family ties also unravels the fabric of society. The royal family Thebes has been ungenerous to its weakest member—the pregnant girl Semele—and through the same failure of reverence, they have fallen out of touch with the people over whom they rule.

At this point I imagine an incredulous reader bursting out "Surely Greek and Chinese reverence belong to different religions. Greeks and Chinese are reverent toward different gods How, then, could they possibly have cultivated the same sort of reverence when they had different beliefs?"

Part of the answer is that reverence is basic to any society and to just about anything that is done in society. Of course it may occur in religion, but it may also occur outside of religion, and its ethical character is not determined by religion (more on this in the next chapter). But classical Greek and Chinese conceptions of reverence bear a common relation to theism: Both conceptions of reverence blossom with the passing away of polytheism and the rise of agnosticism. Reverence survives and flourishes in these circumstances because it is something that human beings need in order to face the most obvious, common, and inevitable facts of human life—family, hierarchy, and death. When rising doubts cloud the certainty of religious claims, reverence is all the more important.

Beliefs have not shown the same power to survive in human history that reverence has; different beliefs can support the same rituals, and it is the rituals that we need, reverently performed. Both Greeks and Chinese insisted on careful disposal of the dead from very ancient times; but they would have given different beliefs, and different beliefs at different times, to explain their insistence on burial. That both cultures chose burial over other means of funeral disposal may be coincidence, but it is no coincidence that both cultures enjoined ceremonies, and that these ceremonies had to be performed reverently, allowing grief its full and proper expression within certain boundaries.

Hierarchy

We can readily see the value to ordinary people of restraining kings and emperors through cultivating *Li;* the trouble is that we can equally well see the value to kings and emperors of cultivating *Li* in ordinary people. It would appear that *Li* develops habits of submissiveness, and this is a common criticism of Confucian ethics. Does

Li give moral support to rulers who suppress the weak or silence dissent? Certainly not as Confucius intends it; *Li* keeps a ruler in check and affects him more than it does his subordinates:

> Duke Ting asked: "How should a ruler treat his ministers, and how should ministers treat their ruler?" Confucius replied: "A ruler should treat his ministers with courtesy [i.e., according to *Li*], a minister should treat his ruler with loyalty." (*Analects* 3.19)

"All right," says the critic. "Perhaps Confucius and Mencius did piously hope that *Li* would hold back powerful people more than weak ones. But in actual experience, restraint through ceremony is inherently bad because it encourages people to sink into bad habits, quietly accepting authority without question." The critic may think that Confucian-based cultures fell behind European cultures in the eighteenth century precisely because they were restrained by ceremony. Unable to question tradition or authority (on this view), Confucian-based cultures languished in a wooden rigidity, while Europe, with its voracious appetite for questioning, its bold impatience with hierarchy, inevitably forged ahead.

That picture is wrong. The restraint that comes from ceremony is never absent, in any culture, from any system of power, whether conservative or revolutionary. As for the Far East, the criticism is belied by history overall and by recent events. China made enormous advances in technology, in social forms, and in other ways for many centuries after Confucian thinking became general. *Li* does not stand against change, but regulates and orders it. Criticism has trouble surfacing in any system, but it has no more trouble in principle under a Confucian system. All cultures seem to run through alternating periods of growth and rigidity; I doubt if there is a single explanation for these. But the age of reverence in Greece was a time of enormous change and creativity; it brought democracy to the forefront for a small moment in history, and it saw reverence as the virtue that best protected this new and vulnerable form of governance.

True, powerful people have used Confucian philosophy as a tool for silencing dissent, but they are in error about Confucianism. A Confucian ruler is supposed to know how to take criticism:

> Zilu asked how to serve a prince. The Master said: "Tell him the truth even if it offends him." (*Analects* 14.22)

But not in public. I have found that a respectful Confucian student is quite ready to correct me as his teacher to my face, but not in front of other students, and in this he follows the example of the Master.

Confucian *Li* often reminds people of their differences in status without obscuring their common humanity. The *Analects* put an emphasis on status because *Li* has more useful work to do within a hierarchy than it does among equals. Equals have less need of internal restraints in acting upon one another than unequals do. Competition aside (and *Li* does put competition aside), there is a natural harmony among peers. But when people find themselves at different levels of power, they are liable to clash.

Li does not impose hierarchy, but where there is hierarchy *Li* makes it harmonious and humanizes the behavior of people at all levels. Respect is reciprocal: great leaders earn the respect of their followers by treating those followers with respect. In a system restrained by *Li*, no ruler treats his subordinates like beasts of burden, and no subordinate fears his rulers as one might fear a beast of prey. Where there are power differences—and there are always power differences—*Li* takes the sting out of obedience for those below, and it lifts from rulers the burden of using force, rather than example, to maintain control.

Hierarchy is not the only context for *Li* as understood by Confucius and Mencius. All human beings, in being human, have the capacity for virtue, and therefore people at all levels of power may cultivate virtue in themselves through education and ceremony. Ceremony does, in the end, celebrate universal brotherhood:

Sima Niu was grieving: "All men have brothers; I alone have none." Zixia said: "I have heard this: life and death are decreed by fate, riches and honors are allotted by Heaven. Since a gentleman behaves with reverence and diligence, treating people with deference and courtesy, all within the Four Seas are his brothers. How could a gentleman ever complain that he has no brothers?" (*Analects* 12.5)

Ancient Greeks would recognize the sentiment and its connection with reverence. In both cultures, thoughts about reverence lead people to ask why privileges should be associated with birth. Confucius prefers to see common people rise to positions of authority, because they are more likely to have been properly trained in *Li* (*Analects* 11.1). And he evidently taught that a noble crosses the boundary of *Li* if, by virtue of high birth, he lays claim to knowledge or virtue he does not actually have.

Power

The power of leaders derives from character, and their authority is essentially moral. The practice of *Li* humanizes power by recasting it as moral authority. But the Confucian point is stronger than that: *Li* simply is the human way to exercise authority:

The Master said, "If you can govern your country with *Li* and deference, what difficulties will you have? If you cannot do so with *Li* and deference, what is the use of *Li*?" (*Analects* 4.13 [see also 8.2, 9.14, 13.4, and 15.33])

This seems to imply that *Li* is the very means by which the ruler has influence over people. At first sight, this seems absurd. How could the mere practice of ceremony secure the power of a ruler? No one who has taken Machiavelli to heart would believe this for a moment; Machiavellians are convinced that it is better for a ruler to be feared than to be loved. But Confucius' teaching does not address the issue between fear and love; above all, his teaching deals with what we would call respect, and the importance of this to leadership.

Reverence is a virtue of leadership because it promotes mutual respect between leader and follower. Leaders generally find that respect is far more reliable than either fear or love for securing obedience. John Locke observed:

He that will have his son have a respect for him and his orders must have a great reverence for his son. (*Some Thoughts Concerning Education* [1693])

A son may love his father and still treat his father's values with contempt; a son who fears his father will seek every opportunity to escape his father's influence. But a son who respects his father has a chance to make his father's values his own. And Locke is surely right: within the family or not, leaders cannot retain the respect of their followers without showing due respect to them in return. Juvenal said that the greatest reverence is due the young (14.47), deliberately reversing the tradition that directs reverence ever upward.

This is one way to explain how power can grow from *Li*—through the respect that gathers around good leadership. But this respect travels both ways in the hierarchy, both up and down, and the emphasis in the Confucian tradition has mainly been on deference to higher ranks, even though it is the very highest rank that has the greatest need to show deference. There is a puzzle here, which I will take up in connection with leadership in modern life. Reverence generally points upward. But if so, how can it help to promote respect that is mutual and goes both ways? And, if reverence points upward, at what does it point? Must the object of reverence be a divine being? And if so, does it matter what you believe about the divine?

Our little systems have their day;
They have their day and cease to be;
They are but broken lights of thee,
And thou, O Lord, art more than they.

We have but faith: we cannot know;
For knowledge is of things we see;
And yet we trust it comes from thee,
A beam in darkness: let it grow.

Let knowledge grow from more to more,
But more of reverence in us dwell;
That mind and soul, according well,
May make one music as before,

But vaster.

—From the Prologue to
Tennyson's "In Memoriam"

7 | REVERENCE WITHOUT A CREED

Reverence is a matter of feeling, and as far as feelings go, it doesn't much matter what you believe. Reverence can occur in ancient polytheism as well as in modern Christianity or Islam, so reverence makes few demands on belief. Otherwise it would not be consistent with so many different creeds.

Reverence must stand in awe of something—something I will call the object of reverence. What could it be? Something that reminds us of human limitations, if we are to stay true to the concept of reverence with which we began. Therefore you must believe that there is at least one Something that satisfies at least one of the following conditions: it cannot be controlled by human means, was not created by human beings is not fully understood by human experts, and is transcendent. Such beliefs are the least you must have in order to be reverent. They do not amount to religion or even to spirituality. For a lover of art, the Something might be a monument of ancient art, since this has passed out of our power to change without destroying. For a reverent scientist, the Something could be the final explanation for the universe, which satisfies the first and third conditions. For a reverent statesperson, the Something might be justice, conceived as an ideal, dimly grasped and much disputed, by which we should try to regulate our poor systems of law. This might satisfy all four conditions. The Something could be nature, or the universe. For many people, the Something will be divine. But if the Something is justice or nature, the reverent person may be an atheist or, as some say, a non-theist.

Small as it is, this kernel of belief makes a profound difference to how people behave and how they feel. We may be willing to sacrifice many of our beliefs to the march of science or to the goal of harmony among religions, but we should never abandon the feelings that keep us humble and respectful of each other.

The Case of Tennyson

No poet has had greater powers for expressing feelings than Tennyson. Although he concluded that science had vanquished traditional religious belief, Tennyson felt that reverence must survive, and he gave us the finest expression of reverence that we have in the English language, "In Memoriam."

The effect of scientific advances since the sixteenth century has been to whittle away at every religious belief that runs counter to the evidence a rational mind must accept. Writing in the 1830s and 1840s, Tennyson had a deep respect for science: "we trust it comes from thee," he says, meaning that scientific knowledge comes from the divine being he addresses. He is willing to give up as many religious beliefs as he must in order to accommodate science, but he is not willing to trim one iota from his reverence; or, in his terms, he will give science the run of his mind but not of his soul.

"In Memoriam" is by general agreement his finest work. It begins as an elegy (or series of elegies) mourning the poet's beloved friend, Arthur Hallam, but it grows to express grief on a larger scale for the loss of faith brought on by science. Tennyson tries to balance the growth of knowledge with a new argument for reverence—an argument that is both new and old, for it harks back to the ancient

Greek idea that reverence grows from acknowledging human weakness. The Prologue continues:

> But vaster. We are fools and slight;
> We mock thee when we do not fear:
> But help thy foolish ones to bear;
> Help thy vain worlds to bear thy light. (29–32)

The light Tennyson finds hard to bear is mainly that of geology, which, at the time he was writing, had been revealing the profligacy of nature. Even before the thought of evolution began to unsettle religious belief, shocking evidence came to light in rocks bearing fossils, evidence that a mind like Tennyson's could not discount. Many animal and plant species had flourished long ago and then died away. To what purpose? Tennyson would like to believe (as Christians do, if they are untroubled by science) that not a sparrow falls but God notices, and that all such events are part of a divine plan. But in the face of the fossil evidence of a vast carnage of species, how can one continue to hold such beliefs? Still, he says, we trust:

> Oh yet we trust that somehow good
> Will be the final goal of ill,
> To pangs of nature, sins of will,
> Defects of doubt, and taints of blood;
>
> That nothing walks with aimless feet;
> That not one life shall be destroy'd,
> Or cast as rubbish to the void,
> When God hath made the pile complete,
>
> That not a worm is cloven in vain;
> That not a moth with vain desire

Is shrivel'd in a fruitless fire,
Or but subserves another's gain.
(54.1–12)

But in the concluding stanzas Tennyson will offer no comfort but reverence. Trust is only a dream, and anything he can say to express his faith is no more articulate than the cry of a baby at night:

Behold, we know not anything;
I can but trust that good shall fall
At last—far off—at last, to all,
And every winter change to spring.

So runs my dream: but what am I?
An infant crying in the night:
An infant crying for the light:
And with no language but a cry.
(54.13–20)

So ends this section of the poem. Later sections sound more hopeful notes, but the poem never clings to articles of faith. The poet does not tell readers what he believes; we must work from vague hints in the poems coupled with much later reports by Hallam Tennyson, the poet's son. And indeed the trust to which the poem returns in later sections has more of the marks of reverence about it than belief. Tennyson harps on how foolish and slight we human beings are when compared to our ideas of God and nature. From start to finish, this poem is an expression of inarticulate reverence—reverence that is too conscious of its own ignorance to make anything but gestures toward the sort of articulate belief that might be stated in a creed.

In place of a creed, we find a hopeful trust running through the poems on two points: First, that "somehow good/Will be the final goal of ill" (54), and, second, that we humans are at least partly spirits or ghosts and "not wholly brain"—that is, we are not wholly material entities, and we may therefore survive in some fashion after death (93, 120). Tennyson is in no position to say what he means by these; indeed, he seems ready to modify them as needed to accommodate science. If they are challenged, he has no argument to give on their behalf; all he can say is, "I have felt" (124), and feelings do not discriminate on points of doctrine. That is why he tends to call his attitude toward these ideas "trust" or "faith" rather than "belief."

We may ask, nevertheless, what sort of theology Tennyson implies by this trust. Certainly it is not Christian. Although many of his peers were uncertain enough about Christian faith to take "In Memoriam" as a reaffirmation of Christianity, Tennyson surely knew what Christians are supposed to believe. There is no sign of specifically Christian belief in the poem, and we know from other sources that Tennyson consciously rejected such doctrines as original sin. The most that can be made of Tennyson's theology is this:

That God, which ever lives and loves,
One God, one law, one element,
And one far-off divine event,
To which the whole creation moves.
(Epilogue, lines 141–44)

The movement of creation to which he alludes is progress (118), both from lesser to greater animal species and from lower to higher moral sensibilities. Tennyson's son, Hallam, tells us also that the poet believes there is a Great Soul, which includes somehow both the creator God and the ongoing principles of Nature, into which the souls of the dead are assumed, and into which the souls of the living can be swept in momentary trances.

For this theology Tennyson has his feelings to thank, but his reason is not entirely innocent. By reason he has found that his faith is less vulnerable to doubt than are most of the standard creeds. Doubt supports faith:

> There lives more faith in honest doubt,
> Believe me, than in half the creeds. (96)

But he does not, like Descartes, test hypotheses methodically against doubt; instead he pins his hopes on the cloudiest of beliefs, beliefs that are too fuzzy to be in danger of being refuted. No one could seriously test Tennyson's hypothesis of a "Great Soul," when he does not say what he means by that. He is so cautious about articulating this belief in the poem that he does not even go so far as to use the expression.

Tennyson's religion has been a puzzle to readers of the twentieth century, which, in response to challenges such as Darwin's, has developed a more precise sense of the demands Christianity should make of belief. "He was desperately anxious to hold the faith of a believer," wrote T. S. Eliot, the sharpest modern reader of the poem, "without being very clear about what he wanted to believe." Confusions in Tennyson's talk about religion led Eliot to conclude that the poet's "feelings were more honest than his mind" and that he was more religious in his doubt than in his faith. But the poem is not about religion in any traditional sense. Its burden is reverence, and this is more in feelings than in the mind. Seen as a poem of reverence, "In Memoriam" is neither confused nor dishonest. Its medium is perfectly in tune with its content. Reverence cannot be expressed in a creed; its most apt expression is in music, which is the most remote of all art forms from the precise representation of content. Tennyson's gift is musical: in his modulation and counterpoint of images, in his metrical variety and close attention to sound, he has given us a heart-rending expression of reverence triumphing over the battle between religion and science. There is no place here for an articulation of belief.

That is why Tennyson has nothing clear to say about the object of his reverence. His trust in a Great Soul is implicit in the poem, and quite vague at that. He never tells his readers what to believe in order to be reverent. How could he teach others, when he does not know what he believes himself? "In Memoriam" is exquisite word-music, not doctrine. It works through sound and rhythm to bring the poet's reverence home to his readers' feelings. The varied cadences of the poem, held in a single verse form, show us how great a distance there is between the articulation of faith and the expression of reverence.

And more: The poem helps resolve a problem that has baffled philosophers about the classic argument from design, which runs as follows: the universe exhibits an awe-inspiring design; therefore the universe had a designer who created it, and that creator we know as God. This is a terrible argument for the existence of God as defined in any creed, and yet it has been enormously influential, even among scientists who claim allegiance to precise and careful thought. How could this be so? The answer, which Tennyson understood, is this: Many of us are awestruck when we contemplate the design we see in nature or the universe, and from awe we find our way quickly to reverence. So far, so good. But if we find our way also to specific beliefs about creation or theology, we can only do so by way of one fallacy after another. Creation is too singular an event to be inferred from the data. Even if it were not, how could we know whether the creator was one or many? Good or evil? Expert or a mere apprentice at crafting worlds? Immortal or perishable? In the eighteenth century, the Scottish philosopher David Hume asked these questions and showed that there is no particular story of creation by a specific deity that we can reasonably infer from our empirical observations. He has never been refuted.

The so-called argument from design is a sorry excuse for an argument. It does not prove a single article of faith; it does, however, brilliantly explain an experience that leads to reverence. Tennyson understood the difference.

Unnecessary Belief

When you begin thinking about this topic, you may be shocked at the religious beliefs of people who claim to be reverent. Yet if you think of reverence as a virtue, you must be prepared to recognize it in religions other than your own (just as you must be prepared to see versions of justice in many other cultures if you think justice is a virtue). Here is an outline of beliefs, widely held in our society, that are not necessary for reverence. If you are worried about these, read on; if not, I suggest you skip to chapter eight, "Reverence Across Religions."

That the Object of Reverence is a unique supreme being

No. Polytheism can be reverent, and polytheism does not hold this belief. (If you do not think polytheism can be reverent, go back and read about ancient Greece in chapter five.)

That the Object of Reverence is a god or gods

Better. But belief in the divine is not universal in Buddhism or Jainism, and people can be reverent in these religions. Reverence is possible for such objects as moral perfection, justice, life, nature, and truth, which are not gods. (For justice as an object of reverence, see chapter eleven on leadership; for truth see chapter thirteen on the reverent classroom.) You may be inclined to attack reverence for something that is not a god on the ground that it is idolatrous, but you would be mistaken. Idolatry is the worship of something other than God. But reverence is not worship. Albert Schweitzer writes eloquently of reverence for life, but he does not propose to worship life, and so by monotheistic standards he is not guilty of idolatry.

That the Object of Reverence Is fearsome

Some people use the expression "God-fearing" as if it meant the same as "reverent," but they are confused. Reverence stands in awe, but awe is not the same thing as fear. Schweitzer was never afraid of life, though life was an object of his reverence. And, in my experience, the people who are the most reverent towards God are the least afraid of Him.

Reverent people may or may not believe *that God or the gods personally intervene in human life, to punish those who violate divine commands.* But anyone who identifies reverence with fear of God must hold that God acts in some way on human life, here or in the hereafter. Tennyson feels he has found evidence that God does not intervene on earth, and still he wishes to be reverent. In fact, fear of punishment is the opposite of reverence; if all you have to keep you in line is the fear of God, then you have denied yourself all of the virtues, including reverence. Virtues are the source of feelings that make you want to do the right things; but fear of God would merely keep you from doing the evil things you would want to do, if you had no virtue whatever.

Reverence is the virtue that makes us feel like not arrogating properties such as infallibility that could only belong to divine beings.

There are at least three different kinds of reasons for observing the "No Trespassing" signs along the fence between the divine and the human: (1) you might be afraid of what the gods do to trespassers; (2) you might dread the violence that arises among human beings when some of them put on divine airs; or (3) you might simply hold that it is morally wrong to trespass, out of respect or awe for those who dwell on the other side. Only the third reason is strictly reverent; reverence is doing the reverent thing for the reverent reason.

Fear is not in itself a moral consideration. Even a vicious criminal can be kept in check through fear. Fear of gods cannot belong to any virtue. Even in cultures that do fear the gods, fear is not the same thing as reverence. In Aeschylus' *Prometheus Bound,* the hero refuses to yield to threats from Zeus and shows no fear of what the god can do to him. He is admirable even so, in his reverence for the unnamed power that will topple the tyrannical Zeus from his throne.

Fear of gods fails other tests than the moral one. From where we stand now, it is easy to see that it is foolish to fear Zeus or Poseidon or Apollo. We know that they cannot harm us, because we know where thunder and earthquake and plague come from. By the end of the fifth century BCE, many Greek intellectuals had given up the old idea that you could bring on fearful disasters by changing or dropping old ceremonies. Ancient travelers saw that different peoples staged different ceremonies to different gods, with no great difference to their chances of prosperity or bad fortune. This meant there was no basis for any group to insist that their gods and their ceremonies were the only ones with real power.

The most telling objection comes from history: Why shouldn't the human story make sense on its own—why suppose that gods intervene? Plague, famine, and tempest come and go, and there is no clear evidence that religious ceremony keeps them at bay. The plague at Athens made no distinctions between those who practiced religion and those who did not.

That the Object of Reverence Is Perfect

Most modern religions attribute moral perfection to the Being they worship, but this is not necessary for reverence. This belief is at least consistent with reverence, but it is not necessary for it. Believers in polytheism often hold that their gods are the source of evil for human beings, without making any attempt to show that their gods are morally good (and similarly for some monotheists). And yet such believers insist on reverence—not because the gods deserve it in some moral sense, but because they demand it, and because human beings will live better and more human lives if they are reverent.

If reverence required human beings to behave in the way they think their gods behave, then worshipping nasty gods would make for a nasty sort of reverence. But reverence actually bars human beings from trying to give themselves divine attributes, and this is especially important when those attributes are thought to be horrible. Again, if reverence always implied respect, and if respect amounted to good opinion, then you would have to twist your values backwards before you could be reverent towards a divinity that you did not believe to be good. But as we shall see, respect is not the same as good opinion. Reverence treats fools and criminals with a measure of respect. The reverent worshipper of an evil god will hold the god in awe and respect, but not admiration.

Reformers who complain about the worship of evil gods are usually showing their failure to understand reverence. From at least the sixth century BCE, Greek intellectuals objected to the immoral behavior of gods in Greek myth. The gods of myth are, among other things, models of what we must not be. It is as if myth says, "Look at all the dreadful things the gods do; they get away with crimes like that, because they are immortal. You, however, are a mortal human being, and you would not long survive if you followed their example. Remember your place, and do not do as the gods are said to do."

Generally, people need not believe in sweet, loving, or even fair-minded gods in order to be reverent.

Unbelief Is Not Irreverence

If I am right so far, cultures that prized reverence should have no complaint to make about lack of any particular belief (beyond the minimum previously discussed). Some modern religions make much of belief and faith. Ancient religions, generally, did not.

Even the Greek poets of reverence were not dismayed simply by lack of belief in this god or that. Pentheus, like many monarchs in Greek tragedy, is a model of irreverence (*Bacchae,* 370ff.). Is this because he fails to believe in Dionysus? Or is it because of positive beliefs that he holds, which the Chorus repudiate (for example, 997ff.)? Although Euripides set the play in long-ago Thebes, he meant it to speak to Athenians of his time, and I believe the play expressed a fairly popular view of reverence—one not influenced by the agnostics or humanists I mentioned earlier.

Athenians held at least three fundamental beliefs: (1) that the gods exist; (2) that the gods pay attention to the affairs of men; and (3) that the relation between gods and men, though unequal, is actively reciprocal. Pentheus, so far as we can tell, does not set himself against any of these beliefs as stated. So far as we know, there are gods about whom he has these three beliefs. He just does not have them about Dionysus. But—and this is a subtle point—Pentheus is not in trouble for not believing in Dionysus. He and his family have never believed in Dionysus, nor have they taken part in Bacchic rituals. Neither has anyone else in Greece, yet only Pentheus and his family are in trouble. Why does Dionysus single out Pentheus and his family for punishment, of all the legions of unbelievers in Thebes and Greece? Their crime is not unbelief; they insulted a god.

Dionysus converts unbelievers, holding them innocent, while wreaking savage vengeance on those who insult him.

Pentheus is in trouble because he explicitly denies that Dionysus is a god and rejects the practices of Dionysus worshippers as a danger to society. He is wrong on both points, as the play shows us. Dionysus introduces himself to us as a god in the prologue, and the Maenads in the mountain are dangerous only when disturbed by men. Pentheus' fears of violence and sexual disturbance are unfounded, so long as he does not try to shut down the practice of Dionysus worship.

Pentheus is in trouble, too, because his family did not listen to their weakest and most vulnerable dependent—young Semele, Dionysus' mother, pregnant, unmarried, and in need. They have turned away from one of their own. These are two impieties in one: violation of family obligation and refusal of a suppliant. If the family has such arrogance towards troubled young Semele, no wonder they are out of touch with the common people of Thebes.

Their rejection of Semele is especially insulting to the gods because it involves particular refusals to believe in interventions by gods in their own lives: the impregnation of Semele by Zeus, the thunderbolt that killed her, the undying fire on the site of Semele's death. Now it is the son of Zeus who has thrilled the women of Thebes into their mountain-dancing. How many times will this family insult the gods and remain in power?

Why did the family reject Semele? Were they seduced by rationalist arguments into doubting that divine intervention occurs? Or did they simply fall into the habit of expecting the normal pattern of events to continue? Unmarried girls often grow pregnant, after all, without any help from Zeus; thunderbolts may strike for no obvious reason, and people fall prey to bizarre religious teachings with alarming frequency, owing to the frailty of the human mind.

Simple belief, however, is not the main point. Dionysus in the *Bacchae* does not spread his religion in order to save souls from damnation, but mainly to secure his own honor. The rest of Greece has up to now lacked faith, but only the Theban royal family has insulted the god by rejecting his mother Semele, and only Pentheus has threatened to put down the Maenads:

> Oh Reverence, queen of gods,
> Reverence, who over earth
> Spreads golden wing,
> Have you heard Pentheus?
> Have you heard the outrage...?
> (Bacchae, 370–74)

And the failure that lies behind this outrage—the failure that the chorus single out for reproach—is Pentheus' failure to recognize his own mortality:

> Wisdom? It's not wise
> To lift our thoughts too high;
> We are human and our time is short.
> (395–97)

> Death makes judgment sound, hears no
> Excuses. When you face the gods, remember
> Your mortality, if you'd live a painless life.
> (1002–4)

To live in the knowledge that you are not divine—that you are mortal—is to have good judgment, and to have good judgment in action is to pull back from every sort of excess, especially from excess of power. Honor is given to gods in many ways, most visibly through sacrifices and other rituals, but also by taking to heart the difference between human and divine. People must not only understand that they are mortal but live in a way that reflects that understanding: they must not be too ambitious, for example, and they must not be too boastful, or they will bring on themselves the anger of the gods. Above all, they must listen to the weakest among them. They should have listened to Semele.

Pentheus puts himself in competition with the god by setting out to take back the minds of the Theban women from the stranger who, he thinks, has addled them. But only a god could compete with a god, and the prize in this case—tyranny over people's minds—is a power no human being may safely enjoy. "The god does not allow anyone but himself to have great ambition"—that is the warning Xerxes has from his uncle (according to Herodotus) when he considers invading Greece (7.10). For a mortal to act like a god is the peak of irreverence (*Bacchae* 395–96).

The Range of Reverence

Reverence crops up in many different systems, with religion or without—so widely, in fact, that there can be no core of required beliefs beyond an inarticulate trust that there is something of which we must stand in awe. Tennyson was right, and so was the mixed group of students I described at the funeral, who longed for a reverence that would not divide them from their friend who had died, and that would not divide their friend from his family. Religions have been in crisis before now, creeds have come and gone, even within Christianity, but reverence lives on.

If you ask the poets of reverence, "What must I believe in order to be reverent?" they will fall silent. But ask them, "What must I not believe?" Then they have an answer: any belief that trespasses on divine ground is the enemy of reverence. Do not believe that you are supreme in any way; do not believe that you alone know the mind of God. These would be troubling violations of the boundary between human beings and the object of reverence. Such violations are common—and are sometimes even considered essential—in some organized religions; that is why being religious is not the same as being reverent. When violence breaks out between people of different religious beliefs, reverence has fled the scene. Reverence—like Tennyson's poem—cannot take a stand on fine points of belief. True reverence does not kill heretics or unbelievers. Reverence knows the limits of human knowledge and never presumes to represent literally the mind of God.

Reverence is not subject to the deaths of men;
They live, they die, but reverence shall not perish.
      —*Sophocles,* Philoctetes *(lines 1442—44)*

Oh ye who tread the Narrow Way,
By Tophet-flare to Judgment Day,
Be gentle when the heathen pray
To Buddha Kamakura!
          —*Rudyard Kipling, epigraph to* Kim

My brother kneels (so saith Kabir)
To stone and brass in heathen-wise,
But in my brother's voice I hear
My own unanswered agonies.
His god is as his Fates assign—
His prayer is all the world's—and mine.
          —*Rudyard Kipling "The Prayer,"*
          epigraph to chapter XIV of Kim

8 | REVERENCE ACROSS RELIGIONS

Religions come and go, but not the needs of our weakness. To these needs, our endless prayers bear witness. Yehuda Amichai, the great poet of modern Israel, insisted that although cultures with their languages and beliefs may perish, prayers do not. Along with prayers, ritual too survives. Often a practice continues with new meanings long after old meanings have been forgotten. Ritual is more robust than belief and has more staying power, but wherever there is ritual, there should be the reverence to take that ritual seriously. Otherwise—and too often it is otherwise—the ritual becomes dry and useless, withers away or becomes a mask for irreverent behavior.

In these fast-changing times, many people feel the ground of religion shifting underneath them. They should be comforted to learn that religious ground has shifted before. Faith changes over history, but reverence remains. We should, therefore, be able to trace reverence back to cultures that have religions very different from modern ones. That's what I plan to do in this chapter, with special attention to religions that seem most repugnant to modern Christian taste. One very hard case is religion that is agnostic, or that places no emphasis on belief, such as classic Confucianism or Jainism. A different sort of hard case is religion that calls for violence in the form of blood sacrifice. If I can show that reverence has a chance of growing on either sort of ground, then we may reasonably expect that it could grow almost anywhere.

If you stand on the ground of your own religion and look at another that is not your own, you may ask how any true reverence could be part of such bizarre practices or such a misguided faith. G. K. Chesterton is eloquent on behalf of Christianity: "Sometimes it would seem that the Greeks believed above all things in reverence, only they had nobody to revere." He believed, apparently, that there can be no reverence that is not about the God of Christians, because He is the only God. Chesterton's view seems to be widely shared—among Christians. Thinkers like Chesterton have a double problem with pagan Greek reverence, or rather, with the gods that pagan reverence is about: It's bad enough (they think) that these alleged gods do not exist, but it's even worse that if such gods existed they would not be reliably good.

But if reverence is a cardinal virtue, then it should be able to team up with a wide range of religious practices and beliefs—and with atheism and neglect of religion as well. That means that we must be able to detach reverence from most features that are distinctive of particular religions. But it's not the case that anything goes with reverence. Reverence will wither away in any movement—religious or otherwise—that arrogates the authority of God to human beings, and it may have little chance to flourish in a movement that has no time for ceremony or ritual of any sort. There is such a thing as religion without reverence; it is frightening and restrictive, as we will see in the next chapter. Here I will bring out some surprising features of religion that are compatible with reverence.

Violent Reverence: Sacrifice

The practices of ancient Greek religion are especially repulsive to modern minds, which see idolatry and bloody sacrifice as at best a set of quaint rituals suitable only for anthropological study. And as for belief, Greek mythology deviates so sharply from morality that even the ancients were shocked. What virtue, you might ask, could be linked to a polytheism that revels in stories of sex, violence, and conflict among the gods? What virtue, besides a narrow and self-interested prudence, could be deployed in transactions with the gods by way of sacrifice or magic? The virtues of a religion centered on sacrifice would appear to be those of a successful merchant or business, virtues you can enjoy without paying the cost of morality: Do what you like and then buy off the gods with burnt offerings. What could such a practice have to do with virtue?

In fact, the performance of sacrifice (like that of any gift or offering) may or may not express reverence. Sacrifice will not protect you if you lack reverence, because the mere performance of ritual will not be enough to win over a god you have insulted. In ancient Greece, ceremonies mattered to the life of the city, of course, but people with good sense knew they could not achieve reverence by the mere performance of ceremony. They did not believe that the gods could simply be bought or crudely manipulated by human beings. The gods of their myths make their own decisions, in their own way.

Sacrifice to the gods is an exchange of honor. Honor is as important to gods as it is to kings, and for similar reasons, as Tiresias argues in the *Bacchae* (317–22). In giving and accepting honor, humans and their gods recognize the special relationship they have with one another and the enormous difference in rank that is bridged by it. Beyond sacrifice, however, the gods demand reverence and justice and soundness of mind from human beings. And what they require they may also grant to those who honor them.

The importance of ceremony to virtue (as we saw in chapter six) is that it is a language of behavior for recognizing a hierarchy and keeping it benign. Without reverence, ceremony cannot do this. With reverence, ceremony shows that one knows and accepts where one belongs, both as a human being in the large order of things, and as a member of structured human society.

Animal rights advocates may wonder how reverence could be deployed in a religion that sanctions the killing of cattle in sacrifice. But evidently the ancients felt that butchery is an arrogant display of power over animals unless it is hedged in by ceremony and tempered by reverence. The priest who brings a proud bull to his knees is reminded at that very moment that he too lives at the mercy of more powerful beings. Workers in today's meat plants have no such ceremonies, no such reminders.

Violent Reverence: Vengeance

Modern taste is especially disturbed by ancient religions that call on their gods for vengeance against their enemies. How could such calls be reverent? One wonders how the Chorus of the *Bacchae* could be reverent, when they scream for vengeance and take joy in the dismemberment of the young king by his mother.

Keep in mind, however, that the vengeance for which the Chorus calls is to be wreaked by the god—not by human beings. Throughout the play, the Chorus observes the essential distinction between what is up to human beings and what is up to the god. "Vengeance is mine," says the Christian God; "vengeance is thine," say the Chorus to Dionysus. This is simply another instance of the main principle of reverence, that human beings should never play at being gods.

If such calls for vengeance still seem irreverent to you, consider the most reverent texts of the scriptures shared by Jews and Christians—the Psalms of David. Here are a handful of familiar passages: "Thou shalt break them with a rod of iron; thou shalt dash them in pieces like a potters vessel" (2.9). "... Thou hast smitten all mine enemies upon the cheekbone; thou hast broken the teeth of the ungodly" (3.7). "Upon the wicked he shall rain snares, fire, and brimstone, and an horrible tempest..." (11.6). "Thou shalt make them as a fiery oven in the time of thy anger: the Lord shall swallow them up in his wrath, and the fire shall devour them. Their fruit shalt thou destroy from the earth, and their seed from among the children of men. For they intended evil against thee..." (21.9–11). "O Lord God, to whom vengeance belongeth; O God, to whom vengeance belongeth, show thyself" (94.1). "And he shall bring upon them their own iniquity, and shall cut them off in their own wickedness..." (94.23).

Agnostic Reverence: Greece

> All that is necessary is that you should not mix a wise moral system with absurd fables, because you weaken through your impostures, which you can do without, the morality that you are forced to teach.
>
> —Voltaire, *Philosophical Dictionary*, s.v. Fraud
> (trans. H. I. Woolf)

Humanists such as Protagoras, Thucydides, and Socrates guarded reverence by taking care not to make unfounded claims about the gods or the heavens or the underworld. Agnosticism is, in fact, a time-honored way of recognizing the limits of human under-standing. An agnostic does not presume to know. We are human, and the wisdom allowed to us, Socrates says, is the wisdom of know-ing our own limitations. If this is right, then the Greeks should never find that an omission of belief by itself is a failure of reverence.

Godless reverence may strike the reader as impossible. But we have already seen that there are several forms of it. In Greece as in

China, the reverence of humanism grows in intellectuals on the wreckage of polytheism. After polytheism has worn thin, or after the fear of violence by personal gods has begun to look silly, many people still believe that they must sustain reverence as a foundation for society. This is the curious and fragile stage that I tried to explain in the chapters on ancient Greece and China.

The arch-humanist of ancient Greece is Protagoras, who is best known for his statement that "a human being is the measure of all things." We do not know exactly what this means, but we do know that Protagoras concerns himself only with human beings and with those elements in the world that have effects on human life. This concern leaves him firmly agnostic about the gods:

> Concerning the gods, I am not in a position to know either that they exist or that they do not, nor can I know what they look like, for many things prevent our knowing—the subject is obscure and human life is short. (Protagoras, Fragment 4).

Despite his agnosticism, Protagoras is the first Greek thinker to speak clearly about the reverence that brings us together. As we saw in chapter four, Protagoras thinks reverence—or something very much like it—is a matter of life or death. No group of human beings can stand by one another without reverence and justice, and if they cannot stand by one another they will perish. The reverence of humanism is a kind of social glue that enables us to survive by helping us to work together. Protagoras is right, I will argue, mainly because reverence marks the difference between stable government through leadership and insecure rule by fear.

Thucydides is the Greek humanist about whom we know the most. His reverence is based on beliefs about human beings. About the gods he is agnostic or atheistic, yet he sets the highest value on reverence, and indeed seems to think that it sums up all virtue, because he treats its loss as the consummate ethical failure of a city:

> [Of the plague] No one was held back, either by fear of the gods or by the laws of men. (Thucydides, 2.53.4)

> [Of civil war] Each party was limited only by its own appetite at the time, and stood ready to satisfy its ambition of the moment either by voting for an unjust verdict or seizing control by force. So neither side thought much of reverence. (Thucydides, 3.82.8)

In order to appreciate Thucydides' loyalty to the classical conception of reverence, one must read with care his entire history of the Peloponnesian War. Thucydides expresses himself rarely through authorial observations, and often through the arrangement of incident, the balancing of speeches, and the tone of suppressed outrage that is unmistakable in such scenes as the final execution of oligarchs on Corcyra (4.47–48). The tragic patterns that the historian arranges, from beginnings in arrogance and overreaching to endings in rage and destruction, are driven not by the anger of the gods but by the anger of men. These are patterns of human history, rooted in the human condition. There is nothing divine about them, but they suffice to bring down the mighty in their pride.

Reverence, in Thucydides, is one of the crucial virtues that, along with justice, has little hold on the minds of men when they are at war with each other or battling a natural disaster. Only in a stable social order can these virtues flourish, and their flourishing serves the order in return, by giving it stability through the satisfied loyalty of all parties to the state. The account of Thucydides I have just given is somewhat speculative—because he does not come out and say it—but is nevertheless the most plausible solution to a number of theoretical difficulties.

What is the particular value of reverence, as opposed to justice? The two virtues govern many of the same situations in Thucydides, but reverence at least gives rise to emotions such as awe, which may in good circumstances have motivating power, while it is hard to see how justice functions at all, except as an abstract idea. I note also that his characters think of justice as mainly regulating the affairs of people or cities who are roughly equal in power, while reverence comes most into play when the strong have the weak at their mercy.

In China, humanism survived the death of Confucius for centuries, at least among intellectuals, but it had little staying power among the ancient Greeks. Traditional religion continued to flourish in Greece despite the power of intellectual criticism, and people continued to fear the gods no matter how hard the philosophers tried to spread peace of mind through their teachings.

Greece had an alternative to humanism, however. Plato was no humanist, but he rejected most of traditional religious mythology and established a pattern of reverence leading beyond the gods. He attacked Protagoras on a number of points and declared that the measure in his system is not a human being but a god (*Laws* 716c). But Plato's attitude towards traditional polytheism is ambivalent. On the one hand, he retains the practices of traditional Greek religion in his ideal state, but only as a device for maintaining order among ordinary people. For philosophers, on the other hand, he will offer a mystery religion in which gods and humans journey together to see the sacred objects. Education, he will say, is like initiation, but the sacred entity that an aspiring philosopher will meet as he is initiated is not anything like the personal gods of traditional myth. Instead, Plato will invest pure justice and every other kind of pure goodness with the attributes of divinity.

Pure justice and goodness are (in Plato's system) examples of transcendent forms, eternal beings that Plato separates from the level on which human beings live. Every moral perfection is truly real, according to Plato—more real than anything we human beings can know through perception. And the things that are most truly real are the transcendent forms. As such the forms are above the gods themselves (in Plato's myth), outside the rim of the heavenly dwelling of the gods. Even the gods must feed their souls on the sight of the forms in order to maintain their immortality. The gods are supposed to be good in every way, but they do not define their own goodness. They have no more control than human beings do over what is just or beautiful or good.

Plato is the first to celebrate *reverence for moral perfection* in place of reverence for the gods. He enlists religion in the support of moral goodness, and indeed he sets moral goodness on the throne which the gods have left. In Plato's system, human beings and gods alike are in awe of moral perfection. Human seekers come to appreciate transcendent justice and beauty with the same sort of awe that they would feel on being initiated into a special relationship with a god. On this Platonic theory, the gods are good not because they are gods; they are gods, rather, because they are devoted single-mindedly to virtue. The gods, then, are examples to emulate, and human beings should practice reverence by trying to live as gods do. How gods live, in turn, is known not by the study of mythology, but by inquiry into the nature of the good. In practice, then, the reverence of perfection is contrary to tragic reverence. The one urges people to emulate the gods; the other forbids them to do so.

Agnostic Reverence: Chinese Humanism

Confucians are silent about the gods, and so they must understand *Li* as reverence toward a Heaven about which there is nothing to be said—probably because nothing about it is distinctly known. *Li* preserves a harmonious relationship between humanity and Heaven by maintaining in human beings a sense of their place in a larger (but unknown) scheme. *Li,* then, is independent of any particular beliefs about the gods and focuses primarily on the expression of reverence in daily life. This is easy to ridicule. Confucius' younger rival Mo Tzu (fifth century BCE) complained that teaching *Li* without belief about the gods was like "making fishnets when there are no fish."

Confucius said of himself that at the age of fifty he knew the will of Heaven (2.4), so we cannot call him agnostic in the strict sense. Some *Analects,* moreover, imply that Confucius thought of Heaven as something like an active and personal god, but on the whole Confucius maintains silence on the subject of Heaven. His silence is itself an expression of reverence, a sign of the awe in which he stands at the thought of Heaven. Generally, reverence requires that one never pretend to powers one does not have. In particular, it is wrong to claim knowledge of the divine:

> The Master said: "I am going to teach you what knowledge is. To take what you know for what you know, and what you do not know for what you do not know, that is knowledge indeed." (*Analects* 2.17)

> The Master said: "I make no claims to wisdom or to human perfection—how would I dare? Still, my aim remains unflagging and I never tire of teaching people." Gongxi Chi said: "This is precisely what we disciples fail to emulate." (*Analects* 7.34)

Confucius, who sets great store by reverence, keeps silent about that which he does not know. He does not speak about the ancient polytheism of China, does not affirm or deny old tales, and says nothing about the effect of ritual on the divine:

Zilu asked how to serve the spirits and gods. The Master said, "You are not able to serve men, how could you serve the spirits?" Xilu said: "May I ask about death?" The Master said: "You do not yet know life, how could you know death?" (*Analects* 11.12)

Perhaps Confucius thinks his students are not ready to hear what he has to say. But in view of his modesty about matters with which he is not acquainted, it is more likely that Confucius would not presume to speak on behalf of the divine. After all, Heaven itself is able to rule without a word to those below:

The Master said: "I wish to speak no more." Zigong said: "Master, if you do not speak, how would little ones like us hand down your teachings?" The Master said: "Does Heaven speak? Yet the four seasons follow their course and the hundred creatures continue to be born. Does Heaven speak?" (*Analects* 17.19)

For this reason, we should not expect articulated theology or even metaphysics from Confucian philosophy. And yet the system supports both ritual and reverence because it brings them down to the human level. Children have parents, students have teachers, administrators serve higher-ups. But however high you rise on your own ladder of advancement, there is always something higher—Heaven, or the Way—that draws you upward even though you cannot say what it is:

Yen Yuan [a student] said: "The Master is good at leading one on step by step. He broadens me with literature and restrains me with *Li*, so that even if I wanted to stop I could not do so. But, although I have done all I can, [the goal] seems to rise sheer above me. I long to go after it, but I cannot find the way. (*Analects* 9.11)

"The goal seems to rise sheer above me. I long to go after it, but I cannot find the way." Awe is inarticulate. A sense of awe comes over us without our being able to say exactly what it is about. Reverence at such a moment forbids any attempt to put words around it. That is why awe is the most reverent of feelings. You feel, when you are in awe, that you are human, that your mind is dwarfed by what it confronts, that you cannot capture it in a set of beliefs, and that you had best keep your mouth closed and your mind open while awaiting further disclosure.

A human being is the measure of all things, of those things that are that they are, and of those things that are not that they are not.

—*Protagoras*

It is the god who is a measure of all things for us—much more so than some human being or other, as has been claimed.

—*Plato*

9 | RELATIVISM

A complete relativist—like a die-hard traditionalist—would tie reverence to tradition so strongly as to make it impossible to break with tradition and not violate reverence. But sometimes it is right to break with a tradition, and in those cases, if reverence is a virtue, breaking with tradition cannot be irreverent.

A good relativist is hard to find. A well-tuned mind cannot overlook the differences in faith and morals between one religion and another. It is not reverent to say that all religions are the same deep down. Well-meaning people who say that they are the same may be setting the issue of belief aside (as would be fair enough for those whose religions do not involve belief). But if they are speaking of belief-based religions, then they are betraying either their own beliefs or the truth. If they don't really care whether their beliefs are true, they betray their beliefs; if they think that every religious belief is true, they betray the truth. The same goes for morals: if you think that every religious system gives equal place to justice, you betray justice.

This judgment may strike you as harsh in view of the rising liberal fashion for passing over differences in religious belief. True, articulate belief plays a small role in most people's actual experience of religion, but when beliefs are stated, they do matter. Anyone who is reverent toward the truth will want to avoid false belief so far as possible, and anyone who is reverent toward justice will want to stand against beliefs that call for violence and oppression. But the moral problem with relativism lies even deeper. A complete relativist would hold that there is a different truth and a different justice in each religion, and that these are true and just in the full sense. But this sort of relativism implies that human beings can create truth or justice as they please on their own, and that is irreverent.

A good relativist is hard to find. There is a logical reason for this as well as a moral one. If you could find any complete relativists, you would never disagree with them, because they would always grant that your opinions are as well grounded as theirs. But in real life we can almost always find something to disagree about. Plato tells us that Protagoras tries to be a relativist, but then Plato shows in a famous argument that even Protagoras cannot keep it up. The instant he defends his relativism against criticism, he implicitly abandons it—because at that point he has to disagree with those who reject his position. Of course, he could pretend he takes no position at all, but if he takes no position at all, he certainly does not take the relativist position. And if he's not prepared to disagree with anyone, he can't really take a position. Perhaps he is not a complete relativist but a skeptic who avoids all commitments of the mind. But we were looking for a relativist, and we now see that this is not what he is.

As a matter of history, we know that Protagoras was not a complete relativist; he defended strong claims on many subjects, and among these was his thesis that reverence could be learned and that learning it was important to the health of society. We do not know what he meant by the enigmatic quotation at the head of this chapter, "a human being is the measure of all things." It comes to us without context, giving scholars a wide-open opportunity to invent interpretations. Whatever it means, however, it is about as irreverent a thing as you can say, and some ancient critics pointed this out, possibly with horrible consequences for Protagoras. Anyone who says that a human being is the measure of what is true or real cannot be reverently aware of human limitations.

The moral point was that complete relativism is arrogant. It tries to offer human beings an immunity from argument and refutation that doesn't fit with human fallibility. Part of accepting your humanity is allowing for the possibility that you may be wrong and acknowledging your vulnerability to refutation. Many would-be relativists miss the moral point altogether, because they think that relativism is tolerant and kind. They think they are doing people a favor by granting them immunity from argument and refutation; they may even think that the moral advantages of relativism outweigh the logical problems Plato pointed out. They are making a mistake. Relativism has no moral advantages. In the world of ideas, relativism cultivates minds that are closed or lazy; in a world of ethical choices, relativism leaves human rights undefended by allowing no place for discussion or debate.

Relativism in Ideas

Relativists in the world of ideas seek a haven from which they need not defend their beliefs. The haven might be silence, or it might be a fast-moving game of words. For students, it is often silence. Most teachers have known a student like Rick, who has nothing to say to the rest of us—not because he is scared to talk and not because he thinks he is better than we are. He is a happy-go-lucky fellow with few cares in the world, not the least bit frightened, and not arrogant in the ordinary way. Early in the year he saw that the members of the class had their own personal views about the issues we discussed and that we all could give reasons for our views. When he realized that hardly any of us ever changed our minds even after hearing each other out, he gave up.

"What's the point?" he asked, when I challenged him to speak. "You have your truth and I have mine. It's not going to make any difference what I say, or what you say. Your truth is still true for you, and mine will go right on being true for me." Rick starts out wrong with his "You have your truth and I have mine." But after that, his reasoning is impeccable. If different people have different truths, then everyone is equally wise. No one has any reason to listen to anyone else, and by the same token no one has any reason to speak to anyone else. On Rick's hypothesis, all communication will be empty between him and me because the same thing will never be true for both of us. Why should I care what is true for him, if I know in advance that it cannot be true for me? And why bother with argument? No matter how well he expresses the reasons he has for his beliefs (he thinks), they cannot become mine.

The best answer to a relativist is no answer at all, because relativists are not interested in answers that are true for other people. "Nothing you could say would be true for me," thinks Rick, closing himself off from the conversation. The best I could do for him is to change the culture of the class so as to draw him into the conversation. Arguing against him is not likely to do this.

A familiar strategy is to lure him into defending his relativistic hypothesis and then show him (as Plato does in the case of Protagoras) that any defense of his position is an admission of defeat. Once he defends himself, he admits that we disagree, and when he does that he has conceded that there is a common truth for us to disagree about. But that is what he was trying to deny. So I would have proven that he is not really a complete relativist after all. This logical strategy is good philosophy but bad human relations. Rick will probably feel that he is the victim of a logical trick and become even more silent. Much better to engage him in a vigorous discussion of some subject he cares about—perhaps the current standing of football teams—and about which he obviously knows a great deal more than I do. Afterwards, I can show how absurd that conversation would have been if there were no common truth about which he could set me right.

Rick will say that he wasn't a relativist about football—just about the subjects that come up in a philosophy class, like ethics. There is no common truth about them, he will insist, but at this point it begins to come clear that he is grasping for reasons to keep his mind out of class. As he develops the patience to see how one argument might be better than another, even on highly abstract subjects, he will take a larger part in the discussion. He has a lot to learn from doing this, and at the same time he will be a better person if he develops a patient and open mind. When he made himself exempt from argument, he made himself exempt from learning. And that is as bad for a young student as it is for an old tyrant or a middle-aged professor. Reverence at any age is open to learning.

Some highly trained intellectuals are as bad as Rick, but with less excuse. It is not that they are silent; far from it, they publish frequently and are often heard at learned conferences. But for them the whole business is a game. They don't think it much matters what they believe, or what *you* believe for that matter.

Take Professor Charles. He may begin an argument, "I happen to like realism on this point," and then draw rigorous inferences from this principle of which the best he can say is that he "happens to like it." His endings are as arbitrary as his beginnings, and the best that I can say of him is that he has learned to play the game he calls philosophy with skill. But ask him whether he thinks realism is true and he will brush you aside gracefully. That question is not for him. Charles says he is content with any theory, so long as the game is well played around it. He won't admit he is a relativist (not, at least, as readily as Rick will), but he is as slow as Rick to engage in a serious defense of his principles.

To do Charles justice, I must admit that he has a rationale for this, and it has something to do with reverence. Claims about truth are too grand for Charles. He is humble about himself and about the limits within which all philosophy must work. No one (except perhaps God) is in a position to declare whether realism is true or false or somewhere in between, and perhaps it is no more than a useful hypothesis for explaining certain results (say, in number theory) that Charles does believe to be true. But Charles' humility carries him too far—really into a sort of arrogance. The immunity he gives himself from argument separates him from other scholars; he is trying to be a community of one. But reverence knows that human beings are vulnerable, and especially so when they are alone.

In fact, Charles is not a very good game-player. He plays a good game until he is seriously challenged, and then he runs off the field. For all I know, Charles is right about realism, but he still owes his colleagues what my students owe each other—full participation in the rituals of ideas. A good game-player does not sit out in the middle of the playing field, silent and inactive, while others try to play around him. No taking the ball off into a corner and playing catch with yourself while the others lose patience. No running off the field mid-game. A good game-player is reverent through and through.

Reverence for truth leads to humility in the face of the awesome task of getting something right. But humility is not despair, and it is not skepticism. In communities that seek learning, it is expressed in the rituals of conferences and peer-reviewed publications. Arguments must be given, and counterarguments must be heeded, or else positions must be modified or abandoned. Reverence is not easy.

Relativism and Tradition

Once you are persuaded that reverence may be found in many different cultures and across many different religions, you may come to believe that the reverence of one culture is just as good as that of any other. Each culture, you might think, should be exempt from criticism. When you visit a society that is new to you, you may believe that you must accept that its way of being reverent is as good for its people as yours is for you. But that too is a form of relativism, and it is wrong. A society has no better claim than an individual to being immune from criticism and argument, and the customs of all societies cry out, from time to time, to be changed.

Consider the case of child-marriage. Suppose a date has been set, the bridegroom selected, and Vaka's parents tell her she should be pleased. Another year and she will be fourteen; at that point the price would go up, because most boys' families would demand a higher dowry for an older bride. The family they have found for Vaka is not bad, considering the poverty of her family. But Vaka is not pleased. Her older brother is still going to the new school during the middle of the day when he is not needed for work, and she would like to continue attending school along with him. Instead of thanking her parents for arranging the marriage, as they expected, she cries all night.

Her parents blame the strangers—young men and women with a poor grasp of the village language who have brought new ideas about irrigation and drainage to the village. Some of those ideas seem to be helpful, but not all, and the new school has been a major threat to tradition—especially by allowing marriageable girls like Vaka to attend class. The elders of the village agree; these outsiders come from a place that has no respect for family and tradition. A girl must be taken into her husband's home by age thirteen and taught the ways of her new family. She must serve the family mother in all things; otherwise, how will the family carry on from one generation to the next? And how will Vaka grow, through reverent observance of family tradition, into a good wife? No responsible parents would let their son marry a woman who had not been brought into his family as a child.

Vaka says that these new people have told her about a god who wants her to go to school and put off marriage until much later. The elders concede there may be a god who makes this odd demand of some people, but they insist that he could not be the right god for their village. The gods of *their* village have supported child-marriage for thousands of years. It is a divinely ordained tradition. They are appalled at even the suggestion that mere human beings set it aside. What could be a greater violation of reverence?

The young teacher is appalled when Vaka abruptly stops coming to school and she hears the reason why. She wants to say: "What arrogance of the village elders to claim that their backward ways were ordained by gods!" And as for passing family custom from generation to generation, that is a charming idea, so long as the customs do not infringe on human rights. But this custom—child-marriage—is tantamount to slavery, she thinks. It violates the fundamental right to choose a partner for life, and it allows the groom's parents to exact untold amounts of unpaid labor, by force, from the bride. Worse, many parents think they have power of life or death over their sons' wives. If reverence supports the village in this abominable sacrifice of young girls, then reverence is an abomination. The teacher would rescue Vaka by force if necessary, but her team leader insists that they not interfere with local customs. They are permitted to open the school to girls, but they must do nothing directly against the wishes of a girl's parents, and they are barred from recruiting girls aggressively to further their education.

This is a hard case for reverence. Each side is appalled at the other's values. The young teacher does not think that the reverence of Vaka's village is a virtue at all, but rather something terribly oppressive, a rationale for slavery. The village elders see no good coming from a school education for Vaka. Apprenticeship in the home, they say, is nothing like slavery; it is reverent training for the role a girl will play as an adult. On the issue between them, the team leader is determined to make no decision. "We have our ways and they have theirs," he says. "Who is to say which of the two is better?" But now Vaka wants to go to school, and the leader's relativism will not help her or the villagers face the pressures that are coming from outside.

The same sort of issue—but this time concerning justice—arose in the debate about chattel slavery a century and a half ago. An abolitionist would complain that the system of justice prevailing in a slaveholding area is no true justice because it protects the rights of the slaveholder but not those of the slave. The slaveholder's counterargument is simple: Justice forbids taking away property by force; slaves are property; liberating slaves is taking property away from their owners by force; therefore, it follows that justice forbids the liberation of slaves. Relativism would declare both sides right: it is unjust to suppress the rights of people who are enslaved, and it is equally unjust to liberate them.

Relativism leads to this dilemma because it allows that justice is a human product, made differently by slaveholders and abolitionists. But no one who has reverence for justice can allow that it is whatever we say it is. Justice is an ideal that is imperfectly realized in codes of law, and it is the ideal—not the imperfect realizations of it—that merits reverence. Reverence is incompatible with relativism. And in the case of slavery, the relativist has made an obvious mistake about justice even as the slaveholder understands it. Slaveholders do not believe that they have simply invented justice to serve their interests; they appeal to justice because they think it is right.

Even slaveholders agree that it is never unjust to return stolen property to its original owner. If you buy a painting from thieves who stole it, and the police track it down, you must return it to the original owner, without compensation unless you can get it from the thieves. By the same token, if you buy human beings whose rights have been stolen by the slave trade, you must return them to their original owners—themselves. Generally, moral dilemmas are only skin deep; there is a right way to get out of them, and there is someone to blame for creating them (in these cases, the thieves and the slave-traders). It only *appeared* unjust to liberate slaves. In truth, emancipation serves justice, even though its cost in social disruption may be very high.

Now back to reverence. For Vaka to stand against village tradition only *appears* to be irreverent. That tradition is just another human artifact. It was not ordained by gods, and it is an act of gross irreverence to claim that it was. The beliefs of the villagers are simply wrong on the main point; no particular human customs were divinely ordained, any more than any particular language was god-given. We all must speak a language, and we all must follow customs, but there is no one language we must all speak or custom we must all follow. We must do our best with the language and customs we have inherited, and we must encourage others to do their best with their legacies. But a legacy can be stolen or fouled in other ways, and we need to know that too. Cultures are always undergoing change, and their guardians must be reasonably open to this, for both moral and practical reasons. God does not tell us how often to sweep a floor or at what age to marry or when it is permissible to split an infinitive. Our needs change, and so must our response to them.

It helps to base ethics on virtues rather than rules. Rules are hard to separate from culture because they are specific, but virtues are ideals of character. The practice of a virtue has to be sensitive to cultural differences, and this is especially true for reverence, which is expressed in a language of behavior. A reverent person will learn how to express reverence in different ways in different places; one who goes shoeless into a mosque should recognize that this behavior might be inappropriate in a Presbyterian church. But the reverence is the same.

Vaka's elders would answer, if I made this case to them, that I am merely speaking for my own culture, and that I have no right to force them to accept these so-called freedoms, which in their eyes are mere rootlessness and anarchy. Perhaps I am right that child-marriage was not ordained by the gods. But for the sake of peace and stability the villagers are better off believing that it was. And if all of the Vakas are allowed to do as they want, the family—the very center of reverence—will begin to fall apart. The elders are right about that, and the teacher has missed their point. But the position I have taken is not exclusive to modern Europeans. The elders are wrong on the larger issue because their attitude will doom their village to poverty and disease, and because they have no respect for Vaka's great potential or her own freely taken choice to develop it if she can. Human potential, too, can be the object of reverent respect.

Vaka is not irreverent to question the tradition in her village, but the elders in her village think their way is the only way, and they have made the common error of revering local custom in place of transcendent ideals. Truth, justice, freedom, God—all these are worthy of reverence. But mere custom—never. Not even the custom of nations.

The team leader has decided, however, so the school will bow to local custom and turn Vaka away, as her parents insist. The best that can be said of this decision is that it puts off a messy confrontation between school and elders and delays a transition for the village that will be painful for all concerned. But it is not a reverent decision or a just one; it serves neither an ideal nor the expressed interests of the person concerned—Vaka. Relativism, here as elsewhere, is an evasion of responsibility.

He's some kind of vagrant.
A tramp.
Not from here
Couldn't be, or he'd never dare
To tread sacred earth!

. . .

Sacrilege! To see someone here.
To hear a voice!

. . .

You've gone too far and trespassed
On a sacred grove where water blends
With liquid honey and flows from lustral bowls.
Beware, stranger, go no further—
Stop now and back away.
Do you hear?
Decrepit beggar.
If you've something to say, say it
But not on sacred land.
Speak to us from a place where words are allowed.
Keep silent until
You have left forbidden ground.

. . .

A stranger in a strange land, poor man,
But he must learn
What offends our city
And what we hold dear.

From the chorus in Sophocles' Oedipus
at Colonus,
translated by Peter Meineck, lines
122–26, 140–41, 155–68, 184–87.

10 | SACRED THINGS

An old man named Oedipus wanders into a strange country, guided by his young daughter Antigone. Neither of them has any idea where they are, except that they are somewhere near Athens. He is blind and crippled, stumbling along, leaning on a heavy stick. He is homeless. Because he carries a curse, he has been hounded out of his own home, and then out of one town after another. He stumbles to a mound of earth, trembling with fatigue, and sits there to catch his breath.

A man who belongs to the place soon turns up. He is horrified at the sight—a homeless old beggar, a complete stranger, sitting on a mound that is sacred to the gods. Of course Oedipus has no idea where he is sitting, but this makes no difference to the gods, or to the feelings of the people who live nearby. This is insufferable. The gods will be angry.

A sacred place is one you may not freely touch, or enter, or trample, or soil.

The horrified native tells the old beggar he is sitting on sacred earth, that he must move before he angers the gods into doing something dreadful to the people here. Other local people arrive, a whole chorus of them, shouting at him to move. They are terrified of the trouble his sacrilege will bring to them if he does not appease the gods.

Reluctantly, Oedipus will eventually shift himself on his heavy walking stick—but only to the boundary of the sacred area. There he will stay. But he must do more than move. The Chorus tell him:

> The goddesses demand ritual purification
> For trespassing on their holy ground. (466–67)

Oedipus realizes he must propitiate the deities whom the local people believe he has offended. Too weak himself, he will have his daughters perform the ceremony on his behalf. So ends the crisis of the sacred place, and so begins Sophocles' last play about Oedipus, *Oedipus at Colonus.*

Imagine ourselves in the place of Oedipus. This is not far-fetched. We often travel to countries we do not understand very well, where places and things are sacred to the natives but not to us. If asked to move, we could move readily enough. Imagine we are tourists, off the beaten track in, say, Turkey. A mosque that has attracted our curiosity is not guarded by English-speaking guides or protected with signs advising those who enter to remove their shoes and cover their naked limbs. In shorts and tee shirts, exclaiming loudly at the beauty of the place, some of us enter—to the consternation of those who are praying within. I refuse to follow the others. "Have some respect," I tell them. "This place is sacred." "Not to me," says one of us flippantly. But he could, and should, respect what is sacred to others.

Now suppose we are in a land of many gods, whose images abound in sacred places. And through some violation of the sacred we have incurred an obligation to perform a ceremony as required by the local gods: we must bow, pour a libation, and light a candle in front of an image. Could we do this as readily as we could remove our shoes and cover our limbs before entering the mosque? Yes, if we have no religious beliefs of our own. But not if we are pledged to honor no other gods but One, and never to bow down to or serve graven images. Not, that is, if we feel bound by the first two of the ten commandments of Hebrew and Christian scripture as these are usually interpreted (Exodus 20:3–5).

But It's Not Sacred to Me!

What is sacred in one culture or religion may be profane in another. Your sacred book may well be my abomination. I might believe that if I treat your sacred book with reverence I would betray the gods as I know them. I cannot bear to do that. But if I profane your sacred book, you may feel that I have insulted or attacked God as you know Him. You cannot bear that. Violence erupts.

The reverent soul tries never to violate sacred things in any culture, out of respect for the people who hold those things sacred. Reverence, remember, is not directly related to any particular faith; it is a quality of character that can be found in any religious community. Reverence belongs to ethics. But ethics cannot require me to betray my own faith in order to treat your sacred things with respect. On the other side, ethics cannot require you to stand idle while I insult your God as you know Him. Violence erupts. What is the reverent soul to do about sacred things?

What Is Sacred?

In a word, sacred things are untouchable. The sacred is what you may not freely touch, or enter, or trample, or soil, or even change. Sacred things include places and times, people and relationships, books and images, laws and treaties, names and words. Almost anything can be made sacred.

A sacred place may be a sanctuary which you do not enter unless you have been duly consecrated—by prayer perhaps, or by washing, or by taking on vestments—or perhaps simply by wearing your starched Sunday best. A sacred time is a time during which you do only what is appropriate to that time: you fast, or you abstain from drink, or you avoid the use of machines. A sacred object is one that you do not touch, or that you touch only with clean hands, or at a sacred time. It might be a sacred book or scroll. A sacred word might be one that you never say or write, or utter only with special blessings.

A sacred relationship may be a treaty sworn between two states with a divinity as witness, or it may be a marriage that has been consecrated by sacrament. Although marriages are now easily marred and broken, they remain for us in the territory of the sacred—how else to explain the intensity of the debate over same-sex marriage? Same-sex couples may be thirsty not only for the legal status of marriage, but for its blessing, its sacredness. And those who campaign against same-sex marriage may be moved by the fear that a sacred institution will be torn out of shape and therefore defiled.

Many believers hold that the world is full of truly sacred things, marked as such by whatever god or gods they worship. They may respect these things out of fear: "What horrible punishment will the gods give us if we violate a sacred day?" More commonly, they may do so in order to prove their commitment: "By respecting the sacred day, we remind ourselves of our faith and cement our bond with God." They respect their sacred things in order to practice their religion.

Some of my readers, however, may think that to call something sacred is to evoke a quaint memory of far-off times—times when magic and superstition clouded people's minds. They are wrong. For many believers, the sacred has nothing to do with magic, and for all of us, "superstition" is an insulting name to call other people's religions. Besides, we will see that even unbelievers—people with no ties to religion or magic—are committed to treating some things as sacred—what I call the secular sacred.

Unbelievers may think nothing of treading on sacred ground, while believers may hold that violations of the sacred are attacks on their god. Other believers may feel a religious duty to trample on what is sacred to someone else's religion, if they believe that religion is an insult to their god. When religious cultures clash and one side tramples on what is sacred to the other, believers may quickly storm into violence. In our time, global communication brings cultures into clashing distance. Sacred things make the world a minefield; no matter how carefully we tread, we may set off an explosion at any moment. And in real life, we cannot always tread carefully. War, famine, the necessity for quick action—any of these can lead to unintended violations. Sacred things are among the world's great dangers.

Reverence can help us face these dangers. Reverent people never erupt in violence on account of things that are merely sacred. Reverent believers know that God is not vulnerable to attack, and they understand the difference between reverent worship and idolatry. On the other side, reverent unbelievers see that sacred things make ethical demands on all of us, whether we are religious or not. I will address the believers in the upcoming section on God. First, however, I will bring out a number of ethical points that should appeal even to unbelievers. The sacred often belongs to religion, but it always belongs to ethics.

The Secular Sacred

The philosopher Nietzsche, who was hardly a believer, nevertheless had enormous respect for the sacred, and faulted scholars for not appreciating the subject:

The way in which respect for the *Bible* has, on the whole, been maintained in Europe might be the best piece of discipline and refinement in manners that Europe owes to Christianity. Books with this sort of profundity and ultimate meaning need the protection of an externally imposed tyranny of authority; this way, they can *last* through the millennia that are needed to use them up and figure them out. It is a great achievement when the masses (people of all kinds who lack depth or have speedy bowels) have finally had the feeling bred into them that they cannot touch everything, that there are holy experiences which require them to take off their shoes and keep their dirty hands away—and this is pretty much as high a level of humanity as they will ever reach. Conversely, what is perhaps the most disgusting thing about so-called scholars, the devout believers in 'modern ideas,' is their lack of shame, the careless impudence of their eyes and hands that touch, taste, and feel everything.

As an unbeliever, Nietzsche is making an ethical point about refinement. Clearly the point is not restricted to the Bible; he is disappointed that only the Bible seems to have this status in Europe. Evidently he would like to see the refinement of respect extended to other areas not restricted to objects related to the Christian God. He is concerned for the survival of the ability to recognize and treat the sacred, wherever it is found, with appropriate feelings. He thinks scholars have lost the ability to do that; they think too much and feel too little. He is asking scholars to have emotions more like those of the uneducated, and to be aware of the emotions they have. Nietzsche does not believe that the Bible is the Word of God, so he can't be asking scholars to worship the Bible as if it were. He can't be asking them to treat it as something transcendent. He is, nevertheless, asking them to respond to the Bible as something sacred.

Things can be sacred without having any connection to God or to anything else that deserves reverence. Secular examples abound outside of what we usually consider the boundaries of religion. Take theater. Performance space for drama is sacred, and the same is true for space dedicated to playing a game. Walking onto the stage during a play, when you are not a member of the cast, is touching the untouchable. So is interfering with the players during a football game—for example, throwing a stone from the stands at the quarterback of the team you oppose, or rushing out onto the field to block a run.

Ethics of the Sacred

By "sacred" in the ethical sense I mean anything that has been given ethical properties by rules that protect that thing—hedging properties. Being untouchable is a clear example of a hedging property. The ethics of a reverent culture forbid us from interfering with the sacred—we should not tread on sacred ground, get in the way of a sacred person, violate a sacred friendship, or abuse a sacred object. To interfere with what is sacred is a failure of reverence—the ethical virtue that calls us to treat other people, and therefore the things that other people care about, with respect. Rules that protect the sacred are often strict, and violations often lead to public disgrace. Think of "don't touch," "do not change," "do not enter," "do not interrupt," and now "turn off your cell phones."

These rules often specify exceptions: "Don't touch *unless* you have washed your hands," or (as in the case of Oedipus) "don't step here *unless* you plan to undergo a certain ritual afterwards" or "*unless* you take your shoes off first," or "*unless* you have been consecrated," or "*unless* you are dressed as a priest, or a player, or an umpire" (depending on the kind of place).

The actions that make something sacred are called sacraments. Some sacraments are so familiar that we do not recognize them as what they are. The anthem before a game, the rising of the curtain, the dimming of lights—any of these can make a space sacred for the time of the performance or the game. And at the end, another action takes the protection away from the space and the time. The last whistle blows, and the fans are free to rush out on the field. The curtain falls, and the audience begins to talk. These actions of consecration and de-consecration are sacraments in the broad sense I wish to use.

A thing does not need to be special in any way in order to be made sacred. A place need not be beautiful or awe-inspiring. A shack can be set aside for praying, a scruffy plot of ground can be a marked off for a game, the ugliest and most disreputable of men or women may be given a sacred role in ritual. There need be nothing about these that makes them untouchable, prior to their being made so by human action. When we make something sacred, we do not make it good or beautiful. Instead, we make it important to us, as many things ought to be, including what is beautiful and good.

Everything sacred is untouchable either literally or figuratively. Breaking an oath that has been consecrated is (figuratively) touching the untouchable, as is violating a consecrated marriage. But not everything that is untouchable is sacred. Human excrement is untouchable in most cultures, but not because it is held to be sacred or cursed. The same goes for a poisonous viper. The danger of its poison alone would make it untouchable (whether or not the viper is sacred in the local culture).

In some cultures, a curse or a dreadful action can make you untouchable. Oedipus has made himself untouchable by killing his father and having children with his mother. It makes no difference that he did not know what he was doing. One can violate sacred things unwittingly, as Oedipus did when he sat on the sacred mound at Colonus. Oedipus also carries a double curse—one that he blindly pronounced against himself as his father's killer, and another that he inherited from his father, Laius. Laius had raped a young boy and received a curse from the father of the boy. The words "cursed" and "sacred" are the same in some languages, and the concepts are closely related.

Generally, cultures have allowed sacred things to be touched under certain circumstances. Some sacred places or objects should not be touched at all; some should be touched only by people who have been consecrated to do so—people who are then, in a sense, sacred. There is a class of sacraments that mark off the people who are permitted to enter sacred space or handle sacred objects. An action that exempts a person from the hedging properties is itself a sacrament. Consecrating priests gives them the status to enter places others may not, and so does suiting up a player and sending him onto the field. On the other hand, we can remove hedging properties and return something sacred to ordinary status. If we follow the rules of the culture, we may lift a curse, transform a church into a shopping mall, defrock a priest, or dissolve a marriage.

The boundaries that define the sacred are not bright; we can identify central examples of the sacred, such as the Sabbath day for many Jews and Christians, or the Koran for adherents to Islam. And then there are cases of the sacred that are further from the center, such as a football field during play, or the stage of the Metropolitan Opera during a performance.

You need not belong to a given culture to recognize and abide by its sacraments. A Christian can feel that it is right to remove shoes before entering a mosque; an atheist can feel that it is right to maintain silence during a mass. One need not believe in anything divine or transcendent in order to recognize the ethical value of the sacred. All you need is the capacity for respect. When you are among people with hedging rules that are new to you, you should be able to recognize that these people are engaged in a common human practice.

They have goals very like your own. You can respect these people and their goals, and you ought to respect them with deep feeling.

We owe respect to people with whom we share reverence for shared ideals. Although it would be false to say that we all worship the same god, it is true that all of our prayers can share the same reverence (as I have argued throughout this book). Shared reverence entails shared ideals, albeit at a high level of abstraction. These people bowing down to this image—however strange it seems to me—have needs and prayers and hopes for the ideal that are very much like mine, whether I am a believer or not. Without sharing their beliefs, I can find that I share enough with them to call for respect. We are all engaged in the great project of human reverence. So I owe respect to their sacred things, respect as deep as what they feel, if I can manage it. This argument from ethics should convince most believers, and all unbelievers as well, if they are reverent.

Sacred Practices

Respect meets its limits at rituals that deny respect to others. Many religious practices are ethically benign and respectful of other people, but some are not. Suppose you find yourself among a people who insist that the gods will abandon them unless they offer up the severed hearts of a dozen people a day. They have made human sacrifice sacred in their culture, but this is a sacred thing that you should not respect. If you respect the people whose hearts are in danger of being ripped out, you should not respect the knife-wielding priests or their lethal ceremonies. That is, the ethics of respect allows you to lay hands on the knives and stop the killing—as you are obliged to do if you can.

The same goes for less-bloody forms of human sacrifice, still widely practiced in our day—physical or mental mutilations. You can sacrifice the lives of young people without killing them. To prohibit a young girl from going to school is to wall her off from most of life's opportunities. We owe the girl respect, and we should prevent her sacrifice if we can, even though this means violating a practice sacred to her culture. Her elders have the power to make things sacred for *them*—that is, to make rules for them not to touch certain things or alter certain rituals. As for us, we should respect those rules out of respect for the elders, if we can do so without denying respect to the girl. We know that her elders cling to their rules because they believe that the gods insist on it. But the elders are human beings, and human beings do not have the power to make their beliefs true. Reverence balks at relativism.

Reverence and Idolatry

We owe respect to all sacred things, but we not owe reverence to anything that is merely sacred. To think that we do is to make the fundamental mistake I call idolatry. Sacred things are not gods. God is not a sacred thing. We call Him holy, but never sacred. We have no power over God, but we do have the power to declare certain things sacred and others not. We have the power to consecrate and deconsecrate, and we know this power is ours whether or not we believe it came to us from God. The sacred ceremonies are ours; we debate endlessly over their design. The sacred books are ours—our translations, our interpretations, our paper, our bindings. We worship God with reverence, but we ought not to worship the things that are ours, the books or the ceremonies. That would be idolatry.

As we have seen, human beings make things sacred by their own actions, and sacred things are sacred within human cultures. In saying this, I am drawing a line between the sacred and the transcendent. I have argued earlier in this book that what we recognize as transcendent is worthy of awe and reverence—God for example, or Platonic Justice. But what falls below the transcendent deserves respect at most.

We humans create images of persons we consider holy, and we may well make these images sacred. But an image is not the same as what it is an image of. An icon of the Virgin Mary may be sacred, and therefore we all owe it a certain kind of respect. But as believers, we would owe reverence not to the image, but to Mary herself. An image is at best a reminder of what we take to be transcendent. Images are things we can make or mar. Reverence is due to things that are beyond our ability to make or mar, while respect is due to human beings and their creations. We have parallel distinctions in ethics and religion: religion condemns the idolatry of worshipping anything of human manufacture, while ethics asks respect for what is human, but for what is divine, it asks reverence.

Reverence is primarily a felt understanding of the difference between the human and the transcendent. So if believers are reverent, they will recognize this difference between their god and their sacred things. Then they will not fall into idolatry—they will not start treating human things with reverence. And they will not feel that an insult to their sacred books or words or names is the same as an insult to their god. The god of a reverent religion is above such insults. Sacred things are dangerous, but reverence reduces the danger and prevents violence. This argument may not convince an idolater, but it should convince a believer who is reverent.

God

But perhaps not. Suppose our reverent believers are convinced that sacred things are not ours—that they are not of human manufacture—that they belong to God—that our puny sacraments are only outward signs of what God has done—that God Himself has made all sacred things sacred, and that to violate these sacred things (or allow others to do so) is a direct violation of God's commandment—that to trample on the sacred is to trample on God. For people with beliefs like these, the danger of the sacred remains in full force, unless they are reverent. Religion often lacks reverence. That is why we have religious wars.

Reverence would temper these beliefs with a full appreciation of the transcendence of God. Reverence knows that God is not vulnerable—that we do not have the power to trample on God, although we trample on the sacred all too easily—that we can desecrate a temple, but we cannot desecrate God—that God is beyond the boundary of what we can pollute. And the same goes for our enemies. Our enemies may insult us and injure us by messing with our sacred things, and we have a right to resent that. But the reverent soul knows that God does not command us to turn to violence. Even if the sacred things are his, his interests are not at stake. God is not vulnerable to human wrongdoing.

Feeling What Is Sacred to Another

Time travel has brought you into the precinct of Dionysus in Athens, about twenty-four centuries ago. Miraculously, you understand the Greek they are speaking here. You are sitting on a wooden bench on the lower slope of the Acropolis, looking across the valley at Mt. Hymettus. On the round dance floor in front of you young men are dancing and singing a prayer to the god they worship. Athens has become a shadow of what it was in its golden age only a generation earlier—weakened by plague, almost leveled by war, desperate for a revival. The young men are enacting a prayer that has nothing to do with the play they have been performing, so it is their own prayer now. They are totally in earnest now as they summon their god to be present in this, his sacred place. The audience is earnest too. They keep sacred silence; once the prayer breaks out they freeze in their seats.

And you, what do you do? Do you stand in your seat and shout out at the absurdity of this? Do you tell them all that Dionysus is really the devil, that they should turn and worship the one true God? Do you instead close your eyes and block your ears? Or do you feel, with a chill at your spine, that this is a reverent assembly of people—that their needs, their prayers, their hopes, their ideals, are not so different from yours? Can you watch and listen to this ritual and not feel respect for the sacredness of the occasion?

If this is too challenging, imagine you are a Presbyterian invited to watch a Catholic Mass. At the moment of transubstantiation do you rise in your seat to tell the celebrants that this is a hoax? That the bread and wine remain just bread and wine? Or do you feel the sacredness of the occasion and respect it? You know by now which of these is the response of reverence.

God of many names,	1115
Glorious child of Thebes,	
Whose mother was bride	
To Zeus' deep thunder!	
It is you who guard the fame of Italy,	
You who look after the embrace, at Eleusis,	1120
Of Demeter, all-welcoming goddess.	
Torches flash through smoke,	
Catch sight of you at Delphi	
High above the twin-peaked crag.	
The Castalian Stream has seen you	
By nymphs of the cave who dance for Bacchus.	1130

The Nysaean Mountains know you too,
The ivy-covered shores, the coasts,
The green tangles of grapevines.
They are sending you to Thebes: Watch over us,
Hear our sacred hymns that sound for you.

And now we pray: Watch over us: 1140
The violence of plague
Strikes all our people.
Come, your presence is healing.
Soar above Parnassus,
Or cross the howling straits of the sea.

O Leader in the dance of stars
That circle across the night,
Breathing fire,
O shepherd of dark voices,
Child of Zeus, let us see you now.   1150
Come, O Lord, with your throng of Maenads
Iacchus, steward of joy,
Grant them ecstasy
To dance all night for you.
(Sophocles, *Antigone,* 1115–1154)

Can you read this without recognizing the reverence that lies behind it? Couldn't you treat it with respect?

You are in danger of losing the empire, and if you do, the anger of the people you have ruled will raise other dangers. You are in no position to walk away from your empire.... You see, your empire is really like a tyranny—though it may have been thought unjust to seize, it is now unsafe to surrender.
                    —*Pericles' last speech, Thucydides'* History 2.63

11 | THE REVERENT LEADER

Pericles is no tyrant in Athens. He is a leader of a people who detest tyranny, who follow him freely because they recognize his wisdom and virtue (2.65). But there is a great irony in the story as the historian tells it: These people who hate tyrants have themselves become tyrants. The Athenians have made themselves masters of an empire by brute force, and Pericles, who led the Athenians to the flowering of their democracy, has now led it to its precarious position as tyrant of an empire.

Leadership and tyranny are so closely tied in our experience that we often find it hard to tell them apart. One man's leader is another's tyrant. When we contrast leadership and tyranny we are dealing in values: Leadership is good, tyranny is evil, though in the tangled world of our experience we may never find a pure example of either one. There may have been moments when even Hitler played the part of a leader, and when even Pericles acted the tyrant. Because good leadership is a moral ideal, no human being should expect to be a perfect leader.

Leadership would be easier to define if we could leave out such talk of moral ideals—if we could simply describe, in a factual way, what leaders do. One familiar strategy is to define leadership by the willing obedience of its followers. This is attractive but unlikely to prove successful. The followers of a true leader are not always willing and not always obedient. There is some truth in the proposed definition, however, because tyrants have reason to be afraid of their followers, and leaders do not. That is why Pericles supposes that Athens is a tyrant, and no longer a leader, to most of the cities and islands of maritime Greece—because Athens must use military force to maintain control, and because it is reasonable for the Athenians to fear that their former subjects would destroy them if they regained their freedom.

Willing obedience, however, is not what a good leader always demands of good followers. True, good leaders must have good followers, but a good follower sometimes disobeys when an order is plainly wrong. And a good leader sometimes takes her followers where they are unwilling to go. The need for a system of discipline is not in itself a sign of poor leadership. This is especially clear in the classroom. Teaching is a kind of leadership, and good teachers should find a way to lead unwilling students to learn. At the same time, good students must know better than to obey good teachers when they are evidently wrong, and when they do obey their teachers, they may do so for reasons that have nothing to do with leadership. Obedience and willingness do not by themselves define the classroom of a good teacher. This sort of definition is no escape, then, from the moral perspective: good leaders and their followers exercise certain virtues. That is what distinguishes them from tyrants and their flocks of sheep-like subjects.

The moral aspects of leadership have come in for much discussion in recent years. This has been very useful, but I believe that it needs to be supplemented by the study of reverence. The recent discussion of leadership has not been illuminated by knowledge of the writers who first made the distinction between leadership and tyranny—the poets of ancient Greece. The writers I have been discussing treat irreverence as the plainest clue to tyranny, and they imply that shared reverence is the mark of good leaders and their followers.

Leadership (as opposed to tyranny) happens only where there is virtue, and reverence is the virtue on which leadership most depends. Public devotion to a lofty goal eclipses the leader's personal interests, if it is a goal that leaders and followers may pursue with equal fervor. Reverence gives leaders the power to treat their followers with respect, and the respect they give is returned by their followers. Tyrants who abuse their followers rapidly lose their respect. Mutual respect—a concept I'll discuss later in this chapter—springs from shared reverence. The ancient Chinese philosophers would have agreed, adding that the reverence of leaders and followers is cultivated by ceremonious behavior between them. We know this, of course, in modern military organizations, which are scrupulous in ceremony between ranks, but we overlook the moral significance of ceremony.

Ceremony joins leaders and followers in a common reverence and reminds them that they hold certain ideals in awe together. Ceremony is especially important among the military—among those who are entrusted with the use of violence. Ceremony marks the difference in virtue between a band of criminals and a legitimate fighting force—and there are other differences between the two, which I shall not address. (I shall take up ceremony later in this chapter; the relation between awe and respect will become clear in chapter 13, "The Silent Teacher.")

Leadership does not serve narrow goals any more than reverence stands in awe of small things. The best forms of leadership are devoted to the highest ideals. If Thucydides is right, the Athenians had only enough virtue for them to cultivate leadership within the walls of their own city. But, if so, they were severely limited, especially since they were trying to be leaders of a group of cities that did not identify with Athens. An object of reverence must be one to which leaders and followers—Athens and its subject states, in this example—can share a certain devotion. Athenians may hold their own power in awe, but this will yield only a mangled semblance of reverence. That is why I suggested in chapter seven that a true object of reverence is one that all people can, in principle, hold in awe—justice, truth, God (so long as God is not supposed to serve special interests). This condition explains why leadership is itself a high ideal.

We can speak of reverence for justice, but we cannot, with straight faces, speak of reverence for a particular law, such as the Gramm-Rudman balanced budget bill. Americans might speak of reverence for the Constitution of the United States, but that is only if they tend to think that the Constitution, unlike any particular law, stands for ideals of justice or the spirit of justice, transcending anything that human individuals could legislate.

Reverence is the mainstay of a leader's good judgment. Good judgment is the intellectual virtue that guides deliberation in the absence of relevant knowledge. Leaders in real life must make decisions without knowing for certain how those decisions will turn out. Later in this chapter, I will show how reverence supports good judgment. The tragic poets of Greece understood this very well.

If you master people by force without reverence, you will depend on force for your very safety; you will become isolated from the people you are trying to lead, and in this isolation you will make mistakes. From the other side of command, people will see you as more tyrant than leader, and perhaps even as the enemy. When you make mistakes, you will be an easy target for rebellion and revenge. Or perhaps you will bring yourself down without help from below.

This could be the summary of a tragic play—of the *Antigone*, for example, in which the new king, brought suddenly to power by a calamitous civil war, imposes his will against reverence without listening to the advice of those around him. Or it could be translated to the stage of history on which empires are built. As such, it is the story of Thucydides' *History*: Athens's growing empire frightened the Spartans into war for the freedom of Greece from empire, while this same growth of empire lulled the Athenians into a series of crimes and errors that led to their defeat. The war began forty-seven years after the Greek allies pushed back the last Persian invasion, and it lasted for twenty-seven years (431–404 BCE). Even afterwards the Greeks continued to war among themselves until the power of Macedonia brought them to heel.

The Tragedy of Empire

The war of Athens and Sparta is really a civil war of Greeks against Greeks. Civil war comes with a breakdown of reverence and the collapse of leadership. Most people side either with Athens or with Sparta; meanwhile, the two great powers exploit their followers shamelessly and sometimes brutally. On a smaller scale, battle is joined between factions in many city-states, and this runs parallel to the great conflict.

Civil war, says Thucydides, means the loss of every virtue, and this he sums up as the breakdown of reverence (3.82–83). It is no good trying to be reverent on your own while everyone around you has discarded virtue, and the same goes for leadership. It is no good trying to be a leader among people who recognize nothing but brute force. Civil war or natural disaster can reduce people to that level; so can tyrannical power. Before they acquire an empire, the Athenians have been among the leaders of the many independent Greek city-states. But they appear to be leaders no longer, as the case of Melos makes clear (415 BCE).

The Athenian warships arrive on the island of Melos with an army sufficient to lay siege to the island's one small city. In a parlay before battle, the Athenians demand that the people of Melos accept the hegemony of Athens or be destroyed. The islanders refuse, saying that they cherish their autonomy—their freedom to live under their own laws—and that they cannot see any justice in the demand of the Athenians. They have hopes, moreover, that if they are attacked they will be saved by their allies in Sparta (5.84–116).

The Athenians are impatient with the Melians' talk of autonomy, of justice, and of vague hopes for help from Sparta. The Melians are certain to have autonomy within limits if they accept Athenian hegemony; but if they resist Athens they have no reasonable hope that Sparta will save them from destruction. Sparta has no navy, and its record for helping out small useless allies is not encouraging. As for justice, the Athenians have only contempt for the Melians' appeal to justice. The subject under discussion, say the Athenians, is not justice but survival—what the Melians must do if they are not to be wiped out by Athens.

The parlay turns out to be a waste of time. The people of Melos cling to their hopes, and the Athenians set out to destroy them. In the end, Athens kills all the men of Melos, enslaves the women and children, and settles its own people on the island. The parlay ends with losses on all sides. Melos loses everything; Athens loses a potential building-block in its empire; and Greece itself—through a long series of such events—loses the opportunity to be united under leadership that could protect it from still-dangerous Persia, from the soon-to-rise threat of Macedonia, and possibly even from Rome.

A favorable outcome for Athens would be for Melos to accept limited autonomy and proceed under the hegemony of Athens. But the people of Melos, along with many of the Greeks who are resisting Athens, are committed to thinking of limited autonomy as a form of slavery. How can one persuade a proud and independent people to accept the hegemony of a state they detest, a state that plainly seeks its own interest above all else and will simply use Melos to further its imperial ambitions by allaying its imperial fears? Why should Melos allow itself to be used in this way? Why not fight for what is right, no matter what the cost?

The most favorable outcome for the Greeks overall would be for Athens to achieve a stable hegemony in Greece. But tyranny is inherently unstable because it provokes internal rebellion. For stable hegemony Athens would have to give up its self-interested greed and fear, and Melos would have to give up its loathing of limited hegemony. It is probably too late for this when the warships come to Melos, but it is worth asking what constellation of ideas would have made it conceivable. The debate we have in Thucydides sets justice and equality, on the one hand, against tyrannical power and the moral equivalent of slavery, on the other, with the result that no one is thinking of limited hegemony at all.

What has gone wrong is simply this: neither side sees the possibility of leadership. The only outcome Athens can imagine is mastery by force, while the only alternatives that Melos considers are total freedom and abject slavery. And so there must be violence. This much is clear, and it is common human experience. But why do the two sides have such narrow vision? Why not think of leadership? This is hard to answer.

Failures must have occurred on both sides, but the greater responsibility must lie with the greater power. The leadership of Melos, to begin with, insists on keeping its followers out of the parlay, for fear that they would soften towards the Athenians. The Melian authorities are afraid to treat their own people with respect. Such isolation of leaders from followers is a first step away from reverent leadership, and this step no doubt helps the leaders of Melos to maintain their narrow vision. Generally, isolation impairs judgment, as we shall see.

The Athenians, for their part, feel that they are bound to use force, here and elsewhere, if they are to retain the empire that they dare not lose. Melian talk of justice strikes them as irrelevant. And indeed it is. Melos is too small and too vulnerable for total independence, with the two great warring powers in the region so close by. Whether or not justice is served, Melos will eventually fall under one hegemony or another. The Athenians cannot easily offer justice to the people of Melos in the context of this war, but they could—if they were not tyrants of empire—offer leadership.

Perhaps the Athenians have too much power to think of leadership. When you have the greatest navy in the known world behind you, it is hard to think of leadership. Command comes easier. But the Athenians have in the past known how to be leaders in Greece—seventy-five years earlier when Greece faced a great danger from Persia, and Athens had more determination than power. As Thucydides tells the story, Athenian leadership of the allies changed over the years and was transformed into tyranny over empire.

Thucydides' version of history cannot be entirely right. A few years after Melos, Athens lost most of its army and navy in a foolish campaign on Sicily. At that point, the Athenians did not seem to have the power to hold their empire by force, and some of it rebelled. But not all of it rebelled, and even in the darkest hours, troops from the empire were willing to die alongside Athenians. For much of the so-called empire, then, Athens was more leader than tyrant. The explanation for this is instructive. Some parts of the empire, at least, must have looked favorably on Athens. In their view, under Athenian leadership and with Athenian power, maritime Greece had virtually eliminated the threat of Persia, brought peace to trade routes on which all depended, and in many cases secured popular government in the city-states. Athenian leadership served peace and prosperity and justice—goals which, in principle, all people can share. On the other hand, much of the empire hated and feared Athens. They saw Athens as having only her own interests at heart, and maritime Greece as the worse for being subject to Athenian power. Thucydides represents their viewpoint.

These two ways of looking at empire illustrate the complexity of distinguishing leadership from tyranny. The people to whom Athens shows the face of leadership find that they are working with Athens toward common goals; the people over whom Athens holds the fist of tyranny believe there is an irremediable clash of interest between them and their masters. But Athens is both leader and tyrant, and this is the tragedy of empire.

How Not to Be a Tyrant

How can anyone lead without becoming a tyrant? "Hegemony" is a bad word as we use it in the early twenty-first century, even though it fits the current position of the United States in much of the world better than any other. "Hegemony" is derived from a Greek word which means, roughly speaking, "leadership." But as we now conceive of the two things, leadership is good, and hegemony is bad. The distinction is roughly the same as the one recognized by the ancient Greeks between leadership and tyranny.

In Euripides' *Helen*, the Spartan king says this about the army he and his brother Agamemnon launched in the Trojan War:

I think the pair of us—I'm not boasting when I say this—
Sent the largest force across by sea to Troy.
And we did not command them with the force of a tyrant;
We were leaders, and the young men of Greece were volunteers.
(393–96)

The play was written in about 412 BCE, only a few years after the destruction of Melos and about the time the imperial power of Athens was starting to come apart. Other texts from the same period suggest that Athenian thinkers were becoming anxious about the precarious tyranny that Athens was trying to maintain.

Persuasion appears to be an alternative to the use of brute force. Pericles was famous for his ability to persuade the people of Athens, and this ability was the basis of his power. But persuasion can be seen as a kind of brute force through the use of words, and Greeks of this period were well aware of the tyrannical uses to which rhetoric can be put. That is one reason why Thucydides, who professes to admire Pericles, attributes the man's success more to force of character than to force of words. Twentieth-century history shows how rhetoric supported tyrannies such as those of Stalin and Hitler. So persuasion is a neutral tool. Tyrants and leaders both use it.

Non-violence looks like an alternative to tyranny, because violent force—or its threat—is used by tyrants everywhere. Perfect leadership, which could occur only in a perfectly virtuous society, could no doubt maintain itself without force or violence. In certain circumstances, non-violent leadership has been effective, mainly as a moral beacon, but behind most authority in the real world are discipline and the threat of force. Force, like rhetoric, is a neutral tool, used by both tyrants and leaders, but tyrants and leaders use their tools differently. Leaders do not simply overpower their followers with the force of words or the threat of discipline. There is something that regulates a leader's use of power, and there is something else that gives a sinister cast to anything a tyrant does with his powers and makes brute force out of force. We will not understand what that is merely by examining notions such as force and rhetoric. The crucial difference must be moral or ethical.

Justice was the key, according to Plato, to the puzzle of sorting out leaders from tyrants. But he cannot be right. Consider again the case of Athens and Melos. The leaders of Melos beg for justice, and the Athenian commanders refuse to consider it, on the grounds that justice never moves people to refrain from doing what they have the power and inclination to do:

For our part, we will not make a long speech no one would believe full of fine moral arguments—that our empire is justified because we defeated the Persians, or that we are coming against you for an injustice you have done against us. And we don't think you can persuade us by saying that you did not fight on the side of the Spartans in the war, though you were their colony, or that you have done us no injustice. Instead, let's work out what we can do on the basis of what both sides truly accept: we both know that decisions about justice are made in human discussions only when both sides are under equal compulsion. But when one side is stronger, it gets as much as it can, and the weak must accept that. (Thucydides' *History* 5.89)

This is the Athenian theory of history. It is brutal enough, but it does *not* say that might makes right. It says, frankly, that what is right does not matter. The only thing that matters is the fact of power, that Athens is strong and Melos is weak. As a matter of history, the Athenian theory is false; power is not the only thing that matters, and the Athenians have sometimes done what is right because it was right.

As moral psychology, however, the Athenian doctrine merely overstates an important and obvious truth: justice has very little motivational power. It is a fairly dry virtue, guided more by judicious thought than by trained feeling. Virtues such as sympathy, reverence, and courage, by contrast, are capacities for emotions, and where they are actively present they move people to act or refrain from action. (That is because emotions are, roughly speaking, feelings that motivate.) So the weak cannot rely upon justice to restrain their powerful overlords because justice, unlike reverence, is not a motivational restraint. Nor can the powerful rely on justice to secure the obedience of their subjects; justice would not convert the Melians into willing followers. Suppose the Athenians had arrived on Melos with good arguments for the justice of their cause, and suppose that on balance those arguments were stronger than those of the Melians. This would have made no difference to the issue of leadership. Had the Melians been defeated in a court of law on grounds of justice, they would still have been defeated, and the defeat would rankle. They would plot rebellion and revenge against their new masters. Justice in a prison system does not take the place of walls and bars; it does not pacify the prisoners, and it does not allow them to think of their keepers on the model of leaders.

Justice does nothing to turn the winner of a contest into a leader or the loser into a willing follower. The trouble with justice is that it allows there to be winners and losers in the first place, and such an outcome is hard for leadership to overcome. Far from being a support to leadership, justice in small matters may actually be an obstacle. For this reason a good leader may not insist on everything that is due him under justice. Agamemnon may have had justice on his side when he demanded compensation for the prize captive he had to give up, but his decision to do so was bad leadership.

Reverence of Leaders

Reverence, not justice, is the virtue that separates leaders from tyrants, as the old Greek poets knew well. In episode after tragic episode, they show how failures of reverence destroy men who are trying to be leaders. Reverence is the capacity to feel respect in the right way toward the right people, and to feel awe towards an object that transcends particular human interests. When leaders are reverent, they are reverent along with their followers, and their common reverence unites them in feelings that overcome personal interests, feelings such as mutual respect. These feelings take the sting from the tools of leadership—from persuasion, from threats of punishment, from manipulation by means of rewards. This is because there are no winners and losers where there is reverence. Success and failure are dwarfed by the magnitude of whatever it is that they hold in awe together. Wordsworth recognizes this in his tale of boyhood races over water in the magnificent Lake District:

> In such a race,
> So ended, disappointment could be none,
> Uneasiness, or pain, or jealousy:
> We rested in the shade, all pleased alike,
> Conquered or conqueror. Thus our selfishness
> Was mellowed down, and thus the pride of strength
> And the vainglory of superior skill
> Were interfused with objects which subdued
> And tempered them, and gradually produced
> A quiet independence of the heart.
> ("Two-Part Prelude," 2.63–72)

A leader who uses persuasion, threats, and rewards reverently does so with respect for the followers. This usually requires two things: the leader does not deceive the followers, and the leader is open to persuasion in return. Leadership involves fairly open deliberation. Openness and honesty are defenses a good leader employs against the danger of bad judgment. Leaders are especially vulnerable to bad judgment when they allow themselves to become isolated. Unfortunately, it is easy to resist this conclusion, and would-be leaders are often given to deceit or other devices that prevent them from taking into account the opinions of their followers. Their excuse is that they know more than their followers. This is often true; they do know more than their followers, but that is no excuse for not listening.

This is odd; I call it the paradox of respect. Why should a leader listen to people who know less than he or she does about the matter at hand? The short answer is that reverent leaders do listen to their followers. The hardest case for the paradox is teaching: Good teachers know more than their pupils; even so, as we shall see in the next chapter, good teachers listen to their pupils, and in this they are reverent.

Ceremony: Acts of Respect

> During his first few weeks in the army the soldier often asks, "Why are drill and ceremonies needed? Why couldn't I use my time more advantageously learning how to fire my weapon?" The answers are that individual efforts alone do not bring survival or victory for the soldier; that the soldier has to learn teamwork and the value of unified and cooperative action …
>
> —Drill and Ceremonies, Department of the Army
> *Field Manual FM-25* (1958)

Why should soldiers march in step on parade? Why should their shoes be polished and their belt buckles shined? Why should their posture be stiff at attention? Why should their clothes be uniform, starched, and pressed? All of this belongs to a kind of military ceremony that may have had some direct utility in the eighteenth century. But why now? The manual makes a brave attempt to explain, but it leaves out the most important point: Drill and ceremonies are an essential part of leadership training. The leader-to-be acquires a command voice and comes to see the power of example as military demeanor is communicated from commander to troops on the parade ground. Most valuably, the leader-in-training finds that good commands are followed, and incoherent ones are not followed or are followed badly—that there are clear limits to what can be commanded—that effective commands on the parade ground must belong to the ceremony that brings leader and troops together. It is the same in real life as it is on the parade ground: effective commands belong to a common enterprise.

Ceremony is present in many areas of our lives, such as the classroom and the home, but it is most obvious in the military because of the way in which elements of ceremony or ritual separate military from civilian life. (We have a way of not noticing the ceremonies of civilian life, unless we are observing cultures we think exotic.) This is because the military has two special reasons for cultivating virtue—military people hold the principal tools of violence, and the military is severely hierarchical. The greater the powers that are put in your hands, the more important it is for you to develop inner restraints against the abuse of power. We used to call it "Mickey Mouse shit" when it became tedious, but that is only because we did not realize how valuable it is for warriors to submit to ceremonious behavior.

Military people wear uniform garments, even in combat, and this is an element in ceremony. Why do they do that? Some troops in Vietnam began to dress like bandits when discipline eroded. Oliver North's first company commander wore a red bandana and allowed himself to be called "Organ Grinder" by his troops; meanwhile North and other platoon leaders grew long hair and mustaches. When Paul Goodwin took command of North's company he would not speak to these young officers until they had gone back to standard military appearance. His explicit reason for insisting on proper haircuts was that "dress is an extension of discipline," but there is a moral aspect to this as well. If you carry guns and dress the part of a bandit, you may find it easier to play the part of a bandit as well (and there were many temptations in that direction in Vietnam). The ceremony with which we surround ourselves in war is part of what makes warriors warriors and not bandits. It's part of what expresses the attitude that is essential to any orderly military force: that the violence they use is not in their own service, but in the service of something larger than themselves—even, in the end, larger than nations.

Ceremonious behavior is a sign of reverence. It also shows respect for other people—a kind of respect that can flow only from reverence. The respect that is shown in ceremony cannot be based on good opinions of the other people involved, because we may not know them well enough to form good opinions, and because, in any case, such opinions are secondary to our larger shared purpose. I do not have to like you or approve of you in order to show respect for you with sincerity. Consider the simplest of ceremonies, the salute. A junior officer salutes the colonel, and the colonel returns his salute. These should be acts of respect. But suppose Junior Officer thinks Colonel is a fool and therefore has no respect for her at all. She has given orders he thinks are absurd. To his peers, Junior Officer says, "When I see the colonel, I salute the rank and not the woman." But this means that his respect is only for an abstraction and not for a person, and his salute is not a sign of respect for her. It is empty ceremony, void of meaning so far as these two people are concerned. She may sense his contempt and return it, along with her equally empty salute. This is not a healthy command relationship.

What has gone wrong? You might answer that the trouble is with the colonel, for being a fool, or, if she is not, with the junior officer for misjudging her. That answer comes from what I call the "good opinion" theory of respect—the idea that mutual respect grows from good opinions people have for each other. This puts an intolerable burden on command relationships, requiring the two parties to prove their value to each other before they can achieve a good command relationship. But the "good opinion" theory is backward. Good opinion in such cases grows from respect, not vice versa. Long before they have any opportunities to test each other, Junior Officer and Colonel must show respect to one another. Respect is given, not earned, and to think otherwise would tear any hierarchy apart. What has gone wrong is that both parties have let their personal judgments of each other undermine the respect on which their entire enterprise depends. What is wrong is that they have lost reverence.

Reverence is a shared devotion to high ideals. Respect—the respect that flows from reverence—requires that we recognize each other's devotion to those ideals. Now suppose that Junior Officer and Colonel recognize each other as being devoted to the guiding ideals of the military. Whatever they think about each other's abilities at first meeting, if they begin with respect they will have a chance of developing good opinions of each other. Junior Officer will try to see *why* Colonel gives commands that he thinks are foolish. That is, Junior Officer will try to see how, in Colonel's view, those commands promote the common cause. And Colonel will see how Junior Officer's cockiness grows from his less mature but equally fervent devotion to the same cause. From such beginnings good opinions grow. Without respect, there is no hope of good opinion rising over personal differences, and there are always personal differences.

The "good opinion" theory of respect entails that whenever I respect you, I believe that you are worthy of my respect. This is dangerous if it forces respect to wait on convincing evidence of individual competence. Such a condition would shoot a crippling confusion into the heart of any organization—the false belief that our success depends simply on each person's being good at his or her job. This is false because, as the field manual points out, success is achieved only through teamwork. And that is true because, as the field manual does not say, even the best of us makes mistakes. A good team is a system for preventing and correcting for individual error at all levels of command. Teamwork of this kind would be destroyed by overconfidence on the part of Junior Officer in his personal judgment of Colonel, whether he thinks she is brilliant or a fool. Either way, overconfidence ruptures teamwork. And overconfidence, as the

Greek poets taught us, is a failure of reverence, a failure that leads often to bad judgment.

Now suppose Junior Officer does salute Colonel with genuine respect. He is now expressing two complementary attitudes—first a sense of awe, and second a sense of his place in the world. His place as a human being is at bottom no different from the colonel's—subject to error, to temptation, and to death. His sense of awe is directed at something more noble and worthy of respect than any human being. A good army serves no single human master, but rather a principle of order and discipline that holds power and violence firmly in the service of the common good.

The same goes for non-military occasions. When I deliver a talk to a learned audience I usually dress as a visiting professor does, with a tie and a jacket, and the audience comes dressed as for an academic discussion—that is, no tank tops or torn shirts. Here too there is a principle that is revered by all present, and it is related to order. Gathering in a room to talk about philosophy, we show implicitly our devotion to the orderly exchange of ideas, from which flows the duty of listening and, when speaking, of attending to the ability of the listeners to comprehend. Genuine discussion serves no human master, but harnesses the force of argument and the power of personality to the common goal of growing understanding.

An act of respect says that none of us is all-powerful or immortal, that no one can play god and get away with it. We will all die; we will all make mistakes. We all together seek to maintain an orderly system that is least vulnerable to hubris, to the violence of mind or action that comes from forgetting our common human limitations. An act of respect represents the thought that I cannot get away with treating you like dirt, no matter how powerful I am. No matter how low, how immature, how foolish, or how weak in mind I think you are, reverence does not allow me to overlook our common humanity and, in the case of a hierarchy, our devotion to common ideals.

Good Judgment

In the *Antigone* of Sophocles, Creon refuses to allow burial for a traitor who has died, Antigone defies him, and Creon's son takes her side. Creon has let his personal judgment outweigh the importance of ceremony, and the result will tear his family apart, especially because he seems to have lost his hearing when he assumed power.

> *Haemon*
> So ease off, relax, stop being angry, make a change.
> I know I'm younger, but I may still have good ideas;
> And I say that the oldest idea, and the best,
> Is for one man to be born complete, knowing everything.
> Otherwise—and it usually does turn out otherwise—
> It's good to learn from anyone who speaks well.
> *Chorus*
> Sir, you should learn from him, if he is on the mark. And you,
> Haemon, learn from your father. Both sides spoke well.
> *Creon (To the Chorus)*
> Do you really think, at our age,
> We should be taught by a boy like him?
>
> *Haemon*
> No. Not if I am in the wrong. (718–28)

The play pairs the themes of irreverence and bad judgment so clearly that no contemporary of Sophocles could have missed the point: if you arrogate to yourself an authority beyond what is permitted to human beings, your judgment will go bad. When your judgment is bad, you will not listen to good advice, and you will bring catastrophe on yourself and loved ones. Creon's mind becomes sound only when he begins listening to ordinary people in his city. In the *Bacchae,* too, a king's failure of reverence leads to a failure of judgment, made plain to the audience through his refusal to listen to those around him. As unmovable as a god in his own decision, King Pentheus plunges down the path to ruin like any number of tragic figures before him, deaf to the entreaties of sages and injured relatives.

Good judgment is the intellectual virtue by which we make reasonable decisions in the absence of knowledge. It is, as its name (*euboulia*) suggests, a virtue that requires deliberation and is most evident in paying attention to different points of view. The ancient Greeks developed a procedure for achieving good judgment through adversarial argument—through debates calculated to bring every possible consideration into play. A wide range of considerations is necessary to good judgment, because judgment without knowledge yields conclusions that are not entirely reliable. Philosophers call such conclusions *defeasible.* In order to make good use of such conclusions, you need to know that they are defeasible and be on the alert for any information or ideas that might open your mind to defeating them. Reverence, by keeping you humble in your opinions, is a bulwark of good judgment, because it keeps you open to new considerations that might alter the course of your reasoning. The example of Haemon shows that it does not matter how young or ignorant the other speakers are. What matters is that they make the best case they can for the position opposed to yours, and that you take the case seriously.

Reverence is not the only conceivable way to avoid error. Perfect knowledge or divine guidance would do even better—if we could be sure we had them. Haemon considers that alternative and dismisses it as unlikely. But it is true that insofar as we have knowledge (and we do on many points) we have no need of good judgment. And surely if leaders received clear divine guidance they would not need to think things through at all; they could do quite well without knowledge or intellectual virtue. But these are deceptive hopes; people who think they have perfect knowledge, or are guided in their decisions directly by God, are usually in for a surprise. Overconfidence is an ever-present danger in a human mind, and the best defense against it is listening to others, with reverence.

I've come, out of compassion,
To ask what exactly you and your poor
Daughter want from us here in Athens.
You can speak freely without shame.
There is nothing you can say so unspeakable
That could deny you a fair hearing.
You should know that I too
Was an exile and had to struggle to survive,
So how could I ever allow myself to ignore
The pleas of one so lost in desperation?
I know that I'm just a man and that tomorrow
May hold nothing more for me than you.
　　　　　　—Theseus, speaking to Oedipus,
　　　　　　Oedipus at Colonus, *556–68.*

12 | COMPASSION

Theseus holds power in Athens. He is a king in myth, but the poets of the democracy honor him as a leader whose power is built on the beauty of his character. For the poets of Athens, he is the model of a reverent leader. He will stand by Oedipus, enabling the old man to live his last day as a triumph.

The play is the last one Sophocles wrote, and it tells the end of Oedipus' story. He has arrived near Athens as an old man, blind, crippled, on his last legs. He will gather power as the day goes by and walk cheerfully out of life, leaving great blessings on Athens and great curses on his ruthless sons. Be careful how you treat helpless people; as the poet shows, they may have extraordinary powers.

The play opens as Oedipus arrives at Colonus, near the city of Athens. Trembling with fatigue, he takes his seat on a sacred mound. This will be outrageous to the local people. They will be terrified of what the gods might be prompted to do by such a sacrilege. The Athenians who live at Colonus see Oedipus not merely as a disreputable homeless beggar, violating their sacred space, but as a man who carries with him a curse on whatever ground he occupies. He has killed his father and made children with his own mother. He did not know what he was doing then, any more than he does now, taking his seat on the sacred mound. But that makes no difference to the gods.

Theseus comes as quickly as he can, out of compassion. He has learned how vulnerable a human being can be, for he has traveled much alone, and he has been helpless. From his own sad experience, he knows there is open season on the helpless wherever there is no compassion. His sufferings have taught him reverence.

Reverence entails compassion, because reverence entails understanding the weaknesses you share with other human beings. When the reverent soul is aware of human suffering, it does not turn away. "That suffering could just as easily be mine," says the reverent soul, and feels accordingly. Then the reverent soul follows those compassionate feelings into action. Theseus will protect Oedipus.

The people of Colonus are good Athenians, but they are not as good as Theseus. They have not had his experience, and they are terrified of what the gods will do to them if they tolerate the sacrilege that this old man has invaded their sacred space with his accursed history. Anger grows with fear. They are like us; they carry a tender garden of compassion inside them, but the garden is easily overrun. When we are frightened, or angry, or simply in a great rush to get things done, we trample on our own compassion like hungry students stampeding across a garden to get to a barbecue. The people of Colonus are not better than we, and they are seriously frightened. They stand around the old man in a threatening half-ring. They don't dare step onto the sacred mound to yank him off, so they wait for their leader, Theseus, to arrive.

Whether a crowd turns nasty or not depends on leadership. If no one is appointed leader, the one with the loudest voice, or the first to be heard, may set the tone and lead the crowd one way or the other, offering the helpless person violence or shelter. The leader who brings compassion may be the lowest-ranking person on a team. The compassionate leader need not be an officer or commander, but a commander ought to be a compassionate leader.

At about six years of age, the poet-to-be William Stafford came home from school "and told his mother that two new students had been surrounded on the playground and taunted by the others because they were black. 'And what did you do, Billy?' asked his mother. 'I went and stood by them,' Billy said." Was that enough to temper the crowd? Probably not. Where were the teachers and the older children who should have been there to speak a word of leadership?

Luckily for Athens, the Athenians have a leader who has the respect of all—Theseus—and he will speak for compassion. Only then will Oedipus tell him what he brings to Athens:

> I have a gift to give you:
> My own broken body—not much to look at,
> But appearances can deceive,
> And it has the power to bring you great good. (576–79)

Oedipus brings a blessing to the place where he will die. If he dies in Athens, his tomb will protect the city from its enemies. But that is not why Theseus felt compassion when he first saw the old man. No one could summon up a true feeling simply to make a profit by it. Theseus responds to the offer of the blessing:

> Reverence forbids me to throw away this gift;
> Therefore I am inclined to allow him to stay
> And incorporate him within our city.
> *(Addressing the people of Colonus.)*
> If he wants to remain here, then you
> Will be responsible for his well-being. (635–39)

He leaves and the men of Colonus treat Oedipus as an honored guest, entertaining him with a lovely ode to the beauty and grace of their land at Colonus. Theseus has set a tone for the way his people will treat the old man. That is what a leader does. If you replace Theseus in the story with a ruthless autocrat, puffed up by hubris, then these same people—who are now kind to Oedipus—will probably drive him off the mound with stones, and then out of their land with sticks. The old man has been driven off by blows before, from everywhere he has gone. Until now, in the vicinity of Athens, where he has found a people who are thriving under a leader who is compassionate—as I believe any true leader must be. Leaders have sources of compassion available to them that may not be open to their followers.

Leaders are responsible for the compassion of the groups that follow them.

That is the most important message of this book.

Sources of Compassion

Compassion is not available to everyone in the same way. The gods of Greek myth were believed almost never to be compassionate. That was because they were immortal and beyond serious injury; they could not suffer the way human beings suffer, and so they could not imagine—as Theseus does in this play—that they would ever be in a position to suffer. By contrast, the Christian God is believed to have lived and suffered as a human being. He did so out of compassion, and, indeed, He suffered into compassion. That is one of the many factors that make Him different from the pagan gods. The Kwan Yin of Buddhism is compassionate because she (or he) is believed to have been a human being, and to have chosen to hold back from Nirvana out of compassion. Compassion rides on experience, real or imagined.

Young adults are like pagan gods. They feel invulnerable. They have not yet learned how easily they may fall through error or accident into doing or suffering dreadful things. Groups of young men are especially dangerous; in fraternities and other organizations they continue to kill and maim each other through hazing. Groups of any age or sex are erratic. Whether they show compassion or not depends a great deal on who sets the tone of the group. The loudest mouth, or the first to act, may turn a harmless collection of folks into a hurricane of violence. Think of a lynch mob.

Wiser heads are needed to call groups to order. The wise heads may be old ones (though not all old heads are wise). Older people have more experience of life. They are in a position to know how easy it is to do wrong, and they may know more deeply what it is to suffer. But wise heads may be young, and some young people must be wise if they are to be leaders in the full ethical sense. For them, education must make up for lack of experience. Every leader-to-be should receive some education for compassion—if compassion is really a good thing.

Is compassion a good thing? You may think this is obvious, but Plato repudiated compassion because he saw it as an insult to justice, and because he confused compassion with pity. Pity is often a bad thing, but it is not the same as compassion. Compassion is the ability to understand the feelings of another, with appropriate feelings, but not necessarily with the same feelings as the other. It is a close cousin of what I have elsewhere called cognitive empathy—a complex response involving both feelings and intellect. The ancient Greeks called it by a word with roots that mean "with-knowledge"—*sungnomosune*.

You may have compassion for someone who has done wrong, and you may still believe that the wrongdoer should be punished. You understand how the thing happened, and your understanding will help you decide what punishment the wrongdoer really deserves. If you understand the feelings that led a criminal to crime, you can come to a more just appreciation of how bad a person the criminal really is—and therefore to a better sense of what justice demands.

Consider Ajax. For nine years Ajax has been the heart of the Greek army at Troy. He is the biggest, the bravest, and the most loyal of all the soldiers. With his shield he is large enough to shelter a number of his comrades. He will fight his way to wherever he was needed and put himself between his friends and the Trojans. In this way he saves many lives, including the king's, at great risk to himself. Agamemnon and Odysseus have both survived thus far because of Ajax. But they have been taking Ajax for granted all along, and he will come to learn that in a most insulting way. After the death of Achilles, his armor—made by a god—is to go to the best of the Greek soldiers. Ajax of course thinks that means him. By any standard measure he is the best. But instead the armor goes to the winner of a debate on the subject, and that is Odysseus, the trickster, the man who fights more with words and ideas than with his spear.

Bitterly shamed by this, Ajax tries to kill his king, Agamemnon, along with his former friend Odysseus, both of whom he now sees as enemies. According to the traditional rules, Ajax deserves to be stoned to death and left unburied for attempting the life of the king. But Odysseus has compassion; he understands how deeply Ajax was hurt by the commander's actions, and so he knows that Ajax is not such a bad man as others think him. Odysseus takes a leadership role and saves Ajax and his family from the worst that could be done to him.

Pity is something else. You could feel pity for Ajax's suffering without the least understanding of what he did or why. And your pity might incline you to let him off the hook entirely—to give him clemency. But that would be a mistake. He has done wrong, and justice requires us to recognize this with a fitting penalty. Philosophers like Plato have held that justice must ignore compassion, because they fear that compassion leads to softening the prescribed penalties—to softening the rules, which they think means ignoring the rules. Softening the rules (they think) would be a breach of justice. That is going too far. Odysseus' compassion helps him see that the rule does not apply well to Ajax in this case. After that, Odysseus' talent at public speaking helps him persuade the others to follow his lead—toward compassion.

Compassion has a role in restoring justice when it alerts the judges to notice how poorly a rule applies to a particular case at hand. What we want from justice is a sustained sense that our community is giving all its members what is due to them. Compassion helps an officer of the law see what is really due in a particular case— and that may not be exactly what the rules prescribe.

Compassion does not call for pity or clemency. It calls for understanding. Understanding is difficult; that is why experience and education help prepare us for compassion. I cannot expect you, possibly obese reader, to feel compassion for me when I tell you I have to work to keep from losing too much weight. You probably cannot imagine what that is like, and you probably do not have a friend with my problem. But I can have compassion for you because I have enough dear friends who have suffered while trying and failing to lose weight. Even vicarious experience can make the difference.

Education for Compassion

The ancient Greeks provided education for compassion. Sophocles' surviving plays, with one notable exception (the *Electra*), all celebrate compassion. In *Oedipus at Colonus*, Theseus sets an example of compassion for the people of Colonus, and he enjoins them to be responsible for the welfare of the homeless wreck of a man who has come among them uninvited. The people of Colonus are old men, but behind their masks they are very young performers— young men just entering the age to be soldiers. Singing and dancing in such a chorus is part of their education as Athenians. Almost all Athenian males had this experience. Through music and dance, they are developing a sense of solidarity with each other and with Athens. At the same time, they are close witnesses to the deepest suffering that a stage can show. This makes up for their lack of experience. And above all, they have been trained as spokesmen for the shared wisdom of Athens.

In another play of Sophocles, *Philoctetes*, the Chorus takes the lead. Faced with a helpless invalid, who is a former soldier in the Greek army, the Chorus members are the first to feel and show compassion. They tell their commander, who is only eighteen:

> Have a heart sir. He's told of such suffering.
> An ordeal I'd wish on no friend of mine.

And the young officer replies:

> It would be shameful for me to seem less
> Considerate than you in helping a stranger in need.

(Sophocles, *Philoctetes*, 507–8, 524–25)

In all Greek tragic plays the Chorus shows compassion for the sufferings of the main characters. In this they take the lead for the audience. Our games today have leaders in cheer, cheerleaders; ancient Greek theater had grief leaders who gave the audience their cues.

The tragic wisdom of the Chorus goes beyond compassion. We have seen earlier how they speak against tyranny and in favor of democratic leadership. Here is a famous example:

> I pray the god will not dissolve
> What is good for the city, our wrestling for power.

(Sophocles, *Oedipus Tyrannus*, 879–81)

The "wrestling for power" is the democratic process that brings now one leader, now another, into prominence. With tyranny, by contrast, there is just one man exulting in power, growing in

power, growing therefore in hubris, and so heading for a great fall
(see p. 86).

In *Oedipus at Colonus,* the Chorus will watch a shocking instance
of the hubris that grows with tyranny. Creon will arrive with an
armed force from Thebes. He will tread on sacred space, seize suppliants by violence, and try to abduct them. He is ruthless, utterly
devoid of compassion, and contemptuous of sacred things. He will
not succeed in this, and the Chorus knows that he will come to a
bad end. Hubris has a high price. Athenians have already seen what
will happen to him in the play *Antigone*—written earlier, but depict-
ing the end of the saga of Oedipus and his children, when Creon
loses his wife and sole remaining child, and comes to see that he is to
blame for his own disaster.

Few people have the opportunity to be tyrants, so the Chorus
must give voice to a wisdom that applies to all of us. Here is the core
of tragic wisdom expressed by the Chorus:

> The bright stars do not linger over mortals in the night;
> Both poverty and wealth shall fade away.
> They move in turn, joy and loss
> Arriving at the same door.
> (Sophocles, *Women of Trachis,* 131–35)

In those few lines are reasons for hope, dread, or compassion,
depending in your position in the cycle of joy and loss.

The young men of Athens perform lines like these and stand
close to enactments of the greatest suffering that a poet could imagine. This gives them the opportunity to learn reverence and compassion, riding on the experience of the poets and the collective
wisdom of Athens. Witness and performance go a long way to make
up for lack of experience. Nothing will force these young men to be
reverent or compassionate against their will, but they deserve an

opportunity to learn, and Athens has given it to them. Their protected young lives would never have given them such an invitation for learning.

So much for ancient Athens. What about us: what can *we* offer by way of education for compassion? Not what we are offering now, in either college or secondary school. Whatever we do offer will have to be powerful enough to counterbalance the increasingly ruthless tone of American civilization, which our students pick up from movies and video games and, worse, from parents and politicians. Education for compassion will probably not come from home or church, and it will certainly not be a by-product of the technical or vocational training that is so heavily supported by politicians.

Everyone is a leader-to-be, because anyone can speak up or make the gesture that could move others toward compassion. As in Athens, everyone should have the education of a leader. To make up for lack of experience—lack of suffering—leaders-to-be should have a broad education in the humanities, including both classic and recent texts. Ancient texts provide a useful distance that opens the most delicate issues (such as incest) to discussion. But whatever they read and discuss, students will have to see it as applicable to their own lives. Most of us who teach in the humanities will have to change our ways in order to meet this goal. Few of our students will have any use for academic disputes about manuscript readings in the Greek plays, but all of them have something to learn from Sophocles' treatment of Oedipus.

We can't make our youngsters play roles in Greek plays, but we can ask that they read the plays, discuss them, and apply them to their own lives. In my experience good teaching never leaves students passive, but engages them. One of the best ways to engage students in the humanities is through performance. When you perform a text, you make it your own, and you are more likely to keep its wealth in the treasure house of your mind.

Whether through reading or performance, the humanities can supply the vicarious experience that grounds compassion. For this reason, we must insist that leaders-to-be are exposed to the best of the humanities and in the best ways.

Second, demand the ability to communicate clearly and with feeling. What good is your compassion if you cannot pass it on to the people you are trying to lead? Speaking ability is essential, but it has been neglected in American education during most of the last century. Few teachers or professors are qualified to teach skill at public speaking, and all too many students think they already have it.

Third, imagination. Theseus could imagine a future in which his position was reversed. His experience helped him do that, but he added a vital ingredient—imagination. Education for compassion should foster imagination through creativity. We are losing ground in this area, as the arts are pushed to one side in favor of the short-term gains expected from technical and vocational training.

Fourth, practice. Leaders-to-be can be leaders now, if they find the right setting in or out of the classroom. In the reverent classroom, students are called on to be leaders, and in their roles as leaders to practice paying attention to each other.

Last, a word about ethics courses. I have little hope that courses in philosophy will make a difference, not as we teach them now. I am optimistic, however, about the use of fine-grained case studies that can give students vicarious experience and, at the same time, provide them with opportunities for practicing decision-making. Such courses are most credible when taught by veterans—people who have lived through situations like those to be studied, have made compassionate decisions, have taken risks in order to live ethical lives, and have succeeded in their chosen careers.

In short, education for compassion is whatever it takes to help people become more like Theseus in this play. But education often fails. Even Theseus will be ruthless, later in his life. In a fit of jealous anger he will call down a curse that will kill his only son. We are human, and nothing we do will make us perfectly good. That is no reason to give up the effort—no reason to forget about compassion. We owe it to each other to do what we can, and part of what we can do for compassion is education. We owe it to each other to give ourselves opportunities to change for the better, whether we take those opportunities or not. Some people do change for the better.

The Idolatry of Virtue

Changing people is very hard to do, and even when people have cultivated compassion in themselves, they cannot be relied upon to stay in character. Your student could become very much like Theseus and still be swept away in a ruthless mob, or reduced by fear and anger to treat human beings like cockroaches, as so easily happens in war. I am human, I succumb to stress, and all too easily I lose my grip on what I thought was my moral character. Part of my vulnerability as a human being is this: I cannot rely on my character to see me through. I too could be too busy to remember my compassion as I hurry down the road, leaving the wounded man to be cared for by the Samaritan.

Chris Hedges, whose background includes service in a ghetto, theological training, and war reporting, writes of his work in Roxbury:

> It was a time I dreamed of being good. But this was idolatry of the self, the worship not of God but of my own virtue. I had to learn my own complicity in oppression, my own sinfulness, how evil lurked within me, how when I was afraid I could turn on the weak and powerless. (Hedges, *Losing Moses* [2005] p. 36)

Being afraid is worst, courage is best, but I have no good within me that is totally dependable. Luckily, I do not have to depend on my own character alone. We have each other, and we can organize—we can set up human systems to slow me down when I am in danger of going the wrong way. Those too may fail, but we must do what we can on behalf of compassion.

Safer Environments

There are two ways to make people safer drivers. One is to change people through driver education. The other is to change the situations in which we put drivers, through engineering. We can change ourselves a little through education, but we can change our situation a great deal through engineering. Better-designed roads and cars have made us safer drivers. That does not mean we should give up on driver education. Education matters. But so do situations.

Similarly, teachers know two ways to reduce cheating on papers and exams. The least effective way is to lecture the students about the evils of cheating. The most effective way is to change the situation. Reduce incentives for cheating, engineer assignments in such a way that cheating becomes more difficult, and help the students learn so well that they feel no need to cheat.

When a commander insists on perfection in every training exercise, her subordinates are likely to lie to her, and the habit of lying taints the military culture. Good commanders do not insist on perfection. Rather than offering academic courses about why you should never lie, they choose to provide a safer moral environment for their subordinates. The subordinates already know they should not lie, but if you insist that they report a perfect operation every time, they will lie to you.

Everyone on a team is responsible for the moral environment in which they operate. But leaders should know that they bear a special responsibility for the moral health of their followers; they should do what they can to make their moral environments safer. Just safer; forget perfect safety. A moral environment is safer when leaders and followers are spurred on by values that they share, rather than by carrots and sticks, when those values bear moral scrutiny. In addition, a safe environment should meet at least these conditions:

1. All team members have the training and resources needed for their jobs.
2. No one is expected to do the impossible.
3. Members of the team communicate with each other.
4. Members of the team help each other catch mistakes.
5. Leaders communicate high standards to the team.
6. Leaders listen freely and without judgment to what the followers have to tell them; no one is afraid to speak up.
7. Leaders are well informed about what the team is doing.
8. Leaders follow up when standards are violated.

A fellow veteran of the war in Vietnam told me that he had an opportunity to kill a prisoner, and he was raging to kill the man in revenge for the death of his best friend. I asked him why he did not pull the trigger, and he said simply that he knew he would have been severely punished had he done so. He felt no compassion at the time, when his mind was rioting with anger and grief. But he knew that his commander enforced high standards, and so, even though he did not *feel* compassionate, he did the compassionate thing. For that he is grateful: one less burden on his conscience. Leadership saved the prisoner's life and the veteran's conscience.

Leaders take responsibility for the ethical qualities of the teams they lead. They do this by example, by specific commands, by training or education, by setting rules, and by following up. In any organization I have served, but especially in military ones, everyone knows which rules matter to the people in charge. "Command emphasis," it was called. In one unit in which I served there was command emphasis on wearing appropriate headgear. Nothing wrong with that—see p. 187. But there was little emphasis on respecting the people of Vietnam, and that was a shame. American civilization can be ruthless.

Failure at Abu Ghraib

We know now that the abuses at Abu Ghraib did not reflect the wishes of the chain of command. But we also know that the command team failed to prevent such abuses. No special training, no clear standards of behavior, no oversight, no follow-up. The Independent Panel to Review Detention Operations reported, "The aberrant behavior on the night shift in Cell Block 1 of Abu Ghraib would have been avoided with proper training, leadership, and oversight." The consensus since then has been that these abuses reflected a monstrous failure of leadership at many levels.

That conclusion did not protect low-ranking individuals found guilty of abuse at Abu Ghraib. They alone were actually punished. No sentences were given the commanders, and some people believed that rank-and-file soldiers were not to blame. I agree that the commanders should have been punished, but I do not agree that the soldiers who committed the abuse should be let off on that account. Individuals are responsible for what they do, and individual malefactors should be punished—no matter how badly the command team fails at leadership.

Philip Zimbardo understood the moral hazards facing prison guards as a result of an experiment he conducted at Stanford. He divided the students in the experiment into prisoners and guards, not anticipating the cruelty that the guards would soon begin to show to their prisoners. He came to believe that the guards at Abu Ghraib were innocent, that it was not their fault they turned bad, and he testified to that effect. Neither the courts nor the military accepted his argument. In defending his view, Zimbardo used a striking image: the abusers at Abu Ghraib were as innocent as cucumbers dropped in a barrel of vinegar:

> Coming from New York, I know that if you go by a delicatessen, and you put a sweet cucumber in the vinegar barrel, the cucumber might say, "No, I want to retain my sweetness." But it's hopeless. The barrel will turn the sweet cucumber into a pickle. You can't be a sweet cucumber in a vinegar barrel. My sense is that we have the evil barrel of war, into which we've put this evil barrel of this prison—it turns out actually all of the military prisons have had similar kinds of abuses—and what you get is the corruption of otherwise good people.

The evidence is against Zimbardo's claim. People are not cucumbers. A human being can retain some sweetness in a sour environment. After all, Joe Darby, another prison guard at Cell Block 1, did object to the abuse, and he did so strongly enough to take the risk of exposing it and incriminating his friends. In other parts of the prison, abuse was absent or much less common. Even in Zimbardo's famous prison experiment at Stanford, some of the young guards behaved well. They were not cucumbers, and they deserve credit for that. The ones who went wrong deserve some measure of blame. But blaming individuals does not let the command team off the hook. The command team put the young people in the barrel without preparation—and then acted surprised when some were corrupted. What did they expect? If you throw dozens of people overboard from a vessel without lifejackets, you must expect some of them to drown. If you throw young, untrained soldiers into a morally corrupting environment, you must expect some of them to go bad. If you throw people overboard, you owe them some means of survival; and if you throw people into prison jobs, you owe them a moral lifejacket. So Zimbardo is right this far: when otherwise good young people are made guards in the prisons that war creates, a good number of them will become abusive. We can reasonably expect, on the basis of research, that this will happen.

I wish we could smash the barrels, abstain from war altogether, and stop detaining people we consider our enemies. But if we do go to war, and if we do detain people in the course of war, then whoever is in command should take responsibility for the moral health of the troops. I have no quarrel with individual responsibility: the guards who were abusive at Abu Ghraib deserved to be punished. But the commanders made criminals of the young people entrusted to them, and making someone a criminal is far worse, morally, than being one. At Abu Ghraib, the commanders were not leaders. They failed to take responsibility for their troops, and they failed to provide them a safer environment, to their shame and the shame of the nation.

Is this an isolated case? I don't think so. When I discuss examples with my students I see that they too—not just the "bad apples" at Abu Ghraib—are infected by the growing ruthlessness of our civilization. We need to look more closely in the mirror.

When Theseus in the play hears about the situation at Colonus, he knows immediately how much depends on him. That is why he rushes to the scene, dropping important ritual business. There he finds the homeless man ringed by frightened, angry citizens. He knows the damage a mob tends to do in fear or anger, because he has felt it himself. So now he gives the orders for compassion, and the crowd does not become a mob. Evoking the beauty of the place, they make the old man at home there, for the last day of his life.

We find in the Veda that when Badhva was questioned by Bashkali he explained Brahman by simply not speaking: "He [Bashkali] asked: 'Sir, teach me.' He remained silent When he was asked a second and a third time, he replied: 'I am telling you, but you do not understand. This self is silent'"

—Shankara,
on the Brahma Sutra 3.2.17

13 | THE SILENT TEACHER

Reverence declares itself through silence, more deeply and more truly than through speech. We hear of the silence of great teachers in many traditions. Confucius is silent about heaven, Badhva about Brahma, and the Buddhist teacher Vimalakīrti too was silent on occasion, though he was famous for his skill in explaining the Buddha's teachings. Su Shih, a poet of the Sung dynasty and a lay Buddhist practitioner, came upon a clay statue of Vimalakīrti, and he remarked that the crumbling statue, nibbled now by field mice, is as good a teacher as the man has ever been:

> Once, when he was alive, someone asked him about the way of
> Dharma,
> And he bowed his head, never to impart a word of what his mind
> certainly comprehended.
> Even now this image remains, impassive in his wordless silence,
> Just as he was in life – nothing added or missing.
>
> ...
>
> Seeing all this now makes one lose a sense of oneself,
> For who can be like **Vimalakīrti**, the master who never spoke?

This is a joke, yes. The wordless teacher is no better than a clay statue. But the point underneath the joke is serious: this teacher may have only a clay shell of a body, but his spirit has survived in his unforgettable silence. That silence was not the silence of a clay pot; great human silences are made inside frames of words, and the silent teacher cannot create a wonderful silence without speaking. If Vimalakīrti had not also spoken eloquently, if he had not been a vital part of a conversation at the time of his silence, he would not have been a teacher. Why should a teacher be silent? Perhaps because words do not suffice to express what he knows in his heart; perhaps because he knows that students must learn the answers for themselves, not from his words, but through their own lives. The silence of a great teacher expresses awe and respect—awe for the enormous subject that is being learned and respect for the students who are learning it under their own power, undiminished by any interference from the teacher.

A silent teacher is not necessarily a mystic. Confucius is no mystic, but he knows when to say nothing. And silent teaching is not specific to Asia. Socrates has his way of being silent, although he is rarely at a loss for words, and his followers too are silent teachers. When Socrates is asked a question, he usually meets it with questions of his own, and when he is persuaded to speak at greater length, without question marks, he plunges into extended metaphors and myths of his own invention, leaving his audience—and Plato's readers—struggling to find out what he really means. But Socrates hides his meanings in inaccessible places. If he knows anything, he rarely admits it. He twists and turns away from the role of a teacher, and if he has answers to the questions he asks, he seldom allows them to be unveiled. Socrates' companions call his behavior "irony," using the Greek word that means "falsehood," *eironeia*, but Socrates' life as Plato reports it gives the word a new meaning, and all the modern ironists from Kierkegaard and Nietzsche to Richard Rorty and Alexander Nehamas are in his debt.

Irony is silence twisted into words that provoke and do not satisfy. Like pure silence, irony shows awe at subject matter that cannot easily be tamed. Irony treats students with more respect than they are likely to recognize. It is Socrates' peculiar way of being reverent toward the goals of philosophy, toward wisdom and the great realities known to the highest wisdom, toward transcendent beauty, goodness, and justice.

A silent teacher need not be a skeptic. Many ancient readers of Plato were struck by Socrates' silence and concluded that he was a skeptic, or at least almost a skeptic, meaning by "skeptic" a philosopher who holds back from committing himself to any substantial beliefs. They were wrong. Socrates has many beliefs, but he is modest about them and conscious of the limitations of the imagery he must use for his lofty subjects.

A silent teacher need not treat lofty subjects. You may think it a trivial fact that seven plus five is twelve, but one may stand in awe of it nevertheless (as has more than one great philosopher). With awe or without, a teacher is well advised to be quiet from time to time about even the most ordinary facts, so that students may have the freedom to make those facts their own.

Respecting Students

When teachers are silent, students must speak—and of course the complement is true as well: students should be silent when their teachers speak. Respect is a gift between teacher and student, freely given on both sides, as it is between any leader and follower. Somehow the teaching must get started before teachers prove their knowledge to their students and before students prove their curiosity to their teachers. Reverent teachers believe that students can match them in hunger after knowledge, that they can learn what they wish to, and that they need to make learning their own. That's part of respect. But the need for respect does not assume that teachers and students are in the same boat. A teacher should not treat students as equals in all things; teachers know things students do not. Still, at every level in the ladder of learning there are human beings perched with astonishing—but limited—powers of understanding and creativity. Obviously they are unequal in attainments; that is why they need to be reminded of the equality they have in reverence for the truth.

Respect is a feeling that goes with sharing a great project, one that has an aim worthy of reverence. You lose respect for people when you cannot see them as joined with you in working toward shared ideals. As a private soldier, you despise a commander who cares so much for personal advancement that he cannot keep his eye on the larger goals that you can share. As a teacher, you will not be able to respect students if you cannot find anything that they want to learn. But people are curious by nature, and the more you bring students' natural curiosity to light, the better you will be able to respect them. Part of good teaching is the ability to discover good things about people who seem to be bad students. And part of being a good student is the ability to discover good things about people who seem to be bad teachers.

Above all, teachers set an example, like any other sort of leader, so that the respect shown by good teachers bounces back to them—in a good class. No one can be a good teacher in a really bad class, just as no one can express reverence well in an irreverent group. What is most important in a teacher's example? Not lecturing at students, because no one wants students to take up lecturing, and no classroom is big enough for two big-mouthed lecturers. Simply this: the most important example a teacher sets is by learning—by showing the curiosity, industry, and open mind that learning requires. That is one reason an exemplary teacher must be capable of learning from students.

Hard she thought it, that penury should force her back into the school-room she was scarce out of, there to champion the sums and maps and conjugations she had never tried to master. Hating her work, she had failed signally to pick up any learning from her little pupils … (Max Beerbohm, *Zuleika Dobson*, chapter two)

On first reading, this account of Zuleika's teaching career may strike you as paradox for the sake of paradox, but with his gentle sense of humor Max has captured two symptoms of bad teaching that often come together: Zuleika cares nothing for the subjects she is supposed to teach, and in consequence she learns nothing from her students. All Zuleika cares about is herself. We have seen this pattern of irreverence before, in examples of bad leadership. Give Zuleika power over her students, but no reverence, and she will be unable to respect those beneath her—not, at least, in the relevant way. Reverence in the classroom calls for a sense of awe in the face of the truth and a recognition by teachers and students of their places in the order of learning. Students should treat teachers loyally as people from whom they have much to learn; teachers should treat students respectfully as fellow-learners. Teachers must not pretend to omniscience, and from this it follows that they must be open to the possibility of learning something from their students. But what could an expert teacher possibly learn from a student? Many things, but at least these: how much the student knows or does not know about the subject, how fast the student is capable of learning, why the student wants to learn in the first place, and what might prevent that student from learning or wanting to learn.

When a teacher refuses to learn at least this much from students, they will say that the teacher does not respect them—and consequently they will withhold respect from the teacher. The virtue that is missing in that case—the virtue that would supply the respect that is missing on both sides—is reverence. In an ideal classroom everyone treats what is to be learned with a reverence that generates mutual respect among teacher and students.

The Irreverent Classroom

The failures of students mirror the failures to which teachers are prone: A noisy student may bully the rest of the class, just as a loud teacher may flatten them all. A silent student may opt out of the class altogether, just as an utterly silent teacher would be no teacher at all, incapable of creating the silences in which learning takes place. Excessive noise and silence both fall away from the ideal of reverence in the classroom. Silence in students is not as harmless as it may seem; somewhere in a silent classroom there is arrogance. Often, silent students are being bullied by an arrogant peer or teacher; often, they are held in check by their own arrogance.

Chris is too good for the rest of us. He is usually silent in class, and on the rare occasions when he speaks, he declares the truth as if from a great height. Luckily for him, and us, he is almost as bright and well informed as he thinks he is. But he is a royal pain in the classroom, and he hurts himself as much as he does the rest of us. He is the class snob, the intellectual snob, and he has no friends. He is not as bright as he thinks he is; if he were, he would know that it takes brains to recognize the intelligence of others. Reverence involves a kind of intelligence that easily recognizes the company of other minds, but snobs like Chris have pushed others into the backs of their minds. The silence of snobs is a failure of reverence.

It may also be a failure of courage; for all I know, Chris is afraid that he might find out he is not the superior thinker he wants to think he is. It would be no surprise for courage and reverence to fail together, since virtues tend to rise or fall together. Chris's failure may also be related to a larger failure in the class. The silence of Chris would be more pardonable if he were in a class that is dominated by a bully, because it is hard to exercise virtue in the neighborhood of those who do not.

The worst violator and the one that is most difficult for teachers to handle is the loud student. Confident in their own brilliance, hugely vocal, and often male, dominant students do not seem to hear what other students or even teachers have to say in discussion, so intent are they on presenting their own views. They speak as if they have nothing to learn from others—or as if the classroom discussion were not an occasion for learning at all. Instead, they take the class as ground on which they can exercise their power to control a conversation. Other students fall into resentful silence (I am afraid I was once such a student).

Sam, in a different class from Chris, is silent from fear. He does not lack reverence, but his class does. When he ventured to speak, early on, he was put down traumatically by a loudmouthed peer, Lila. Now he never opens his mouth. A put-down from the teacher could have had the same effect. Sam knows he should have more courage, but knowing that is no use to him. Nor can a teacher help him by telling him how bright he is. He knows that already. What might help is changing the ceremony of the classroom. When the seminar is split into groups of three, Sam finds he can talk eloquently in the smaller setting about a clearly defined problem. In time, he might work up to addressing the larger group. When the teacher gives voice to Sam's ideas by reading parts of his papers to the class, they realize that Sam is the best writer among them.

Lila is harder. Easily the brightest student in the room, well-read, articulate, and monumentally unaware of those around her, Lila does not feel she can allow another student to express an opinion. She knows better than the others, and because she knows better she sees no reason why she should have to hear them out. On the rare occasions when she does allow a fellow student to complete a sentence, she has no trouble seeing the flaws in what was said, and she will bring those flaws to the attention of everyone, with scornful elegance. The rest of a class containing Lila usually sags into sullen silence. Teachers feel redundant in a classroom with Lila. So effective is Lila's control in a classroom that she can steer a class entirely off the subject of the syllabus if she does not find it interesting or is not prepared to discuss it (not having found time in her busy schedule to do the reading).

Both the bully and the silent snob have failed in reverence, and both can be neutralized by ceremonial improvements to the operation of the class. A good teacher might not let Lila speak until she has been recognized, and then not let her speak again until the silent students have had their say. This might dampen Lila's voice enough that the class can proceed, and it may give voices to Chris and Sam, but it won't address the deeper problem. Ceremony without reverence is never enough for anything. Lila and Chris will have to develop a sense of their own limitations, and they will have to learn this themselves, not from discipline so much as from a growing passion for learning. They will not have learned reverence until they begin to feel how far they have to go to achieve a goal that is now theirs and not merely the teacher's.

Why Not Dominate, If You Are Right?

Without reverence, Chris will still think, "These people aren't worth my time." And Lila will say to herself, "If I know the truth, why shouldn't I speak out about it? And if the other people are so stupid and ignorant that they keep going wrong, why does the teacher let them speak at all?" Their superior knowledge has let them forget what they have in common with the beginners in the class, and they are unable to resolve what I call the paradox of respect—the surprising truth that a wise person will show respect for a fool, if both are reverent. Then sage and fool will have equal reverence for the truth; they will need each other, and each other's respect, in the rugged practice of learning and teaching that forms the life of anyone who cares about the truth. For a sage will be dissatisfied with claims to knowledge that have not been tested against every kind of objection—even the kind of objection that looks foolish.

The great Dr. Johnson was well aware of his own greatness. But, after refuting several generations of Shakespeare scholars, he quotes Achilles' lines to Lycaon (p. 84): those who slay enemies on the battlefield know full well that they too will be slain. Every honest scholar knows that he too will die, that future generations will know more than he, and that someone will sooner or later refute him on some point or other. Knowing this—really knowing it in a way that enables you to feel respect for the faltering efforts of beginners in the field—is reverence.

A loud student like Lila needs to come to understand that she has been abusing power—in this case the power of her mind and personality. Her weapons are a loud voice, willingness to interrupt without compunction, a ready way with words, and perhaps a few very good ideas. She may eventually grow up to be a professor. In the meanwhile, however, she does not know enough about her subject to speak with authority. But she is unaware of her ignorance, at least at the conscious level. She is, in short, ignorant of her own ignorance, and this second-order ignorance is what allows her to behave as she does. Reverence should temper the loud student's ego and soften her voice. But how is she to learn reverence?

Why not begin by proving to her that she is ignorant? Easier said than done. This problem student sees the classroom as a place for contests of power. If she is bested in argument by the teacher, she may recognize this as a defeat, but she will attribute her defeat to being outgunned and overpowered by the teacher. She may fall silent, but hers will be an angry and rebellious silence, not one in which she absorbs learning from classmates and teacher. Power games don't support education, because learning and teaching are not about power. Neither, in the last analysis, is leadership. A wise leader, remember, avoids situations that call for force, knowing that the more she has to use force, the less secure is her leadership. It is the same with teaching. Socrates refutes people roundly, but he never says he is a teacher, and most of his defeated companions walk away from philosophy in anger. A true teacher avoids outright refutation in a battle of wills, knowing that defeated students do not learn. Rather, like defeated rebels, they stop listening and plot revenge.

The silent and the noisy student both need a rising passion for learning, along with a growing reverence for the truth. They will not acquire these easily or in a short time, and their best hope is to have a teacher whose example is contagious. Why, after all, do expert teachers curb themselves with ceremony, hold their tongues when ignorant students speak, allow contrary views to come into the light of discussion? Lila may think at first that her teacher is a relativist, that he listens to students because he thinks their truths have got to be as good as his. But we have seen that relativism and reverence do not mix. Great teachers listen because of their great passion for learning. Reverent teachers are in awe of the truth, and they care about it (unlike Zuleika) even as they know they are more expert than their students on their subjects. But at the same time they are fully conscious of their own limitations. They don't think themselves to be in full possession of the truth. They know they could not be in awe of the truth if they thought of truth as merely a personal possession.

The Paradox of Respect

Earlier I asked which way reverence points in a hierarchy of leadership—up or down? On the one hand, reverence seems always to be directed above, from child to parent, from student to teacher, from people to sovereign, and from earth to heaven. On the other, it seems to look downward because it holds back the stronger from brutalizing the weaker—because, in effect, it humanizes hierarchy. It seems to do this through respect, by ensuring that a reverent leader is able to respect his or her subordinates. But respect for subordinates is a strange idea.

Reverence, remember, is the capacity for certain feelings where they are due, and among these is respect. Respect comes in three degrees of thickness: too thick, too thin, and just right. Thick respect is a judgment of quality and is supposed to be due only to those who deserve it. Thin respect expresses only equality, and is due to every human being. But the respect that flows from reverence is a felt recognition of a connection growing out of common practices. You owe reverent respect to anyone who satisfies two conditions—he or she (1) belongs to a practice in common with you and (2) recognizes his or her position in the practice.

Let us begin with thick respect, which I am supposed to owe only to those who are better. I owe thick respect in sports to the better athlete, in class to the better student, and so forth. On this account, I should respect my subordinates if they are better than I am. For example, if I am a teacher, I should respect only those students who know more than I do; but if they know so much that they deserve my respect, why should I not change places with them? Should I be their student? Quite right. Reverence entails knowing my place and accepting it: if I recognize that you are my better, I should accept a position below yours in the relevant hierarchy. The point is obvious if the hierarchy is educational: if I set out to teach you Greek, but find that your Greek is better than mine, then I should ask to become your student. In no case, on these grounds, should I respect you for your knowledge of my subject, unless you should be my teacher.

Socrates sets up his conversations with that in mind. He cannot be your teacher because he is aware of his own ignorance on the matter at hand. But he hears you say that you know the subject. If so, he will become your pupil and encourage others to do so as well. But first he will insist on checking to see whether you really do know what you say you know. None of Socrates' companions ever pass the test, with the result that Socrates never finds anyone to whom he will give the respect he thinks a teacher deserves. And if there is no one for Socrates to respect, then what opportunity is there for him to cultivate reverence? We must ask the same question of ourselves if we follow Socrates in this. Indeed, the central belief of reverence—the belief in human imperfection—would imply that no one deserves full respect from anyone else if respect is a judgment of quality.

Thick respect cannot be all there is. Respect cannot depend wholly on judgments of quality, because some respect has to come before judgment can be fair. If I do not respect you, why should I trouble to understand your reasons for doing as you do? And if I do not take the trouble, I will not judge you fairly. To make matters worse, if respect is a judgment of superior quality, then I will never have a good reason to respect anyone who has a good reason to be my student. And my students—not knowing my subject—will have no good grounds for respecting me. They would have to master the subject before they could judge my work, and only then, on this theory, could they have reason to respect me. But how will they learn the subject if they do not respect their teacher? Perhaps they will be able to make do with ungrounded respect for their teacher until they know better. But this is an unpalatable result; we want to be able to say that they are right to respect their teacher. The problem arises for leadership of all kinds: it is reasonable for leaders and followers to respect each other before they can have good reasons for judging that they deserve respect. So it cannot be thick respect that develops between student and teacher, and we will keep our minds clear if we distinguish respect from judgment.

Thin respect is no more helpful in understanding teaching and leadership. It treats all human beings with respect for no other reason than that they are human. In you I find the same capacities and the same weaknesses—the same mortality and the same desire to live—that I know in my own case, and so I treat you with thin respect. But who would care to earn and keep my respect if I offer it to everyone? If there were nothing that would cause me to take back my respect? True, we may have a kind of thin respect for each other in view of our human capacities alone. But in the richer, more usual uses of the word, "respect" is for something that can be rightly given or withheld. Equality is a fine ideal, but it is fatal to a rich conception of respect, as philosopher Harry Frankfurt has shown.

The respect that belongs to reverence and expresses a moral character is neither too thick nor too thin. It is a feeling that is built into special relationships. Your respect, if you are a leader, helps your followers feel that they belong in the group and are part of what the group is doing. Your contempt makes them feel left out, overlooked, irrelevant. To understand respect in a given society, you need to look closely at how groups work together in their culture.

Confucians develop respect in the family from early childhood. Family relationships, they believed, were undermined by the idea of universal love (a classical Chinese variety of egalitarianism taught by Mo Tzu). In much the same vein, Aristotle complained against Plato. Plato had proposed making family love universal in the ideal city, by replacing the nuclear family with a citywide family in which all men of the guardian class shared all the women as wives and all the youngsters as children. Aristotle thinks Plato has made more than a mistake in scale: Family and city are not just different sizes, they are different sorts of social entities altogether and require different sorts of ties among their members. But the whole of humanity!

What could it mean to show equal respect to everyone? Can universal respect be respect in the true sense?

Equal respect for all leads to a bare flat sea. Thick respect, grounded in judgments of quality, led to a rocky headland. The entire voyage so far has been misguided because it left behind the compass that points to objects of reverence. When respect flows from a virtue it flows from reverence, and reverence is *for* something. We need to set out again. This time, instead of asking simply, "To whom is respect due?" we should ask, "What are the objects of reverence in a family? In a military unit? In a classroom? And how does this reverence determine when respect is rightly given, and when rightly denied?"

Reverence in the family expresses a sense of family unity, that these people belong together, in the various roles assigned them under their culture, relative to the function of the family. In modern cultures, the function of the family is vastly diminished, and with it the importance of family ceremony and the internal system of respect that ceremony represents. No surprise there. But family still counts for something, and it is still possible to lose your place in the family—not simply through rebellion, but through the kind of self-absorption that takes you out of the orbit of family function altogether. It might be through self-imposed isolation, or through drugs, or simply through leaving home altogether. And indeed, that may be a good thing to do, if you are lodged in a home in which you receive no respect and are treated like a slave. Home, as we'll see in the next chapter, can be a mixed blessing.

In a sports team or military unit, we easily see how respect is distributed and why. Soldiers and officers, players and coaches respect each other insofar as they are serious in the way they approach their work, if they hold up their end and if they are not simply out for their own promotions. If, in other words, they work smoothly as parts of the team. They share a common goal, and in the best case they are passionate about it. Team spirit, patriotism, and, at the highest level, a passion for justice and peace—these are the feelings that allow respect to grow strong. Toward the end of the war in Vietnam, U.S. Army units showed a precipitous decline in respect for officers; this came in exact parallel with the loss of the idea that the aims of the war included peace or freedom or justice—just as the theory of respect from reverence would predict.

Leadership training in the military of the 1960s included a strong injunction never to admit that you are wrong when you are in a position of authority. An officer, we were told, is never lost, never ill informed, never without resources to complete a mission. "Can do, sir!" was the refrain of an officer in those days. We were taught, in other words, to deceive those above us and below in a systematic way, as if a mask of deceit were essential to good leadership. It isn't. True, soldiers will not follow an officer who is clueless or who leads them into disaster. But in a healthy unit, soldiers can respect an officer who makes unfair decisions, if they recognize in him or her a common commitment to fairness, and they can respect a reverent leader who makes an occasional mistake. They will actually respect their officers all the more if they do not catch them hiding their mistakes or blaming them on other people. A reverent leader is devoted to ideals such as freedom and justice. A reverent leader need not pretend to be godlike; the ideals are godlike enough.

Now we know what to say about the classroom. There, teachers and students will respect each other insofar as they recognize that they belong together in a common effort—trying to understand something that it is important to understand. Teachers and students can both go wrong—and be honest about it—without breaching mutual respect. Teachers can handle a totally ignorant class, but they face an impossible task if they are assigned a thoroughly irreverent gaggle, in which the desire to learn has been rooted out. That is just a roomful of students, not a class, and there is no basis for respect in being merely a roomful.

Now we see why even the best student in the room will not be able to respect a self-absorbed teacher who comes late to class, forgets to grade papers, or interrupts office hours for private business—no matter how much the teacher knows about the subject. And for the same reason, the teacher will find it hard to treat with respect a student who knows the subject better than anyone else in the class but who comes late to class or misses it altogether, turns in assignments sporadically, and alternates between contemptuous silence and scornful speech. Neither the bad student nor the bad teacher is part of the sort of common effort that gives rise to respect.

Reverent respect cannot grow just anywhere or for just anyone. What it needs in the classroom is not knowledge, which is always unevenly distributed, but the desire for it, which can, at least in principle, be shared by all. That is the answer to the paradox of respect. The silent teacher shows the highest respect for students when sitting in reverential awe while the questioning voices fall into silence. The silent teacher truly respects students, but not because they are who they are. What lies behind the teacher's respect is devotion to the truth, and it is devotion to the truth that, at this moment, draws teacher and students into the circle of mutual respect.

Still, as the spiral grew,
He left the past year's dwelling for the new,
Stole with soft step its shining archway through,
Built up its idle door,
Stretched in his last-found home, and knew the old no more.
—Oliver Wendell Holmes,
from "The Chambered Nautilus"

The Things We Do To Make It Home
—Book title by Beverly Gologorsky, 1999

14 | HOME

Earlier in this book I presented a frightening image—the widening gyre in Yeats' poem, a dizzying spiral out of control (p. 31). I end here with a spiral that has all the comforts of home: This poet imagines an animal—a mollusk—growing in its "ship of pearl" and finding itself at home in each larger chamber that it builds. The image is startling because it is absurd: Animals do not really have homes, and what we mean by "home" is tied to the way human beings live. We tend to be frightened of homeless people, out of an ancient fear that without homes people may behave like animals. As adults, we are amused by children's stories that give homes to animals, along with most of the fixings of human life, but we know better. A solitary beast like a mollusk cannot do the sorts of things we do to make a shelter into a home.

Countless small acts of ceremony make a shelter into a home—ceremony at mealtime, at day's end or beginning, at games or entertainments, often shared silently among those for whom the place is home. You do not make a home by yourself. If you live alone, and are at home, you are linked to ancestors or to absent children by things you do or by relics that you honor. Home holds reminders of the rise and fall of families—a picture, an old toy, great-grandmother's table—but whatever it contains a home is the center for a web of respect across generations. The ceremony that makes a home is an expression of reverence; ceremony that does this cannot be an empty routine, and, for reasons we will see shortly, it cannot be rigid and unchanging.

A shellfish hangs no pictures on its walls, and we cannot imagine a mollusk standing in reverent awe of the wholeness that families seek when they make a home. Still, the image of the nautilus is powerful. The chambers grow smoothly, each out of the smaller one that is left behind, and the whole history of the animal is carried in the shining spiral of its home. The things we do to make a home out of a shelter may form a linked succession as we outgrow our old quarters and stretch into new ones. In this image, there is nothing confining about home; it is not a prison or a cage. The poet says nothing to imply that a home could hold back its resident until his last line, when the animal has left its "outgrown shell by life's unresting sea" and moved beyond the physical plane altogether. Home is a place to expand, or to expand in, and to expand smoothly, not in the violent manner of more common images, such as repotting a plant.

Think what happens to plants that are root-bound. They will break through barriers in the ground unless they are clipped and trimmed—or else plucked up and transplanted to a larger space or a wider flowerpot. This more brutal image is the one we use in daily speech—we say we are uprooted ("deracinated") when we move on in the hope of finding space in which to expand. The image of uprooting is painful. We are not plants, and we do not need roots.

We need reverence, and indeed we know reverence first hand wherever we are truly at home—but the knowledge is rarely conscious. Reverence at home is so familiar to us that we are hardly aware that this is what it is, and we may have to visit homes of a different culture before we recognize that the places where family pictures hang, or where grandmother's unused teacups gather dust, are shrines.

To enlarge a shelter you push back walls or add rooms, but this is not what it is to expand a home. We have no trouble spreading our accumulated junk or the contents of our shrines into larger quarters, and we can easily conduct old ceremonies in new places. The challenge to a home comes when someone leaves, when someone new arrives, or when someone returns—especially when someone returns from a transforming experience. A baby is born; children grow up and leave; a soldier comes home shattered from war; children drift back from college with new tastes and ideas; one spouse is transformed by a moment of epiphany—whatever it is, the change throws the home off balance. The women of Gologorsky's book (*The Things We Do To Make It Home*) never succeed in making homes for their men who have come home from war, morally devastated by what they have seen and done.

At such times we speak of the need to reestablish routines, but mere routine is hollow. The repetition of routines by itself does not bring home out of chaos. It reminds us, instead, of what we have lost. If routine is all there is at the place that used to be home, that place has come to be a trap for those who are lodging there—a trap that is either as vacuous as a prison cell or tortured with bad memories. We turn our backs on it and on the people who are there. Home breaks.

The house of empty rituals is not a home. It is not a home because it is a house that has lost reverence. When ceremony becomes rigid, when it declines into routine, it has lost its power to express reverence. Home is the clearest illustration of my thesis that reverence cannot be a conservative virtue. Making a place home, through all the changes that strike a family, is a dynamic process: adjusting ceremonies and creating them, breathing reverence into them, finding new ways to show respect as old ways lose meaning or become less appropriate. If you wish to be at home with your father, you will change toward each other as you age. When you are grown up, you are not at home in a place where you must address your father in exactly the terms you used as a child.

Reverence gives us the power to make changes toward each other, changes in attitude and ceremony that allow us to go on being at home with new or changing people, or in the absence of loved ones. Reverence allows us to escape from dying rituals without losing direction—smoothly, continuously, as the nautilus blends chamber against chamber in brilliant mother of pearl.

Home Virtues—and Vices

> The author lives in Austin, Texas, with his wife, their two daughters, two dogs, and two cats.
>
> —Possible book-jacket blurb

A blurb about the author's address is supposed to reassure a casual shopper: This writer is all right, he is one of us, a domesticated man with all the virtues that support the settled life. Woe to the homeless, the unsettled, the wanderer, or the one whose sexual preferences are not welcome in the suburbs. Such writers are dangerous, and their lives are best omitted from the jackets of books for the general market. Domesticity is a sign of virtue, particularly of reverence, which tells you to know your place as a human being. And where is the place of a human being, if not at home? Home is the place to look toward, to dream of. Home is the place to be sick for. It is the focus of return and of all the connections we must remember in order to be fully human—to remember who our parents are, our children, our wives or husbands.

Home is not always comforting. It is the place where failures of reverence are most devastating. Secret things happen at home, things cloaked in reverent silence if they are good—like lovemaking—or in fearful silence if they are bad. True, we admire domesticity, but we also applaud anyone with the courage to leave a home that has become a trap. We are of two minds about home, whether it is good or bad. Must we be ambivalent about reverence as well? We know that reverence, like any virtue, can be abused and exploited, as when a tyrannical parent takes advantage of respectful children. Long after childhood, dreams of home may be uneasy. Home may have been dreary and stultifying. It may even have been a locked-in world of violence against powerless women and children.

The cruelty of bad homes does not make reverence any less a virtue. The bad home is not a reverent one. I would argue that it is not a home at all, just as a bad leader is not really a leader. Both "leader" and "home" are normative words when we reserve them for good cases, as we often do. True homes are reverent, and their reverence restrains the exercise of power. In ancient Greece, the people who have the most power and the most freedom to leave home are men. But reverence keeps powerful men mindful of their homes, of the respect they owe to others in the home, and of gaps in their own good judgment. Reverence holds men back from enjoying the liberty of wild animals. But reverence is easy to forget. Leaving home enables men to forget their humanity. Homer pictures the Greeks at Troy living casually on the beach with stolen women. At best, they are camping there like people on holiday, but in battle they are like animals, a point Homer makes in metaphor after metaphor. But he shows the Trojans in warmer images, frequently in the embrace of family.

So much for men. What does reverence require of women in regard to home? Reverence gives to those who are oppressed the promise that there are powers greater than human ones, and that there are limits that no one should be permitted to overstep, no matter how big or strong or deep-voiced the oppressor may be. Reverence cannot always look to a home address. No virtue could be so simple as to ask you always to respect your home. Courage sometimes calls troops to advance, at other times to retreat, and still other times not to enlist at all. What is courageous is not always the same thing. So it is with reverence; what you call home may or may not call for respect. The ancient Greeks held that home is where a woman should stay—for the most part. But even the earliest poets recognize the pain of being homebound, and later poets give it full voice. Euripides' Chorus in the *Bacchae* celebrates the release of women from the home, when they revel in the mountains in honor of Dionysus, each visualizing herself as a fawn that has escaped the hunt:

> To dance the long night!
> Shall I ever set my white foot
> So, to worship Bacchus?
> Toss my neck to the dewy skies
> As a young fawn frisks
> In green delight of pasture?
>
> She has run away now from a fearful
> Hunt, away from watchful eyes,
> Above tight-woven nets—
> While the dogleader cheers
> The running of his hounds.
>
> She strains, she races, whirls and prances
> On meadows by rivers, delighting
> In absence of men
> And under shadow-tresses
> The tender shoots of the wildwood.
> (863–77)

Away from home, in the mountains, there is freedom, joy, and the presence of Dionysus. Here is a paradox: If reverence calls us to know our places, then how can reverence for Dionysus call women out of their homes? The answer is obvious: Home is not—or at least not always—the place to be, and reverence does not simply bow to a traditional assignment of roles. The call to adventure away from home is not necessarily a call to abandon reverence. There need be no contest between reverence and adventure.

There is a contest, however, between adventure and reverence in romantic poetry and romantic fiction, but it is a strange contest, not really between equals, and even the strongest partisans of adventure cannot manage to support it wholeheartedly. The most famous spokesman for adventure in modern literature is Tennyson's Ulysses, and the ancient paragon of reverence is the hero of Homer's *Odyssey*—two versions of the same hero, representing opposite ideas about the place of reverence in a well-lived human life. Each hero has a foil. Ulysses' foil is his son Telemachus; Odysseus' foil is the high king, Agamemnon.

Telemachus: Homebound Virtue

In "Ulysses," Tennyson's hero turns away from the virtues of home life. After becoming a name "for always roaming with a hungry heart," Ulysses has come through his many adventures to Ithaca; he is home again with his wife, his grown son, and his job as king. But he is not happy. He "cannot rest from travel"; he will soon be off to sea again, leaving the management of Ithaca to his son, Telemachus:

> Most blameless is he, centred in the sphere
> Of common duties, decent not to fail
> In offices of tenderness, and pay
> Meet adoration to my household gods,
> When I am gone. He works his work, I mine.

Telemachus is domesticated, and Ulysses has no use for the boy's virtues in his own life. He recognizes their value for the life his son is living, but he cannot wait to put broad waters between him and those virtues forever. Readers are charmed by Ulysses' restless energy; they buy posters with quotations from the heroic verses Tennyson writes for his home-hating Ulysses, and they hang them—where else?—in their homes.

Ulysses: The Call of Adventure, the Siren-song of Death

If Tennyson's picture is right, there are two kinds of virtue—one for daredevil Ulysses, and one for his stay-at-home son. Ulysses is pulled away from home by his restless virtues, "beyond the sunset and the baths of all the western stars"; Telemachus is governed by his quieter virtues, mainly reverence, to keep up a humdrum life at home. If there really are these two kinds of virtue, and if reverence belongs to the class of virtues that lead only homeward, then Ulysses is right, and heroes should shake the dust of their homes from their heels. In doing so, they must put reverence behind them. And then reverence would not be a virtue for all seasons, but only for cycles of return to the home.

Tennyson has actually turned the old story backwards. In ancient myth it is Achilles who chooses the glory of battle over a safe homecoming, and it is Ulysses (Odysseus) who prizes home above all, while his son dares a long journey to find his lost father. Above all, Tennyson's Ulysses belongs to a different moral universe from Homer's. Unlike Homer's characters, this Ulysses makes a stark choice between two systems of value. "He works his work, I mine," says Tennyson's Ulysses. Different work, he must suppose, calls for different virtues—so different, it seems, as to be incommensurable.

Tennyson's picture must be wrong. If there are any cardinal virtues, they are not seasonal or relative to a job at hand. Cardinal virtues are needed for human life itself, no matter what conditions obtain. Courage? No doubt Ulysses will need courage on his voyage, but so will Telemachus on the home front when times are hard and he is tempted to cut and run from trouble or to shirk from standing up for what is right. Why should reverence be any more dispensable than courage? Won't Ulysses need reverence on his voyage? Doesn't every leader need reverence? Telemachus and Ulysses will need each other's strengths. It is a pity that they must separate.

The picture is very wrong. Only a great poet could have made it as attractive as it is in this gripping poem. True, battle-scarred veterans never do find their homes to be as they left them, but only the mentally ill push off afterwards with no destination. The dog dies, the children move away, but a veteran rekindles a hearth fire somewhere, renewing marriage or making a new one. Home itself is no more static than the fire that is its symbol. Tennyson is right about the anger and alienation of the soldier who comes home from the war, but he is wrong about where that anger leads. War cures old soldiers quickly of hunger for adventure.

In any case, Ulysses does not simply choose to follow adventure in this poem. At one level beneath the surface of the verse, we see that Ulysses is flirting with death and casting it in his mind as adventure. This is a very young man's poem, one of many that Tennyson wrote in mourning soon after the death of his beloved friend Arthur Hallam, and it reflects a young man's semi-conscious dream of standing on the shore between life and death. His Ulysses has nowhere to go. Life has lost meaning for him. Why else would he talk of setting out at day's end, as Tennyson has him?

> The lights begin to twinkle from the rocks:
> The long day wanes: the slow moon climbs: the deep
> Moans around with many voices.

Ancient sailors rarely put to sea when the long day waned; they preferred to sail in sight of the coast. But when they ventured into the open sea they preferred to sail at night because they depended on stars for navigation. In this poem, however, navigation is not at issue: The long day is over for Ulysses; he has nothing to do and no reason to set course for any particular destination. From here on he will not need courage or reverence or any other virtue. Virtues are for the living, for living well. But there is only dying ahead of Ulysses.

Among poets writing in English, Tennyson is our greatest witness to depression, but Homer knows more about war and the love of home that lingers in a warrior's mind. Homer understands that in wartime reverence pulls two ways, both homeward and away. War is painful. War does not allow its human playthings to make their own choices between glorious death and happy homecomings. A warrior's path is split by war into a tragic tension for which there is no healing. Not even death will bring peace to the warrior's soul; not even victory can promise him the homecoming that is his cherished dream. A sword, flaming in the warrior's own mind, stands between him and the home he left when he went to war. He will never be the same, and neither will his home. The poet can give him everlasting fame, but his sweet home, had he never left it, could have given him a human life.

In "Ulysses" Tennyson writes a paean to adventure at the expense of reverence, but the paean is set against a counterpoint of grief expressed in a great weight of imagery and funereal stateliness of rhythm—so much so that the prevailing sentiment of the poem emerges as an unquiet acceptance of death. Tennyson's enthusiasm for adventure is equivocal. We find no such complexity, however, in the poet from whom Tennyson took his character. Homer would never side with adventure against home, and he would never side with anything against reverence.

Agamemnon: The Love of Honor

Agamemnon is the worst case of irreverence in Homer's poems and in the myths that came down through other sources about the war. This is not surprising, because Agamemnon is the supreme commander of the Greek forces at Troy. Irreverence is most likely to occur among people who have authority, for reasons we have seen, and among those to whom it does the most damage and is therefore easiest to identify. Agamemnon's irreverence is due to his love of honor (*philotimia*), which leads him into one violation of reverence after another. He is so eager to leave his home and begin the war that he is willing to summon his own daughter to be sacrificed for a fair wind to Troy. During the war he continues to be driven into irreverence by his passion for honor.

Most of Homer's men love their homes, but some love honor more. Love of honor pulls hard against reverence, but love of honor is not a virtue. Sometimes, love of honor works like a virtue to keep a hero on the path to glory, fighting bravely and avoiding shameful retreat. But sometimes love of honor leads to useless sacrifice, as in the death of Hector, who was ashamed to take cover behind the walls of Troy. And sometimes love of honor works like a vice. It can be destructive of community, of leadership, and of life itself.

Later Greek poets saw the point clearly. Here is a mother, Jocasta, speaking to her son:

> Why do you follow the worst of deities my son—
> Love of honor? Don't do it; she is an unjust god.
> Many happy homes and cities have had her in—
> And out—to the destruction of those who pursue her.
> (Euripides, *Phoenician Women,* 531–34)

The young man will not give up honor; he will follow it where it leads, to civil war, which is a calamity for his people, and literally to killing, and being killed by, his own brother. That is irreverence. Like the poets, Thucydides sees the love of honor as a cause of civil war, and of this the chief moral symptom is a loss of reverence. The poet and the historian are writing during the great age of the sophists, when many thinkers have been questioning the heroic values of their ancestors. At one point in my study of these themes, I believed that Euripides and Thucydides are revolutionaries in rejecting the love of honor. But, no, Homer has been there before them. Reverence overrides all other values for Greek writers before Plato—starting with Homer.

Agamemnon, as leader of the Greek army, ought to be reverent. He ought to exercise the virtues of leadership, but he is the man who angers Apollo by holding prisoner the daughter of his priest, and he is the one who is so jealous of his honor that when he gives the young woman back to her father, he takes another from Achilles, driving a bolt of anger through the forces under his command. We know that Agamemnon cannot win the war without Achilles' help, but Agamemnon is confident:

> Go ahead and desert, if that's what you want!
> I'm not going to beg you to stay. There are plenty of others
> Who will honor me, not least of all Zeus the Counselor.
> (*Iliad* 1.173–75 [Lombardo 1.183–85])

And so confident is he of his special relationship with the god (a sure sign of irreverence) that he is willing to use his power in the most brutal way:

> I'm coming to your hut and taking Briseis,
> Your own beautiful prize, so that you will see just how much
> Stronger I am than you, and the next person will wince
> At the thought of opposing me as an equal.
> (1.184–87 [Lombardo 1.194–97])

This is not leadership. Because of his own love of honor, Agamemnon has failed to honor the best Greek of them all. Now we see how the love of honor vitiates reverence: Reverent leaders respect those who serve under them, but they cannot do that if they are too jealous of their own honor.

Achilles, too, is jealous of his honor, and readers both ancient and modern have found him to be the principal foil for Odysseus. But this is misleading. Give both men a choice between honor and a homecoming, and both (as Homer represents them) would choose to go home. True, love of honor holds Achilles out of the battle after Agamemnon insults him; but honor is not Achilles' ruling passion. Friendship alone moves Achilles when the generals try to persuade him to arm again. And Achilles really wants to be safe, he wants his beloved friend to be safe, and he wants to go home. In the end, it is grief for the one he loves most, Patroclus, that shatters his dream of homecoming. He tells his mother:

> My friend is dead,
> Patroclus, my dearest friend of all. I loved him,
> And I killed him...
> You will never again
> Welcome me home, since I no longer have the will
> To remain alive among men, not unless Hector
> Loses his life on the point of my spear
> And pays for despoiling Menoetius' son.
> (18.80–82, 89–93 [Lombardo 83–85, 94–98])

Achilles has lost the desire to live, no matter what happens with Hector. He now believes he is certain to die at Troy, and he accepts this fate (19.329–32). He has not had the luxury of choice, he has never chosen battle over homecoming, and he has never shown contempt for reverence. He will lose all human reverence in the grief-stricken rampage that follows, but it is a brief loss, and we know he will recover. Tennyson picked the wrong hero for his poem. Achilles, not Odysseus, is the man who loses all taste for life when his beloved friend dies. Hallam is to Tennyson as Patroclus is to Achilles. There is no Calypso for Achilles or Tennyson, no captivating island goddess as there is for Odysseus—only the memory of lost glory and grief for a lost love.

Odysseus: Looking Homeward

Odysseus too has his flashes of irreverence in the *Iliad*. The safe path he follows leads him to kill a prisoner, for example, and sometimes to treat his friends with disrespect. In the *Odyssey,* off the battlefield, he is as crafty as in the *Iliad,* but his craft is now bent wholeheartedly on his return. The epic begins with Odysseus as a love-slave to the divine nymph Calypso, who has offered him ageless immortality, but he spends his days weeping on a headland, where Calypso finds him when she goes to tell him Zeus has ordered her to let him go:

> Calypso composed herself and went to Odysseus,
> Zeus' message still ringing in her ears.
> She found him sitting where the breakers rolled in.
> His eyes were perpetually wet with tears now,
> His life draining away in homesickness.
> The nymph had long since ceased to please.
> (5.149–54 [Lombardo 148–53])

The last line is our only hint that he had ever been satisfied with Calypso. What could have made him change his mind? She is beautiful, she is immortal, and the scene of life in the cavern is so lovely that even a god is enraptured by it, spellbound (5.74). She has been kind to Odysseus, there is nothing wrong with their sex life together, and she offers him the endless life and youth of a god. But Odysseus longs for home, even though he has no hope or plan of leaving. Evidently he sees his fling with the goddess as an interruption of his human life.

To be reverent is to take care never to play the part of god or beast. Odysseus knows he has no business playing at immortality with Calypso, and with Hermes' help he is able to resist the charm of Circe that turns men into pigs. He is human, and his place is home. This knowledge is one of the many signs of his reverence. To it we should add the care and respect he shows to his men, his refusal to eat the cattle of the Sun, and his understanding of human weakness—shown, for example, when he recognizes that he cannot resist the sirens' song unaided.

Odysseus has spent his life either at home or looking homeward. When he arrives on Ithaca with his treasure he does not recognize the place, and no one recognizes him—no one but the dog. This, the poet tells us, is a contrivance of the goddess Athena, but how could it be otherwise after so long an absence? Any veteran knows. The young soldier is now grizzled and scarred, his tiny son is now a young man, his dog can barely rise to its feet. And a riot of hostile men is taking possession of his house, with the hope of marrying one of them to his presumed widow, Penelope. Still, Odysseus does not flinch from making the place his home again. He is cunning, violent, and deceptive in his homecoming, but he does come home.

The Summer Day

Who made the world?
Who made the swan, and the black bear?
Who made the grasshopper?
This grasshopper, I mean—
the one who has flung herself out of the grass,
the one who is eating sugar out of my hand,
who is moving her jaws back and forth instead of up and down—
who is gazing around with her enormous and complicated eyes.
Now she lifts her pale forearms and thoroughly washes her face.
Now she snaps her wings open, and floats away.
I don't know exactly what a prayer is.
I do know how to pay attention, how to fall down
into the grass, how to kneel down in the grass,
how to be idle and blessed, how to stroll through the fields,
which is what I have been doing all day.
Tell me, what else should I have done?
Doesn't everything die at last, and too soon?
Tell me, what is it you plan to do
with your one wild and precious life?

—Mary Oliver (Reprinted by permission of
The Charlotte Sheedy Literary Agency Inc.)

15 | EPILOGUE
RENEWING REVERENCE

I never planned to give anyone advice on how to live. That way lies hubris, and I am conscious enough of failures in my life to know better than to tell others how to conduct theirs. But since writing about reverence I have been asked again and again what people could do if they wish to take reverence more seriously. Conversations with Dr. Harry Wilmer, of Salado, Texas, helped me form my ideas on this. I dedicate this epilogue to his memory.

Reverence is easily lost; it seeps away from me like water from a lightly cracked bowl, a bowl so beautiful that I am blind to its cracks.

Every success, every victory, is an opportunity for overconfidence. The victory of the United States in the Cold War contributed to our entering wars in a Muslim world that we did not understand, after 2001, with absurd hopes. Success in the Cold War also led to our unblinking trust in unregulated capitalism, and this overconfidence led to the financial collapse of 2007–08. That is why a reverent mind is suspicious of victory. Only a spoilsport would look around every silver lining to catch sight of a dark cloud. But if I wish to be reverent, I should always guard myself against the thought that one success promises another.

Even my efforts to maintain reverence weaken it. Suppose we set up rituals to build reverence into our lives and make them our routine. Then the routines can lose meaning and become chores, and chores are not conducive to reverence. Routines can also give us the confidence that we are among the reverent people on earth, and such confidence leads to hubris. Reverent people like me (I might think to myself) can do no wrong. Routines are not enough. As we are always leaking reverence, so we must always look for new ways to replenish it. I cannot rest on my reverence. Reverence begets reverence. But believing too much in my own reverence will slay whatever reverence I have ever had.

I offer three ideas for renewing reverence: pay attention, speak the languages of reverence, and ask the right question. I end with a reminder of why this is so important: reverence saves lives.

Pay Attention

I write to you from a place of extraordinary beauty. Anyone could feel awe here. The bay and the sky are speaking blue to each other. A gull with a glistening white head alights on water that is barely ruffled by a southerly breeze. Now she rises and perches on the stem of my dinghy. In the distance, to the northeast, a rise of small mountains shows a deeper blue against the sky, which will soon take on light pink as the sun descends to the west. The islands around the harbor, where I am alone with my brother, have knees of white and pink granite. Above the tide line is a tangle of spruce, opened occasionally by the windfall of great storms. Tall grass grows green in the openings. Under the spruce boughs, broad cushions of moss sponge dew from the sea air, and fallen branches are bearded with lichen.

This is an easy place to flex the emotional muscles I use for reverence. Awe comes easily in the presence of beauty that anyone could see. But only a reverent eye sees every opportunity. The reverent writer Barry Lopez, walking in the Arctic, found himself bowing to a horned lark he saw staring back at him. Not everyone would have seen the bird's stare as connecting to him. Lopez has a well-developed capacity for awe.

I do not have to travel far to see wonders. Stepping by accident into a polluted mud puddle, I may see an iridescent rainbow. Looking up when I hear an infant screaming, I may recognize the tenderness of a mother's face hovering over the child. Or as a mosquito prepares to draw blood from my forearm I may be struck by the delicacy of design in a creature so light and powerful. When the moon sets long before morning on a clear night, I may rejoice in the wonder of a dome of stars arched over by the cream of the Milky Way.

I need time and patience to see things in this way. The mud puddle seeped into my shoes, chilling my feet, the crying child interrupted a conversation I wanted urgently to finish, and the mosquito threatened me with a tropical disease. The setting of the moon could be the signal for an enemy attack, hidden by darkness, on our compound (this before infrared goggles had been invented for troops). I can't always pay attention to beauty. Still, I pay attention when I can, at whatever opportunities my life gives me to exercise my sense of awe.

Paying attention is something I can do alone, though it goes better with a loving partner, as I have had the good fortune to learn—whether the partner loves me or the things I care about. I see only where my eyes are pointing, but you, looking another way, can call my attention to something I should see. Bird watchers are not solitary. Many eyes see more, if they communicate.

"Paying attention" is a way of referring to mindfulness, which is at the core of ethics in every ancient tradition. I have much to be mindful of, besides all that is awe-inspiring around me. I need to pay attention to other people, for example—to their needs and feelings. I need to pay attention to myself as well—to what I am actually doing (which may not be what I think I am doing), and to my feelings and needs. This is obvious enough.

The Languages of Reverence

I feel reverence through awe, but I never find words to express what awe feels like, so my language of reverence cannot be a mere offering of words that you would understand. Nor could it be a set of sounds that only I can understand. A language is not a language unless it is shared. If we can grow a language of reverence, it will bring us together.

Music can be a language of reverence. We have many traditions of music, and many ways of being reverent and expressing reverence through music. Here's mine. Often when I try to play a Bach sonata on my cello I am aware of nothing but my personal struggle to sound each note before the next one demands its turn. But every now and then I slow down, time seems to hold its count, and I feel as if my intercourse with Bach and the cello has been an act of worship.

To give sound to music as a language of reverence, I have to play with reverence, patiently, and with a focus on the beauty Bach has captured, with no thought of myself or my clumsy left fingers or my awkward bow hand. This I can do alone. But forgetting myself in music is easier when I am with others; for example, when joining them to bring out the music in a Hayden quartet—something none of us can do alone, since the individual parts are not the music Hayden wrote.

Poetry can be a language of reverence. I may be gathered with like-minded lovers of poetry, forgetting myself, setting aside for the moment the temptation to prove that I know more about Keats or John Clare than you do—reading, listening, sharing poetry. To appreciate poetry, we let our minds play freely together, beyond the plain meaning of words. Settling reverently into poetry, we are speaking a language of reverence.

The traditional language of reverence is ceremony. Simple gestures of greeting and recognition are tokens of respect. They can be more than that. If uttered with reverent feelings, these gestures belong to a language of reverence. A sincere good morning, a warm handshake, the appropriate use of the eyes (different in different cultures)—these say, "Here we are together, where there is something more important than either of us, which we care about, and which we try to point to by means of these courtesies." Confucius insisted that it is never enough to perform the rituals without feeling, and that the rituals need not be letter perfect. But they do need to be expressed with reverence.

Sacraments (as Christians have insisted since the early Church) can be effective whether or not they are carried out with the right feelings or beliefs. But sacraments serve only to make things sacred, and sacred things do not deserve reverence (see chapter ten). Sacraments do not help us renew reverence in our hearts unless we perform them in a reverent way.

Liturgy—the formal practice of worship—may be a language of reverence, but I am afraid that formal practices of worship often undermine reverence, especially if they reassure the worshippers of their elite status, or if the forms themselves become objects of worship. We fall so easily into idolatry of ourselves or of the things we do.

Ask the Right Question

The reverent soul does more good by asking questions than by answering them—questions for myself, questions for others.

A good question for myself is this: Can I do this thing I am planning to do in a reverent spirit, reverently? I call this the adverb question.

See how different it is from the noun question: What action does reverence tell me to do now? The noun question has no answer. Reverence generally does not tell me what to do; it tells me how to do the things I choose to do. But if I can't see how to do that thing reverently, I should not do it at all.

Over forty years ago, as a young army lieutenant, I had this choice: Continue active duty in a war I thought wrong, become a deserter, or seek conscientious objector status. A reverent soul could have made any one of those choices and carried it out reverently, and many chose each of these three courses. But I could not. As it happened, I would have had to lie to be accepted as a conscientious objector, and I do not believe that I could have lied in a reverent spirit. Nor did I think I could reverently have broken my pledge by deserting. I chose to serve, and most of the time I think I did so reverently, but I had underestimated the character-destroying effects of warfare. Before serving, I had believed that I could change the army more than it would change me. That was hubris, and I was wrong. I finished my tour with the guilty knowledge that I was not as good a human being as I had thought. That was, at least, a lesson in reverence. I should also have asked the next two questions:

The second question for myself: Am I fooling myself? Do I really know what I think I know? Am I forgetting my ignorance, overlooking how prone I am to error? This is Socrates' question for himself, and it is crucial to his lifetime project of avoiding the hubris of claiming knowledge he does not have. The reverent soul probes itself.

And the third: Am I actually doing the things I think I am doing? And not doing the things I think I am not doing? For example, in the classroom am I leading my students toward learning or am I showing off? A mindful teacher would know the difference. The reverent soul knows what it is about.

Questions for others. These may help others see the way to reverence. I assume (as Chinese classical ethics assumes) that human beings have the sprouts of all the virtues in them by nature. A sprout may be hidden, deeply buried, or even starved to death, but even the nastiest tyrant started with a sprout for reverence. The right line of questioning, in the right circumstances, could lead anyone to be aware of this treasure deep inside.

Here is a dialogue I remember from over ten years ago, before the United States attempted to remake the Middle East by toppling Saddam Hussein in Iraq—a time when many of us were trumpeting the importance of projecting the power of the United States around the world. I was in an airplane next to a young man who had just graduated from a military academy. Of course I had certain advantages—he had nowhere to go to escape me, and I was older than his father. We talked a bit about his education, and I asked him about his ethics courses—knowing that all the military academies try to teach ethics, but seem to fail.

PAUL: Were your ethics courses effective?

YOUNG OFFICER: No. Waste of time. The people who teach ethics do not understand that ethics has no place in military life. Our job is to project our nation's power into the world, and that has nothing to do with right and wrong. Ethics is a waste of time. What we do is all about power.

He went on to say that he had read a little Thucydides at his academy. He believed the Greek historian corroborated his view that power is all that matters to people. He made the point emphatically. When people talk about ethics, he thought, they are just blowing smoke— as Thucydides says. Thucydides does say that, I knew, but he also shows how failures in ethics lead to catastrophe. So I tried another line of questions:

PAUL: By the way, did you have leadership training at the academy?

YOUNG OFFICER: Yes, we sure did.

PAUL: So I guess you plan to be good at being a leader.

YOUNG OFFICER: I do. I hope I have what it takes.

PAUL: How can you tell whether you're a good leader?

YOUNG OFFICER: That's easy. People follow you willingly.

PAUL: Willingly? Why do they do that?

YOUNG OFFICER: You have to know what you're doing, be an expert. They won't follow you if you're an idiot.

PAUL: That's all it takes to be a leader? Be an expert?

YOUNG OFFICER: No. They have to trust you, too. They have to see that you are an expert.

PAUL: Does that mean you have to trust them as well? In the army they taught me that trust was mutual, that it goes both ways. The troops won't trust you if you never trust them.

YOUNG OFFICER: Yes, of course.

PAUL: So if you trust them, then you pay attention to them, listen to them when they have something to tell you.

YOUNG OFFICER: Of course.

PAUL: So you don't assume that you have all the knowledge. You are not the only expert.

YOUNG OFFICER: No way. A leader leads a team. That's why you have a team. Some of them will know things I don't. Be able to do things I can't do.

PAUL: I am sure that's right. Does a leader treat the team fairly?

YOUNG OFFICER: Yes, of course.

PAUL: I noticed there's one word you have not used so far— "power." As a leader do you use your power to make people do what you want?

YOUNG OFFICER: Yeah, an officer has power all right. I will have a lot of power over them.

PAUL: But then, if you depend on your power over them, are they following you willingly? Does power make you a leader? You said a little while ago that nothing matters to people but power. Do you still believe that? Is power all that matters between you and the troops you lead?

At that point the pilot interrupted us, announcing our landing, and after that the young officer changed the subject. I suppose he could have drawn a distinction between the ethical way he wanted to work with his own troops and the non-ethical way he wanted to treat others. Then I could have asked him whether he could divide himself in that way, and whether that division would leave him with a satisfactory sense of who he is. But that would have been too much for a short plane ride.

I will never know whether he remembered the conversation. I will never know whether it made any difference to him in the long run. But I gave him a chance, at any rate, to think more deeply about his values, and although I never used the word "reverence," I was creeping up on the idea, and surely I had found in him some sprouts that could grow into reverence. I hope so, because he will have power as he gains in rank, and the more power he has, the more he will need reverence.

Reverence Saves Lives

Reverence is the virtue that protects the helpless. That means it is also the virtue that protects me, when I am powerful, from abusing those who are helpless.

The company commander. A friend commands a company in a sweep of the Vietnamese countryside, and they have detained two women, one with a little girl, in black pajamas. The women have been carrying ammunition, supplies, and messages to the enemy. Through his interpreter, my friend has extracted what information he could in the circumstances. He calls for a helicopter to take the prisoners to the interrogation center, but the operations officer tells him over the radio that no choppers are available. "But I have to move out and I can't take them with me," he says, in effect. "And I can't leave them here. They'll tell everyone where we are. Request disposition instructions."

"Destroy the contraband supplies," says the officer. "And if your prisoners happen to die of malaria or some other disease by morning, we will understand." He is using a familiar code to give my friend an order to shoot the prisoners, even though they are unarmed civilians pressed into service by the enemy. The "we" implies that the battalion commander approved the order. My friend turns to his executive officer, "I want you as a witness to what I am doing. I have just been given either tacit permission or an implied order to kill these two women. I am not going to do it."

Luckily for all concerned, my friend has a rock-solid character. The captives do not die of malaria or any other disease that night. The company commander scares them and releases them. In doing so he is not adding to the danger his troops are in; the local Vietnamese people already know where his troops are, how many and how armed. My friend had the power to commit a crime and get away with it. Only his character—his well-developed reverence—stood in his way. I hope it would be the same for me.

That night, after releasing the two women and the child, he marches his company ten hours over difficult terrain; at dawn he surprises an enemy headquarters and captures a North Vietnamese officer. On the officer's map he finds his position from the previous evening, accurately marked. The enemy knows where he has been, and the information probably did not reach them by way of the women he released. There would not have been time.

I have used this example in ethics classes, telling the story up to the coded order, then asking the students what they would do. One

ROTC cadet, destined for a nursing career, proposed to cut out the tongues of the women, so they could not give our position away. Others thought they would shoot the captives, but one clever lad, who balked at killing them directly, said he would tie the women to trees and call in artillery after our unit moved out—hoping thereby to escape responsibility for their deaths. In that particular ROTC class, not one student chose my friend's solution—which I believe is the right answer. That appalls me. These young people were being prepared to hold positions of power—not only to command others, but to call up awesome levels of destruction.

Too often I find that young people are trained to hold power by teachers who forget how great is the moral danger that comes with power. Perhaps the old Greeks were not much better, but they at least were exposed to Sophocles and Aeschylus, and they had seen on the tragic stage how power leads to hubris, hubris to blindness, and blindness to glaring failures of humanity. They also sealed the lesson by training young men as a chorus to perform hymns to reverence in the plays.

Because war gives some commanders extraordinary powers, warfare demands an especially vigilant reverence. But quite ordinary people in peacetime often find themselves with the power that must be tempered by reverence.

The teacher. Teachers, especially of young children, have enormous powers that can be used for abuse. Sometimes the abuse is subtle. Sometimes not.

Suppose I have in my classroom the seven-year-old brother of a boy I taught a few years ago, who was one of my stars. This one learns slowly by comparison. He frustrates me, and so I make the comparison almost every day: "Your brother could add and subtract at your age, why can't you? Why aren't you as smart as he is?" I am teaching him that he is stupid and reinforcing the lesson ceaselessly. Sad to say, he will learn this—though it is not the case. A more reverent teacher would find this boy's brilliant core (it truly is there) and teach to that. But I would have to take time to listen to the boy, to pay attention to him, to find out what he does well and build on that. But I might say to myself: "Why bother, when I already know how to teach? I succeeded with the boy's brother, so I must be a fine teacher, and the fault must be the boy's." This would be a false conceit of knowledge. In this way, hubris, even in a small matter, could have a devastating effect on a life. But there is worse, as we all know.

Suppose I am a teacher or a preacher alone with a very attractive teenager who has no family looking out for his or her interests. The teenager has enormous respect for me and will do what I say and keep quiet about it. And besides, a youngster without a healthy family life is desperate to be loved by someone. I could do what I want and (at least for a time) expect to get away with it. Let's hope I want nothing harmful. Such young people are helpless and I am powerful. Only my character protects them. And me.

The nursing home aide. Suppose I am an aide in a nursing home. We have a lot of demanding old people here. Often I am alone with one of them. She has lost most of her mind. I could do anything I want to her, and no one would ever know. Let's hope I do not want to do anything bad to her. She is so helpless and I have so much power in her world. Many of us will have power at one time or another, but all of us were helpless babies, and most of us will be helpless in illness or old age. Then we will have lost the beauty of infants, along with their promise of growth and change for the better. As we advance into old age—which has a beauty of its own that few can recognize—we will depend more than ever on the reverence of others.

In Place of a Conclusion

The last word on reverence? Not here, and the last question isn't here either. Not on any reverent page. Yes, our best hope when we are weak is that our rulers are reverent. And our best hope when we rule others is that reverence will keep us safe from abusing the weak. But isn't that a frail and distant hope? How can we, when we glory in success or power, remember reverence?

Even if this book lay by the bed of every potentate or military commander, every senator or member of a national legislature, what good would that do? Reading never put reverence in a soul, not reading by itself. Would a national conversation help? Perhaps, if it brought good examples to light—lives lived in reverence, attractive, beckoning for us all to follow.

And you, reverent reader, do you dare to set an example? You would have to live your life in a certain way, making choice after choice with a view to reverence. If you could lead such a life, could you do so in a way that might start a chain reaction? You would have to touch other lives as you strive for reverence. You would have to live in such a way that those you touch would feel, as you do, that the ceremonies of reverence are necessary—in spite of the urgencies of work and war and poverty. And when people take you for an example, could you remember how far you are from achieving reverence?

You would have to take risks gladly. Could you embrace the risk of loss that follows on compassion? Could you shrug off the worry that others will take advantage of your compassion? When we are at war, and our enemies threaten terror, could you see more hope than danger in compassion, even then? Could you honestly look these dangers in the face and still have the confidence to lead others toward compassion?

The seeds of reverence may sprout in any soul, but they are easily trampled or starved. When you set this book down, what will you do to guard and nourish the tender gardens of reverence?

NOTES

All translations in this book, including the epigraph on the title page, are my own except where indicated in the text or notes. The notes that follow are grouped first by chapter and section, and then by page number for notes that apply to specific statements. Books are identified by author's last name; a short title is supplied for authors of more than one cited work.

Preface to the Second Edition

"Part of what you criticize": Stafford (2003, 36).

Chapter One: Introducing Reverence

As far as I know, there has been no other general study of reverence as a virtue. This is the first. Garrison, however, has published a fine study of *pietas*, the analogous Roman virtue, and its descendants in literature through the eighteenth century. The revival of interest in virtue ethics has produced a sizable bibliography, which I introduce in the note to chapter four.

p. 3. "The one great western philosopher who praises reverence is Nietzsche": See below, p. 161–62.

p. 4. "If we find a common thread in Greek and Chinese ideals": See chapters five and six; for a defense of my claim that reverence belongs everywhere, see chapter nine, "Relativism," with references.

p. 5. "Cardinal virtue": A virtue of such importance to satisfactory human life that it is honored in many cultures and is essential to a complete virtue ethics.

p. 5. Defining Reverence

My approach is based on my understanding of Aristotle on courage and other virtues, especially *Nicomachean Ethics*, Book 3, Chapter 7. A general discussion of ancient virtue ethics comes at the start of Annas (1993); important studies of Aristotle's ethics relevant to this task are by Cooper, Sherman, and White.

p. 6. Awe and respect: See chapter seven for awe and chapters eleven and thirteen for respect.

Chapter Two: Without Reverence

p. 13. God Votes in a City Election

See pp. 151–55 and chapter thirteen, "The Silent Teacher." The ancient Greeks observe a strict line between gods and humans—gods know things that humans do not. And yet they respected a class of prophets who did claim to speak for the gods. How is this possible? (1) They knew that human prophets could get the message wrong; (2) when the prophet got it right, they gave credit for that not to him but to the god; (3) they apparently believed that reverent prophecy was difficult to read—that prophecy may be true, but not in the way human beings tend to understand it. All these stand between the giving of prophecy and the sort of arrogance I have illustrated in this section.

p. 15. No One Votes at All

On social choice theory, see A. K. Sen's classic work (1970), especially pp. 192–96 for the problem about voting, which has not been resolved since then from within the theory.

p. 17. Trees Are Merely Cash and Sawdust

Thanks to Paul Domjan for showing me how valuable virtue ethics (especially the ethics of reverence) are to environmental issues.

Steinbeck (1962) writes: "The redwoods, once seen, leave a mark or create a vision that stays with you always. No one has ever successfully painted or photographed a redwood tree. The feeling they produce is not transferable. From them comes silence and awe. It's not their unbelievable stature, nor the color which seems to shift and vary under your eyes, no, they are ambassadors from another time. They have the mystery of ferns that disappeared a million years ago into the coal of the carboniferous era. They carry their own light and shade. The vainest, most slap-happy and irreverent of men, in the presence of redwoods, goes under a spell of wonder and respect. Respect—that's the word. One feels the need to bow to unquestioned sovereigns."

In chapter seven I will ask what sort of thing can be an object of reverence. These are the conditions I suggest for consideration: An object of reverence (1) should not be in our power to change or to control; (2) should not be fully comprehended by human experts; (3) should not be a human product; and (4) should be transcendent. The trees satisfy the first three, but not the fourth. Those who insist on the fourth may wish to think of the trees as inspiring awe because they represent to us the power of God or of Nature, considered as transcendent. A tradition or way of life satisfies only the first two conditions at best; it can't be changed very much and still be what it is, and it is pretty hard to understand; but it is made by human beings, and human beings can replace it. It is, therefore, much less worthy of reverence than the trees are. Trying to have reverence for tradition is dangerous; on this, see chapter nine.

p. 20. "Socrates' famous belief": Plato's *Crito* 47 de.

p. 23. "the ambiguity of ritual": Kertzer, especially p. 77. On political party conventions and Galbraith's view of them, see Kertzer, pp. 182–84, citing Galbraith (1960).

p. 26. We Know the Enemy Loves to Die

"Studies have found that such armies are reluctant to shed their civilian ethics": Grossman, especially Section 1.

p. 28. "(That is one of the lessons of post-traumatic stress)": Shay, p. 32–35, Grossman, 281ff. The point was dramatized by Bertolt Brecht long before these studies in "A Man's a Man."

p. 29. There Is No Reverence

p. 30. For Aristotle on learning virtue, see his *Nicomachean Ethics*, book 2 chapter 4; for Mencius, see Ivanhoe, *Confucian Moral Self-Cultivation*, pp. 18–22.

p. 34. Plato's objection: See p. 272–73. (note to p. 95).

p. 34. "We shall see, however, that justice does not suffice for a healthy society." See p. 138 and the treatment of justice in my recent book, *The Ajax Dilemma* (2010).

p. 35–36. *Analects* of Confucius: I have modified Legge's translation, printing "*Li*" for his "rules of propriety." Legge's otherwise excellent translation misses the point: it is not the rules of *Li* that take the bustle out of respectful courtesy, but a spirit or underlying attitude of reverence. See also *Analects* 2.7, 3.3, and 17.11. Different translators take the last clause differently: "If you are upright but lack ritual you will become inflexible" (Slingerland).

Chapter Three: Music and a Funeral

The string quartet and the funeral are not actual events but composites of events that I have shared in or witnessed. The overlapping terms "ceremony" and "ritual" in this discussion must be understood fairly loosely. Part of the reason we lose sight of reverence is that we reserve these words for grand events in our own culture and trivial ones in others. But shaking hands is ceremony, and dining out usually involves ritual.

p. 39. Philip Larkin's "High Windows": title poem in a book published by Farrar, Strauss and Giroux (New York: 1974) and Faber and Faber (London:)

p. 45. Reverence Across Cultures

This section summarizes material explored at greater length in chapters seven and eight.

Chapter Four: Bare Reverence

p. 50. Protagoras was the first teacher in ancient Greece to call himself a sophist and the most famous teacher of his time (fifth century BCE). Only a few sentences have survived from his writings, but several other sources purport to give us the gist of his teachings. Plato is the chief source, but he is unreliable on the history of philosophy. Plato reports that the statement "a human being is measure of all things" was equivalent to the relativist position: "what you believe is true for you, while what I believe is true for me" (Plato's *Theaetetus* 152a, with subsequent context). Other evidence shows, however, that Protagoras could not have been a consistent relativist (Woodruff, 1998). For a translation of the surviving work of Protagoras, see Gagarin and Woodruff (1995, pp. 173–89).

p. 51. "According to Plato, Protagoras held such a view": Plato's testimony on historical matters is not as reliable as we would wish, and there is no consensus among scholars as to whether the historical Protagoras held the view related in this chapter. Still, we have good reason to think that views of this kind were in the air among humanist intellectuals of the later fifth century BCE.

p. 52. Protagoras is not alone among humanists who support reverence: See my remarks on Thucydides, pp. 136–37.

Agamemnon's failure of reverence: Homer does not use the concept of justice at all. For a more detailed discussion of this issue, see chapter eleven on reverence as the virtue of leaders.

p. 55. A Philosopher's Questions

Modern work in virtue ethics has been much influenced by MacIntyre; I was myself deeply affected by my colleague Edmund Pincoffs. For recent work in the field, see the articles printed in Crisp and Slote; Crisp; Braybrooke in his chapter 12, "No rules without virtues, no virtues without rules"; Casey; and Hunt. McDowell has been especially helpful to me in showing how the knowledge that is virtue is internal to practices. An excellent introduction to virtue ethics is Annas (2011).

p. 55. Plato presents a scene: The opening of his dialogue, the *Charmides*.

p. 57. *Do virtues replace rules?* See Onora O'Neill for a systematic approach to ethics that complements rule-based ethics with a theory of social virtues very like the theory of virtue I am laying out here. See also her eloquent warning against the danger of pushing virtues that support social structures in the absence of rules protecting human rights.

"A sense that there is something larger than a human being": "larger" here is a figure of speech; I explain the idea more fully in chapter seven, p. 113.

p. 58. *What is the difference between reverence and ceremony?* On ritual, see the discussion in Burkert. Many students of ritual would disagree with my claim that the meaningfulness of ritual depends on attitudes and ultimately on the presence of virtue. Ethology has found "biological" explanations for human rituals in comparable behaviors in primates and other mammals.

p. 58. "Faith is not a virtue": See Bennett's *The Book of Virtues*, however, where he does represent faith as a virtue.

p. 59. "Nietzsche says that European Christian culture shows its greatest nobility in respect for the Bible": *Beyond Good and Evil*, section 262. See also p. 161–62.

p. 60. On respect, see Woodruff (2013).

p. 61. "Does reverence carry compassion? Yes." This is especially clear as the ancient Greeks understood reverence and compassion. See the notes on the ancient Greek attitude toward suppliants (p. 227 with p. 194).

p. 62. Compassion understood in this way is compatible with justice. On compassion and its relation to justice, see my *The Ajax Dilemma* (2011), pp. 99, 102–07, and 140–58.

p. 62. "Even an atheist or a non-theist may be reverent": for example, see Ursula Goodenough, *The Sacred Depths of Nature.*

p. 68–69. "The prevailing trend in Confucian philosophy, developed by Mencius, was to suppose that every human being is endowed with the seeds of virtue": For Mencius on learning virtue, see Ivanhoe, *Confucian Moral Self-Cultivation*, pp. 18–22.

p. 70. "Hardly anyone who takes virtue ethics seriously, whether ancient or modern, thinks it worthwhile to wait for external foundations to be secure": Aristotle does not. For a modern defense of an internalist approach to grounding talk of virtue, see McDowell, "Two Sorts of Naturalism." For an argument that internalism does not have to lead to relativism, see Nussbaum, "Non-Relative Virtues" (1998).

"Can a reverent person do evil?": Confucius thought that he was not secure in virtue until he was seventy, because only then did his desires accord with the will of heaven (*Analects* 2.4). Is it a paradox that the diminution of some of our powers makes virtue easier for us? In both Greek and Chinese traditions, virtue is not a triumph over harmful desire; it is freedom from harmful desires.

Chapter 5: Ancient Greece

All translations in this chapter are mine, except for the translations from Homer, which are by Stanley Lombardo. Both his and mine are used by permission of the Hackett Publishing Co. For the content of the epigraph, compare the poem "What are Years?" by Marianne Moore (*Collected Poems* [1951, originally 1941], p. 99.)

A brief discussion of sources and methods

The ancient Greek concept I wish to explore is named by both *hosiotēs* and its near synonym *eusebeia*, which is frequently translated as "piety." It overlaps substantially with *aidôs*, which is untranslatable but usually rendered as "respect" or "shame."

For this subject we must depend more on literary sources than most historians of religion are willing to do. The *Bacchae*, for example, cannot be treated as a source for actual Dionysiac cult practices in Athens or anywhere else. Fortunately, we have non-literary evidence bearing on cult practices, but this will not help us understand the ideas that lie behind those practices. I have argued elsewhere that Euripides' *Bacchae* represents through the chorus a religious spirit known to the Athenians from their experience in the Eleusinian Mysteries (in my *Bacchae* [1998], and at greater length in my manuscript *Godless Wisdom*).

Understanding a concept such as reverence is difficult because it is most apparent in religion, and religion has too much to do with inarticulate loyalties to yield much from a close study of concepts. In the experience and practice of religion, the fine distinctions that matter to philosophers will seem irrelevant to most worshippers. Religion in ancient Greece is a complex of different kinds of worship in different places and for different groups of people. Time travel to the fifth century BCE might acquaint us with a number of different concepts of reverence. Even the majority of the jury that condemned Socrates would probably not have agreed with each other about precisely what reverence requires.

This chapter discusses *a* prominent concept of reverence; I make no claim that the concept is typically or widely held in fifth-century BCE Greece. It is not *the* concept of reverence. In its rough outline, I think most Athenians of the period would have recognized it as theirs, but once it is closely defined, its proper home is only in the texts from which I have derived it. Here I am working from three kinds of texts: Homeric epics, Athenian tragic plays, and the histories of Herodotus and Thucydides. In all of these, I believe, the same concept of reverence is at work. The writer who does most to challenge this traditional notion of reverence is Plato, whom I will treat briefly in a note at the end of chapter five.

I have found no good general studies of the ancient Greek concept of reverence. Yunis, *A New Creed* (1988), is helpful on the new emphasis in the latter fifth century on beliefs about the gods. Belief, however, is not my subject.

Ancient Greek customs of reverence

1. **Treatment of the dead.** Violations of the dead call for the greatest outrage from poets and historians alike. Creon's crime in the *Antigone*, according to Tiresias, is to bury a living person—Antigone—while withholding from burial a person who is dead—her brother—and who belongs to the gods because he is dead (lines 1064–1071). Thucydides does not explicitly treat this as a matter of reverence. But see 2.52, 2.53, and the general importance of revering the graves of the dead from the Persian war to the debate at Plataea.

2. **Laws of war.** The rules for starting and waging war fall under reverence. "Reverence allows one to repel an aggressor" (Thucydides 3.52). War frequently involves oathbreaking (see #4) and the rejection of suppliants (see #3). Thucydides sums up his long catalogue of virtues lost in civil war under the rubric of reverence (3.82).

3. **Suppliants.** Prisoners of war are suppliants; reverence requires that they not be killed (Thucydides 3.58, cf. 3.81). As often with ethical matters, Thucydides lets us see that no one can honestly expect others to behave ethically: the Thebans extract oaths to protect their suppliants (MacLeod, 1977, p. 233). But respect for suppliants is plainly honored as an ideal. We have seen that the actions that mark Achilles' inhumanity most clearly are his refusals to honor the requests of suppliants, and the sign of his recovery is his protection of the suppliant Priam.

4. **Keeping oaths.** Reverent people keep oaths even when doing so does not appear to be to their advantage. This is often cited as a requirement of justice also, but it is a requirement over which the gods particularly watch, and it has a more intimate connection with reverence than with any other virtue. (Thucydides 3.82, cf. 2.71, 2.74. 3.53, 3.58; cf. Xenophon, *Memorabilia* 1.18, Philodemus *De Pietate*, col. 51, 79.)

5. **Ritual.** "Those accused of irreverence sometimes defend themselves by saying that they have at least done what was required by way of religious

ritual." This is Xenophon's defense of Socrates (*Memorabilia* 1.2) and Philodemus' defense of Epicurus (*De Pietate*, col. 51). Creon, for example, will do the ritual minimum for Antigone by leaving a token of food for her in her living burial (lines 773–80), but he has contempt for the idea of reverence, because he holds the rationalist view that the gods are too good or too powerful to be affected by our actions. "I am certain no human being has the power to pollute the gods" (lines 1043–44).

6. **Respect for sacred rituals, objects, secrets, or places**. Athens tried several well-known citizens on charges of profaning the Eleusinian mysteries; the city recalled its best general, Alcibiades, from a campaign to face charges of defacing sacred statues; Thucydides was shocked by the profanation of temples in plague or civil war.

7. **Harmony.** A reverent society will not go to war with itself; when a society does fall into civil war, the moral casualties end in a loss of reverence (Thucydides 3.82). That is because reverence is an attunement of awe and respect and shame among people of all ranks. If you are shameless, or if you lack respect for others, or if you are incapable of standing in awe of the divine, then you are out of tune with society. And that is one of the symptoms of irreverence. Reverence makes you feel like subordinating your interests to a higher good of some kind; reverence keeps selfishness at bay. The effect of reverence on society, then, is to dampen the sort of mean-spirited desires and ambitions that would lead to factionalism and civil war if left unchecked.

Notes on ancient authors

Euripides. Much has been written about Euripides' treatment of religion. The main influence on my thought on this author has been Seaford (1994 and 1996), which is controversial. See especially the critical comment in Segal (1997). My edition of the *Bacchae*, with notes on the matters and texts discussed in the present paper, is published by Hackett (1998).

Socrates. The best account of the issues behind Socrates' trial is now Parker (1996), which otherwise offers little help on my subject. I await eagerly his projected thematic study of Athenian religion. McPherran (1996) presents an account of Socratic piety. His view that Socratic piety reforms traditional *do ut des* religion with the result that human duty to the god is subsumed under virtue is largely due to the teachings of Vlastos. On Socrates, see Smith and Woodruff (2000). For Plato's wider theory, see Morgan (1990).

Thucydides. This historian's rationalist attitude towards religion was scarcely noticed in antiquity (with the exception of *Vita Marcellini* 22); modern scholars have paid it more attention, but it is neglected in recent works on the sophists. The consensus is that Thucydides' neglect for Greek religion is an important feature of his history, but scholars have been reluctant to commit themselves as to the nature of Thucydides' personal beliefs. An important article by Hornblower (1992) indicates how much Thucydides declines to tell us about events that were related to religion.

Marinatos reviews and criticizes modern scholarship on the subject. She defends Thucydides on the charge of atheism, showing that Thucydides does show respect for the practice of religion (which she wrongly thinks is all that mattered to the ancients), and concludes that "his affirmation of the social and moral validity of the religion of Greece is certain" (1981, p. 65).

Notes on specific passages

Line numbers refer to the Greek texts. When the translator counts lines differently, that count is given in brackets.

p. 79. Pindar's famous line "Custom is king": Fragment 169; the poem is quoted often in antiquity. See Plato's *Gorgias* 484b and Gagarin and Woodruff, p. 40.

p. 82. "Achilles plays the beast": Achilles is not the only fighter who is likened to a beast in the *Iliad;* Menelaus is frequently seen as a lion. Generally, the Trojans are more reverent than the Greeks and are pictured as more human and domestic. Hector, in particular, is more tamer of animals—horses—than he is animal. On domesticity, see chapter fourteen, "Home."

p. 83. "The most violent sociopath may, in some sense, remember that he is human—indeed, he may remember that he is a sociopathic human at the very time he commits the most odious crime." I owe the point to Edwin Delattre.

p. 85. "Most ancient Greek thinking about ethics starts with this inference from the 'is' of vulnerable human nature to the 'ought' of virtue." Alasdair MacIntyre builds on a similar inference in his *Dependent Rational Animals.* G. E. Moore is responsible for the widespread view that it is the Naturalistic Fallacy to derive an "ought" from an "is." Annas (1997) has criticized ethical naturalism on the grounds that it is often abused, in "Ethical Arguments." I defend ancient Greek-style naturalism in my "Natural Justice." On the subject, see McDowell's "Two Kinds of Naturalism."

p. 86. "Hubris grows from tyranny": Some editors prefer to translate this as, "Tyranny grows from hubris," which is supported by the manuscripts but does not fit the context. On the issue, see Meineck and Woodruff, *Oedipus*, Introduction p. xxvi and the note to the passage (the first antistrophe to the second stasimon).

"Oedipus' irreverence belongs mainly to the way he rules his people": For a longer discussion, see my Introduction to *Oedipus* (Meineck and Woodruff). Note also that he, and his father before him, thought they could thwart a prediction of the oracle.

p. 88. "Creon proceeds like a tyrant, confident in his judgment": Plato's Socrates is in line with the conventional notion when he says he found that "in reality it is the god who is wise . . . and human wisdom is worth little or nothing" (*Apology* 23a). Thinking yourself wise puts you in danger of thinking yourself equal to a god. Protagoras claimed to teach good judgment, probably by teaching students to argue on both sides of an issue—and thereby to see both sides of an issue. This is the skill Creon and other tragic figures notably lack. See my "Euboulia as the Skill Protagoras Taught" (2013).

p. 89. "Megaphones into hearing trumpets": Stafford (2003), 36.

p. 95. Plato's joyful reverence: Although Plato gives expression to joyful reverence in a number of texts, he breaks with tradition and with the poets on the importance of reverence as a virtue. Plato transforms reverence in two ways, making it subordinate to justice and detaching it from its role in promoting social harmony: according to the *Republic*, justice is the foundation of social harmony; it is the first principle of statecraft, and reverence follows after. In Plato's work, generally, reverence is eclipsed by justice. Justice is what Socrates cares about above all. In the *Euthyphro*, he considers reverence to be a part of justice and asks how we can identify the part of justice that it is. Evidently, it is the part of justice that obtains between human beings and gods. But since Socrates thinks the gods need no service from human beings for their own sake, he concludes that we cannot owe them anything in the way in which we might have debts to each other. Nevertheless, if justice is anything like paying debts, what could it ask us to do for the gods? In the *Euthyphro*, Plato leaves us wondering what Socrates thinks reverence really is. Some scholars have supplied this answer from the context: reverence is serving the gods by promoting justice and the other virtues.

If reverence consists of promoting justice and other virtues, then it is not a virtue with its own moral content. That would explain why Plato's Socrates omits reverence altogether from his lists of virtues in the *Republic* and other dialogues likely to have been composed after the *Euthyphro*.

In the ideal states of both the *Republic* and the *Laws*, Plato retains traditional temple religion with all its rituals and ceremonies, but with a refined theology that will not countenance the old stories of wickedness on the part of the gods. The ritual that survives in Plato's ideal states is independent of the belief that bad people can buy off the gods by giving sacrifices. The judgments of Plato's gods are inexorably just. In both ideal states, religion serves to stabilize the state, and reverence supports this project.

Religious reverence in the *Republic* and the *Laws* is more a quality that rulers should foster in their subjects than a quality they should cultivate in themselves. As a result, these rulers look suspiciously like the rulers we read about in tragic poets—kings like Creon of *Antigone*, who think they know what is best for their people, and therefore do not think they need to listen to those below them. Plato thinks he must reject the tragic view of reverence insofar as it predicts disaster for rulers who take this attitude. The philosopherkings do know what is best.

Chapter Six: Ancient China

p. 98. The translation of the poem by Meng Zhao is my joint effort with Xiusheng Liu; we have brought out its structure by rendering it nearly word for word.

The Confucian conception of Li

My account of *Li* as both ceremony and reverence is based on the *Analects* and the *Book of Mencius* only; it does not purport to represent *Li* in the Chinese tradition overall, or even as it is found in the other classics. I have followed Confucius and Mencius partly because they are central and partly because they emphasize the capacities of individuals for appropriate feelings—capacities that are virtues by the definition developed in this book.

I am well aware that these two classics give only a partial understanding of the ancient Chinese view of *Li* and that not all Confucians agreed with Mencius. As with the Greeks, I am simplifying. What I present here is *a* Confucian concept of *Li*, not *the* Confucian concept. Generally, other ancient texts bring the *rules* of *Li* into prominence, whereas these two classics, as I read them, insist that rule-following is of no value if not in accordance with virtue. Nevertheless, a full study of Li would survey also the *Li Ching* (classic about *Li*), which deals mainly with detailed instructions for *Li*.

As with the ancient Greeks, we are dealing here with a cluster of related concepts: ceremony with reverence (*Li*), filial piety (*xiao*), obedience to older brother (*ti*), respect (*gong*), deference (*rang*). I take it that *Li* refers by turns to proper ceremony and the virtue that lies behind it; *xiao* and *ti* are particular elements of *Li;* respect and deference are the feelings that one should have to carry out any expression of *Li* in a virtuous manner.

Scholars of Confucianism

I depend especially on two secondary works that bring out the interiority of *Li* with useful clarity: Tu Wei-ming and Benjamin Schwartz (especially pp. 67–75). I have a debt also to A. C. Graham's elegant survey, and Ivanhoe's work on Confucian theories of virtue and virtue education.

On the *Analects* of Confucius and the *Book of Mencius* I am at the mercy of translations, but I have had a great deal of help from two friends and teachers: T. K. Seung and Liu Xiusheng. I have often used Simon Leys'

Analects because they are good idiomatic English. I have also consulted James Legge, D. C. Lau, and Chichung Huang. In preparing the second edition, I have consulted Slingerland, who provides not only a fine translation but useful quotations from the ancient Chinese commentaries. In numbering the *Analects* I follow the numbering scheme that now appears to be canonical in D. C. Lau and others.

Translations

These are often composites produced with the help of Xiusheng Liu, but I have used Huang for 2.7 and Leys for 6.27, 9.3, 12.5, and 14.22.

p. 100. *Analects* 2.7. Cf. Mencius 4A.12.

p. 102. *Li* and the absence of external restraint: The view I have expressed is that of Mencius; it may seem to be contradicted by 12.1 but here the restraint is internal; it precedes and makes possible the correct practice of ceremony (Schwartz 1985, 77):

"To restrain oneself and return to *Li* constitutes Humaneness" (ancient maxim quoted in *Analects* 12.1).

The metaphors "inside/outside" carry no metaphysical weight in Chinese philosophy; they make no assumptions about what it is to be a person or to have a conscious mind.

On the inner qualities on which true *Li* depends: *Analects* 1.3, 3.3, 3.12, 3.26, and 17.11. See Schwartz 1985, p. 72ff, esp. pp. 75 and 81. The feelings supported by Li include sympathy, shame (*Analects* 2.3, 5.7), reverence, and respect. For *Li* and right attitudes, see 3.3 (on *Ren*) and 3.26.

p. 103. "Different sorts of advice on same topic": *Analects* 2.5–2.8, with Leys' note, p. 115.

"Rules restraining powerful people from usurping the dignities of the Son of Heaven": *Analects* 3.1, 3.2, 3.10; for a lower-level usurpation, 3.22.

p. 104. No competition for virtue: Plato (*Republic* 1.349), Confucius (3.7, 3.16, 6.30); no value in taking power by force of conquest (3.25, with Leys' note, p. 129).

p. 105. *Analects* 8.2.1 and 8.2.2. The first is translated after Legge, on which see the note to 35–36. The second is Leys' translation. Many scholars hold that the second is a separate selection.

"How, then, could they possibly have cultivated the same sort of reverence, when they had different beliefs?": Belief, on the whole, was different in the two cultures. In ancient Greece, agnosticism was a flash in the pan, but something like agnosticism was at the center of Chinese secular philosophy. I will ask in chapter seven how reverence can flourish in the absence of specific beliefs about the divine.

p. 106. "When rising doubts cloud the certainty of religious claims, reverence is all the more important": There may be a see-saw here. Indomitable faith seems to support some people who have no talent for reverence (extreme Protestants who eschew all ceremony), while deep reverence seems to ground some people who have no faith at all (atheist scientists who live in awe of the truths that are investigated by science). T. K. Seung has suggested to me in conversation that the rise of reverence in cultures that are losing faith is a sign that they are clinging desperately to the trappings of that faith as it erodes (my paraphrase). But I will argue in the next two chapters that reverence is not at all a trapping of faith.

p. 107. "The restraint that comes from ceremony is never absent, in any culture, from any system of power, whether conservative or revolutionary": For a detailed and compelling study of the role of ritual in politics, see Kertzer (1988).

"Li does not stand against change, but regulates and orders it." This is explicit in a text from another author in the Confucian tradition:

> Through rites [Li] Heaven and earth join in harmony, the sun and moon shine, the four seasons proceed in order, the stars and constellations march, the rivers flow, and all things flourish; men's likes and dislikes are regulated and their joys and hates made appropriate. Those below are obedient, those above are enlightened; all things change but do not become disordered; only he who turns his back upon rites will be destroyed. (Xunzi 19, third century BCE, also known in English as Hsun-tzu. This translation is from Watson, 1963, p. 94.)

p. 108. "The example of the Master." On speaking truth to power, but with deference, see also 7.31 with Leys note (p. 155) and 4.18.

p. 110. Juvenal, *Satire* 14.47–49:

> The greatest reverence is due to your son; if you
> are fixing to do something disgraceful, even your baby boy
> should block you from sin. Don't think he's too young . . .

Here *reverentia* is not simply respect, but an attitude in the presence of something holy that keeps one from sin. Juvenal is arguing that children are easily influenced by the moral example of their parents, especially of the same sex.

Chapter Seven: Reverence Without a Creed

p. 113. "That there is at least one Something . . . that is not controlled by human means, was not created by human beings, is not fully known by human experts and is transcendent." I have placed them in descending order of importance for the concept of reverence. Reverence towards something in your power is always wrong, but some human products—great buildings, paintings, or string quartets—strike us with awe and may be objects of reverence. They belong so much to the past that they cannot be changed without irreparable loss, and therefore they satisfy the first condition. One may feel reverence for natural human powers, or even for a flash of human genius, like Mozart's. Such things are not in our control or due to our conscious efforts, nor do we understand them fully.

By "transcendent" I mean completely independent of the world as we experience it, otherworldly. We can be reverent without believing in transcendence, if we are reverent toward nature, for example. But readers who wish to reserve reverence for transcendent objects may respect non-transcendent objects for representing to us the majesty of otherworldly powers (as a great tree might be thought to represent the majesty of God).

p. 114. Tennyson's reaction to science: In 1837 he read Lyell's *Principles of Geology* (fourth edition, 1835) with a number of his friends. See Mattes in Ross, pp. 120–26, "The Challenge of Geology to Belief in Immortality and a God of Love."

p. 115. "Still, he says, we trust": See Mattes in Ross, p. 120ff.

p. 117. "Tennyson consciously rejected such doctrines as original sin": Martin, p. 1.

"Tennyson's son, Hallam, tells us also that the poet believes there is a Great Soul": Ross, p. 61, n. 6; cf. pp. 131ff.

p. 118. "he was more religious in his doubt than in his faith": T. S. Eliot in Ross, pp. 176–77.

p. 120ff. For the outline of beliefs related to reverence I am indebted to T. K. Seung.

p. 121. "if all you have to keep you in line is the fear of God, then you have denied yourself all of the virtues, including reverence": Thanks for this point to Reuben McDaniel.

p. 123. "source of evil": Reverence does not entail that you believe only good things about the gods. The late Epicurean philosopher Philodemus defends Epicurus against a charge of irreverence by quoting his remark that "A person is reverent if he preserves the immortality and consummate blessedness of the god" (Philodemus, *On Piety,* col. 40, Obbink), but this defense evidently has not succeeded. Why is it not irreverent to believe that the gods have done wicked things?

p. 124. "Athenians held at least three fundamental beliefs": Yunis (1988). Pentheus would be irreverent if he thought his power was a match for a god's, but he does not believe that Dionysus is a god.

Chapter Eight: Reverence Across Religions

p. 130. Epigraphs: "The Narrow Way" is an allusion to Matthew 7.13. The Song of Kabir is also called "Song of Kahir"; Kahir was a fifteenth-century Hindu religious reformer.

p. 131. Yehuda Amichai, *Open Closed Open*, p. 39.

p. 132. G. K. Chesterton, The Everlasting Man, p. 125.

p. 134. The *Bacchae* and Athenian audiences: Because Euripides wrote the play while abroad, he may not have intended it for Athenian audiences. My hypothesis for interpretation, however, is that this is a very Athenian play. The attitudes of the Chorus are strikingly Athenian.

p. 134–35. The Psalms: Quoted from the King James Version.

p. 135. "The wisdom of knowing our own limitations": Plato's *Apology* 23ab.

p. 136. On Thucydides: see p. 7, and my *Justice, Power and Human Nature,* for an abridged translation with introduction and advice on further reading.

p. 138. On Plato: My account here is controversial, and based mainly on my reading of Symposium, Phaedrus, and Republic. Plato argues for the existence of a cosmic god in Laws 10, and prescribes serious penalties for impiety at *Laws* 10.909. See p. 272ff.

p. 139. Chinese Humanism: Some Analects seem to imply that Confucians thought of Heaven as something like an active and personal god (*Analects* 3.24, 7.22, 9.5); others, that Heaven is an impersonal force of nature (17.19). See Schwartz, p. 117ff, especially p. 122.

By contrast with Confucians, Mo Tzu plays down ceremony and plays up belief in intervention by gods and spirits on behalf of Humaneness: "To maintain that ghosts do not exist, yet learn the sacrificial ceremonies is like learning the ceremonies for guests though there are no guests, making a fishnet though there are no fish" (Graham, p. 48, using Y. P. Mei's 1934 translation).

Chapter Nine: Relativism

p. 144. Epigraphs: "A human being is the measure": Protagoras, quoted in Plato's *Theaetetus*, 152b.

"The god is a measure": The Athenian in Plato's *Laws*, 716C. Oddly, the Athenian does not use such a measure in developing his political theory.

p. 145. "When beliefs are stated they do matter": Philosophers generally take the verb "believe" as synonymous with "believe to be true"; but some religious believers understand their beliefs as metaphorical rather than true. Whatever this means, it does not disarm the point about relativism because two metaphors may be incompatible. For example, if you believe the world is a sort of garden given by God to humankind, you cannot believe both that humans are charged metaphorically with tending it and that they are told to make it over for their own exclusive use. Metaphors can lead to moral difficulties as well as logical ones.

"Plato tells us that Protagoras tries to be a relativist, but then Plato shows in a famous argument that even Protagoras cannot keep it up": *Theaetetus* 152ab and 169d–171c.

"But we were looking for a relativist, and we now see that this is not what he is": Of course milder forms of relativism may be held; and there is a form of skepticism that resembles relativism but takes no position of any kind. On alternative relativisms, and on Protagoras' non-relativism, see my "Rhetoric and Relativism" (1999). For Protagoras' view on reverence, see chapters four and eight.

p. 146. "A complete relativist": For simplicity's sake, this chapter considers only the most extreme forms of relativism. There are more palatable forms; indeed, we must recognize that many things are what they are relative to others (as a theory is relative to the language in which it is expressed), and some skeptics adopt versions of relativism that do not assign truth in the full sense to competing positions.

If reverence is a virtue, there must be a core idea of reverence that is at least potentially universal. If certain emotions, such as fear, are recognized in most cultures, then we would expect that various capacities to feel those emotions would also be recognized across cultures. Then, if the conditions of human life are similar enough across cultures, we would expect that certain capacities, such as courage and reverence, would be widely recognized as virtues, while others, such as cowardice, would be widely recognized as vices. The anthropology or cultural psychology to support this hypothesis is beyond the scope of this book.

On the universality of certain emotions, see Paul Ekman and Richard Dawson, *The Nature of Emotion* (1994). Nussbaum has argued persuasively that an Aristotelian theory of virtue can reach across cultural boundaries, mainly because virtue concerns issues of character, rather than the precise ways in which moral character is expressed in one culture or another (1988).

p. 147. "horrible consequences for Protagoras": Plato certainly thought Protagoras irreverent; some sources tell us that the Athenians prosecuted Protagoras for irreverence, but many scholars doubt the tale.

p. 150. "A good game-player is reverent through and through": David Reeve points out to me that Charles may be considered a good game-player who sets up the rules of the game and then sees no reason to discuss them further. That would be fine if the game were a contest like chess, for which the goal is simply victory of one side over the other. But it is not fine when the purpose of the game is to advance human understanding.

Relativism and Tradition

For Vaka's case I am indebted to Roshan Ouseph, who was and remains deeply worried by it. Such cases tempt Europeans and Americans to feel superior in their culture, but such temptations should be resisted. Oppression knows no boundaries. On the complexity of the issues related to this, see the essays from different points of view in Okin (1999), particularly Nussbaum's "A Plea for Difficulty" (1999). For the broader issues relating to human development, see Nussbaum, *Women and Human Development* (2000), especially pp. 48–49 on relativism. On reverence for tradition, see above, p. 65.

p. 153. "But no one who has reverence for justice can allow that it is whatever we say it is": See the discussion of objects of reverence above, p. 113 with the note to p. 17 on p. 263. One may, nevertheless, revere justice as an ideal that is internal to, and corrective of, widely shared practices. Justice need not be a Platonic form in order to be worthy of reverence.

"Justice is an ideal that is imperfectly realized in codes of law, and it is the ideal—not the imperfect realizations of it—that merits reverence.": Levinson argues that the U.S. Constitution as it was framed, with clearly implied support of chattel slavery, is not worthy of reverence, and shows how writers who do express reverence for the Constitution are thinking more of the moral ideal than of the literal text (pp. 60–87, particularly in his conclusion, "Against Idolatry," pp. 87–89). I think, however, that he blurs the distinction I want to make between reverence and respect. I would add that reverence is not due to anything that it is in our power to change; but that it is precisely because we have respect for the Constitution that we do want to change it, and not simply shrug it off, when it is wrong. See pp. 223–25 for the distinction between thick and thin respect.

p. 155. "But the position I have taken is not exclusive to modern Europeans": The ancient Greeks knew that it was irreverent to insist on human traditions as if they were god-given. Two great tragic poems prove the point: in Euripides' *Bacchae*, Pentheus is shown to be irreverent because he tries to enforce the tradition that kept women in the homes, excluding them even from religious festivals. When a new religion comes to town, old customs must bend, and it is not reverent to hold onto them rigidly. In Sophocles' *Antigone*, Antigone goes overboard defending burial customs. Such customs were never as rigid as she says they were, and her claim that the gods are on her side is outrageous. She appeals to an unwritten, unvarying law of Zeus concerning burial customs, which Creon and the chorus rightly recognize as a serious threat to any existing political order. The concept of divine unwritten law is new in the mid-fifth century and arrives, not surprisingly, along with a set of revolutionary challenges to tradition. Sophocles' *Antigone* illustrates how easy it is, once people start going off the rails of tradition, for their opponents to go just as badly astray in defense of what they claim to be the old ways. As far as we can tell, it was never part of the ancient Greek tradition that tradition could not bend. (And indeed we see that Antigone herself is willing to bend the law she cites, except in the case of this brother, for whom she has a perverse longing.)

It is somewhat the same in ancient China. Although Confucianism (like many religions) became a rock of stability, resisting many tides of change, neither the *Analects* of Confucius nor the writings of Mencius reflect such rigidity. Confucius insists on maintaining to the letter the rituals that curb the arrogance of minor kings, but otherwise his emphasis is on having the right attitudes in ritual and this clears room for a certain flexibility, which later Confucianism gave up under threats from other cultures (above, p. 103, p. 108–09 with note).

Chapter Ten: Sacred Things

For my understanding of sacred things I am indebted to John Meyer and Reuben McDaniel, as well as to anonymous readers for the journal *Ramus*, who made useful criticisms of a draft of my article, "Theater as Sacrament" (Woodruff 2013). I have used the material I developed for that article in this chapter. Bill and Weslie Janeway steered me to Mary Douglas and gave me time and space to write the meat of my new chapters at Hancock Point. For that I am most grateful.

p. 159. The first two commandments: For a reverent understanding of these commandments, one which should entail an ethical response to diverse religious traditions, see Hedges (2005, pp. 9–52).

p. 160. "When magic and superstition clouded people's minds": See Douglas, *Purity and Danger*, on nineteenth-century views of taboos, under the influence of scholars such as Frazer and Robertson Smith (Douglas 2002, especially pp. 12–35).

p. 162. Nietzsche on respect for the Bible: Nietzsche, *Beyond Good and Evil*, Translated by Judith Norman in Horstmann and Norman 2002, 160, section 263. Other translations use "reverence" where this one (rightly in my view) uses "respect." I am grateful to Christopher Raymond for help with this passage.

p. 165. "The words "cursed" and "sacred" are the same in some languages." The prohibition implicit in the idea of the sacred is carried by the meanings of the Latin root for our word "sacred": *sacer*. Along with "sacred" and "holy," the word means "accursed" and "detestable." So the word seems to carry two values, but just one prohibition: do not touch. For traditional anthropological views on this, see Douglas (2002), pp. 9–10.

p. 166. "We owe respect to people with whom we share reverence for shared ideals." See above, p. 000.

p. 168. "What we recognize as transcendent is worthy of awe and reverence": p. 168.

p. 169. "God is beyond the boundary of what we can pollute." In the *Heracles* of Euripides, the hero—who has polluted himself with a great crime—hides his head from the sky so that he will not pollute the heavens. His best friend pulls the covering off his head: "You are only human," he says, in effect. "You cannot pollute what is divine." Euripides, *Herackles*, p. 1233.

Chapter Eleven: The Reverent Leader

For recent thinking on ethical leadership, see Ciulla, especially her introduction, "Mapping." The volume includes a helpful foreword by James Mac-Gregor Burns, who is the parent of recent discussion of ethical leadership. See also the chapter on leadership in *The Ajax Dilemma* (Woodruff, 2011, pp. 185–201).

Thanks to Paul Burka who, as a commentator on politics, helped me to understand Thucydides' Melian dialogue as a failure to recognize the possibility of leadership.

p. 176. "if they tend to think that the Constitution, unlike any particular law, stands for ideals of justice, or the spirit of justice, transcending anything that human individuals could legislate": See the note to p. 153 on p. 281.

p. 183. "the Athenian theory is false": See my *Power, Justice*, pp. xxx–xxxii.

p. 187. Paul Goodwin and Oliver North: for the episode, see Timberg, pp. 142–43. It is not surprising that Goodwin did not articulate the moral case for discipline. Reverence is hard to talk about.

p. 187–88. "that the violence they use is not in their own service, but in the service of something larger than themselves—even, in the end, larger than nations": Hence, I believe, the consensus that aggressive war (which may serve the interests of a nation) is wrong and demeans the soldiers asked to take part in it. In real life, in the military and elsewhere, acts of respect are usually done from habit, to smooth social interaction, to avoid censure, or in the hope that they will be returned. But I am writing about the ideal these acts are supposed to serve.

p. 189. The "good opinion" theory of respect: For a review of current theories of respect, see my recent article, "Respect," in the *International Encyclopedia of Ethics* (2013).

Chapter Twelve: Compassion

p. 194. "I've come, out of compassion": This and subsequent quotations were translated by Peter Meineck, from Meineck and Woodruff (2003).

p. 197. "I went and stood by them": a family legend told by the poet's son, Kim Stafford (Stafford, 2003, 7; see also his poem, "Serving with Gideon," 95).

p. 199. "Pity is often a bad thing, but it is not the same as compassion." I have argued that compassion is compatible with justice (although not with fairness). Pity, which is often mistaken for compassion, may be a serious threat to justice. See *The Ajax Dilemma* (2011), pp. 99, 102–07, and 140–58.

p. 199. Cognitive empathy: See my *The Necessity of Theater*, pp. 181–85.

p. 200. "Consider Ajax": I have written an account of this story and the issues it raises in *The Ajax Dilemma* (2011).

p. 201. "The ancient Athenians provided education for compassion." True, as shown in this play, but not perfectly effective. As Thucydides shows, the Athenians could be ruthless. But, as Sophocles shows, they understood the value of compassion, which is a theme of almost every one of his plays. On failure in moral education, see later in this chapter.

"Sophocles' surviving plays, with one notable exception, all celebrate compassion": The exception is his *Electra*, which is shocking for the absence of compassion; although the Chorus expresses some compassion for Electra, they do not celebrate it or urge her to compassion. In *Antigone*, Creon suffers for his lack of compassion; in *Ajax*, compassion wins the day. In *Philoctetes*, compassion vies with ambition and almost wins the soul of a young hero (but ominously fails in the long run). In *Oedipus Tyrannus*, Oedipus wins our sympathy in the first scene with his monumental display of compassion, even though it is laden with hubris. We have seen what happens in *Oedipus at Colonus*. *Women of Trachis* ends with a plea for compassion from the surviving main character: "grant me/For doing this, great compassion/And also see the ruthlessness/Of the gods in these actions" (1264–67).

p. 203. "The bright stars do not linger": my translation in Meineck and Woodruff (2007).

p. 205. Imagination: Violent responses generally show a failure to imagine what will come of violence, as well as a failure to imagine the stories of the other people involved. "Going to war shows a lack of imagination" (Stafford, 2003, p. 153).

p. 206. The idolatry of virtue: "It was a time I dreamed of being good." Chris Hedges (2005, p. 36).

p. 207. "Education matters. But so do situations": On the responsibilities involved in what they call "choice architecture," see Thaler and Sunstein, *Nudge* (2009).

Character vulnerable to situation: See Doris (2005) and Zimbardo (2007). Doris, Harman, and some others have argued that vulnerability to situation renders virtue ethics untenable. Classical virtue ethicists such as Plato, Aristotle, and Confucius have always understood this vulnerability and reckoned it into their thought, developing political and social theories that aim at environments that are relatively safe for virtue. For accounts of virtue ethics that are compatible with the data on situations, see Annas (2011) and Kamtekar (2004).

p. 209. "American civilization can be ruthless." See the example in chapter fifteen, "the company commander." Not one student I have taught—and not one student taught by the commander in the story (who later became a teacher of military ethics)—has ever shown compassion for the detainees in the case. When asked why not, they cite lessons learned from parents or grandparents. They might also mention Spielberg's movie, *Saving Private Ryan*, in which sparing the life of a prisoner leads to the hero's death.

On the range of opinion on such ethical issues, see Olson (2006).

On the history of treatment by U.S. forces of prisoners and detainees, see Doyle (2010). His chapter on Abu Ghraib is very telling (pp. 310–33). I regret, however, that he says almost nothing about the horrors attending the detention of civilians in Vietnam during the war of 1965–73, aside from a brief mention (pp. 285–86).

American civilization has not always been ruthless with prisoners. George Washington generally required relatively decent treatment for British and German prisoners of war (Doyle, 2010, 30, cf. 332). I know from family legend about the other side of the story: Two of my ancestors, New Jersey militiamen, barely survived British prison hulks. They were the lucky ones. Many died. For the conditions in Civil War POW camps, see Doyle: "A Very Uncivil War," pp. 8–112.

p. 209. "The abuses at the prison at Abu Ghraib": the best introduction is still Hersh (2004).

"The aberrant behavior on the night shift": Schlesinger (2004): Final Report of the Independent Panel to Review DoD Detention Operations, August 24, 2004, p.13.

The Stanford Prison Experiment. See Zimbardo's account of this in his book, *The Lucifer Effect. Understanding How Good People Turn Evil* (2008).

p. 210. "Coming from New York": From Zimbardo (online interview), "You Can't Be a Sweet Cucumber in a Vinegar Barrel: A Talk with Philip Zimbardo." http://edge.org/3rd_culture/zimbardo05/zimbardo05_index.html

"Another prison guard": SPC Joe Darby, saw the photos on a fellow guard's computer, found them disgusting, and turned them over for investigation. Schlesinger, p. 39. For Darby's subsequent history, see the June 10, 2013, article in the *New York Times*, http://world.time.com/2013/06/10/10-notorious-leakers-and-how-they-fared/slide/abu-ghraib-photo-leak/

"The abuse was absent": "The vast majority of the detainees . . . were treated appropriately." (Schlesinger, p. 18). I suspect that this overstates the case, but at least some of the cucumbers in the barrel at Abu Ghraib did not go sour.

"Some of the young guards behaved well": Even the good guards, however, felt bad about their failure to stop the brutality (Zimbardo, 2007, pp. 188–89, cf. 457–59).

Chapter Thirteen: The Silent Teacher

On reverence in the classroom, see now Rud and Garrison, *Teaching with Reverence* (2012).

p. 213. The passage from Shankara was translated and given me by Patrick Olivelle. The poem is an excerpt from "The Idol of *Vimalakīrti*, a Clay Sculpture by Yang Huizhi of the Tang Dynasty, in *Tianzhu* Temple," Translated by Chiu-Mi Lai for this edition. *Tianzhu* (lit. Celestial Pillars) Temple is located northeast of Fengxiang (in modern-day Shaanxi). *Su Shi shi ji* (Beijing: Zhonghua shuju, 1982), 1.110–111.

p. 221. Dr. Johnson, after refuting previous scholars, admits that he will be refuted in turn: "The opinions prevalent in one age, as truths above the reach of controversy, are confuted and rejected in another, and rise again to reception in remoter times. Thus the human mind is kept in motion without progress. . . . How canst thou beg for life, says Homer's hero to his captive, when thou knowest that thou are to suffer only what must another day be suffered by Achilles?" (Johnson, 1765, p. 99; Homer's *Iliad* 21.106–14). On the passage in Homer, see p. 84.

p. 222. "The Paradox of Respect": I owe this puzzle to E. De Lattre.

p. 225. "Equality is a fine ideal, but it is fatal to a rich conception of respect, as philosopher Harry Frankfurt has shown." See Frankfurt's elegant defense of respect in his 1997 essay, "Equality and Respect," especially pp. 150, 153.

p. 227. "Team spirit, patriotism, at the highest level a passion for justice and peace—these are the feelings that allow respect to grow strong": Not all respect is due to virtue. The respect that flows from reverence would have to be related to an ideal higher than the victory of this particular team. If the team's ability to give respect stops at their own boundaries, then their respect is not admirable. They need to respect players on other teams and, above all, umpires.

Chapter Fourteen: Home

Thanks to T. K. Seung for pointing out to me the importance of the *Odyssey* as expressing a myth of reverence.

p. 232. "but this is not what it is to expand a home." Oliver Wendell Holmes makes plain in the last lines of the poem that he is writing about the growth of the soul away from the body and towards heaven—a Platonic idea that I will not pursue in these pages.

p. 236. Dionysus: With nice symbolism, he replaced Hestia, goddess of the hearth, in the Athenian list of principal gods, about a generation before Euripides wrote the play.

p. 237. Tennyson's "Ulysses"

On interpreting "Ulysses," see Ricks, pp. 113–19, and Kincaid, p. 42 n.14. I am grateful to William Gibson for setting me straight about Telemachus. Tennyson's Ulysses is a man who does not need to have a home; as such he is unconceivable to the ancient Greeks, for whom Aristotle spoke when he said: "He who is without a homeland (*polis*) by reason of his nature and not by some accident, is either a poor sort of being or else a being higher than human" (Aristotle, *Politics* 1.2). Only beasts or gods would be without a home—unless beset by accidents of the kind that keep Ulysses away from Ithaca. On the ancient model, the adventures of Ulysses are obstacles or trials on a journey that is never in doubt. Homer's audience would never agree that the journey was worth more than the destination.

The idea that Ulysses prefers adventure to knowledge—following "knowledge like a sinking star"—is at least as old as Dante (*Inferno*, Canto 26). Tennyson acknowledged that he followed Dante, but we should note two important differences: Dante's Ulysses knows that he is leading his men to their deaths; and Dante's Ulysses is speaking from Hell, where he is being punished

for his lies—and possibly also for his irreverence in chasing knowledge beyond
the limits set for men by the Gates of Hercules, and in neglecting his duties to
his home:

> Not fondness for my son, nor reverence
>> For my old father, nor the due affection
>>> Which joyous should have made Penelope,
> Could overcome within me the desire
>> I had to be experienced of the world,
>>> And of the vice and virtue of mankind.

To his men, before sailing into forbidden waters beyond the Gates of Hercules,
he says:

> "Oh brothers, who amid a hundred thousand
> Perils," I said, "have come into the West,
>> To this so inconsiderable vigil
> Which is remaining of your senses still
>> Be ye unwilling to deny the knowledge,
>>> Following the sun, of the unpeopled world.
> Consider ye the seed from which ye sprang;
>> Ye were not made to live like unto brutes
>>> But for the pursuit of virtue and of knowledge.
> —trans. Henry Wadsworth Longfellow

p. 239. "War cures old soldiers": So I believed in 2001. Now, in 2013, reflecting
on post-traumatic stress, I realize that old soldiers often miss the excitement, and
most of all the close fellowship, of war.

p. 240. "Among poets writing in English, Tennyson is our greatest witness
to depression": T. S. Eliot said of him that he was "the saddest of English poets,"
(in Ross, p. 178).

p. 241. "Hector, who was ashamed to take cover behind the walls of Troy":
Iliad 22.99ff.

p. 242. Thucydides: 3.82.8; see also 2.65.7 and 8.89.3.

Chapter Fifteen: Epilogue: Renewing Reverence

p. 246. Mary Oliver, "The Summer Day." From *House of Light* by Mary Oliver, Published by Beacon Press Boston. Copyright 1990, Mary Oliver. Reprinted by permission of The Charlotte Sheedy Literary Agency Inc.

p. 248. Barry Lopez: *Arctic Dreams*, Preface, p. xx, xxix.

p. 249. Mindfulness: I am grateful to Ursula Goodenough and Reuben McDaniel for conversations on the subject. Goodenough (1998) shows the wonders of nature at the microscopic level. Goodenough and Woodruff (2001) explores mindfulness in relation to reverence. Langer's account (1989) is basic reading; and Weick and Putnam bring out the differences between western and eastern approaches to mindfulness (2006).

p. 251. "We fall so easily into idolatry of ourselves and the things we do": See Hedges on the first two commandments (2005, pp. 9–52).

p. 254. "People follow you willingly." I argued in chapter eleven that having willing followers is neither necessary nor sufficient for good leadership. A leader may need to find a way to move unwilling followers. At the same time, followers may be willing to follow for reasons that have nothing to do with qualities of leadership.

p. 255. "A friend commands a company." Story told me by William Gibson, used here by his permission. He reminds me (as I knew myself) that many high-ranking officers held their troops to high moral standards. But some did not. Gibson has taught ethics and used the story in ethics classes; like me, he receives mostly lethal solutions from his bloodthirsty students.

p. 257. "Hymns to reverence in the plays": see p. 126, pp. 201–04.

WORKS CITED

Annas, Julia. *The Morality of Happiness*. Oxford: Oxford University Press, 1993.

Annas, Julia. "Ethical Arguments from Nature: Aristotle and After." In *Beitrage zur antiken Philosophie; Festschrift für Wolfgang Kullman*, edited by Hans-Christian Günther and Antonios Rengakos, pp. 185–98. Stuttgart: Franz Steiner Verlag, 1997.

Annas, Julia. *Intelligent Virtue*. Oxford: Oxford University Press, 2011.

Amichai, Yehuda. *Open Closed Open; Poems*. Translated from the Hebrew by Chana Bloch and Chana Kronfeld. New York: Harcourt, 2000.

Beerbohm, Max. *Zuleika Dobson*. London: W. Heinemann, 1911.

Bennett, William, ed. *The Book of Virtues: A Treasury of Great Moral Stories*. New York: Simon and Schuster, 1993.

Braybrooke, David. *Moral Objectives, Rules, and the Forms of Social Change*. Toronto: University of Toronto Press, 1998.

Brecht, Bertolt. *Baal, A Man's a Man, and the Elephant Calf*. Translated by Eric Bentley. New York: Grove Press, 1964.

Burkert, Walter. *Greek Religion*. Translated by John Raffan. Cambridge, MA: Harvard University Press, 1985.

Casey, John. *Pagan Virtue: An Essay in Ethics*. Oxford: Clarendon Press, 1990.

Chesterton, G. K. *The Everlasting Man*. London: Hodder & Stoughton Limited, 1925.

Ciulla, Joanne B. *Ethics: The Heart of Leadership*. Westport, CT: Praeger, 1998.

Cooper, John M. *Reason and Human Good in Aristotle*. Cambridge, MA: Harvard University Press, 1975.

Crisp, Roger. *How Should One Live? Essays on the Virtues*. New York: Oxford University Press, 1996.

Crisp, Roger, and Michael Slote. *Virtue Ethics*. Oxford: Oxford University Press, 1997.

Doris, John. *Lack of Character: Personality and Moral Behavior*. Cambridge: Cambridge University Press, 2005.

Douglas, Mary. *Purity and Danger: An Analysis of Concept of Pollution and Taboo*. Orig. 1966. London and New York: Routledge & Kegan Paul, 2002.

Doyle, Robert C. *The Enemy in Our Hands: America's Treatment of Prisoners of War from the Revolution to the War on Terror*. Lexington: The University of Kentucky Press, 2010.

Ekman, Paul, and Richard Dawson. *The Nature of Emotion*: *Fundamental Questions*. New York: Oxford University Press, 1994.

Frankfurt, Harry. "Equality and Respect." (1997). Reprinted in *Necessity, Volition, and Love*, 146–54. Cambridge: Cambridge University Press, 1999.

Gagarin, Michael, and Paul Woodruff. *Early Greek Political Thought from Homer to the Sophists*. Cambridge: Cambridge University Press, 1995.

Galbraith, John Kenneth. "Conventional Signs." *The Spectator* 6892 (July 29, 1960), 205.

Garrison, James D. *Pietas from Vergil to Dryden*. University Park: Pennsylvania State University Press, 1992.

Goodenough, Ursula. *The Sacred Depths of Nature*. New York: Oxford University Press, 1998.

Goodenough, Ursula, and Paul Woodruff. "Mindful Virtue, Mindful Reverence." *Zygon: Journal of Religion and Science* 36 (2001), 585–95.

Graham, A. C. *Disputers of the Tao*: *Philosophical Argument in Ancient China*. La Salle, IL: Open Court, 1989.

Grossman, Dave. *On Killing*: *The Psychological Cost of Learning to Kill in War and Society*. Boston: Little Brown and Company, 1996.

Hedges, Chris. *Losing Moses on the Freeway: The 10 Commandments in America*. New York: Free Press, 2005.

Hersh, Seymour M. "Torture at Abu Ghraib: American Soldiers Brutalized Iraqis. How Far Up Does the Responsibility Go?" *New Yorker,* May 10, 2004. http://www.newyorker.com/archive/2004/05/10/040510fa_fact

Huang, Chichung. *The Analects of Confucius*. New York: Oxford University Press, 1997.

Hunt, Lester H. *Character and Culture*. Lanham, MD: Rowman and Littlefield, 1997.

Ivanhoe, Philip J. *Ethics in the Confucian Tradition: The Thought of Mencius and Wang Yang-Ming*. Atlanta: Scholars Press, 1990.

Ivanhoe, Philip J. *Confucian Moral Self-Cultivation*. 2nd ed. Indianapolis: Hackett Publishing, 2000.

Johnson, Samuel. "Preface" to Shakespeare (1765). *Yale Edition of the Works of Samuel Johnson*, Volume VII, pp. 59–112, edited by Arthur Sherbo. New Haven: Yale University Press, 1968.

Kamtekar, Rachana. "Situationism and Virtue Ethics on the Content of Our Character." *Ethics: An International Journal of Social, Political, and Legal Philosophy* 114 (2004), 458–91.

Kertzer, David I. *Ritual, Politics, and Power*. New Haven: Yale University Press, 1988.

Kincaid, James R. *Tennyson's Major Poems: The Comic and Ironic Patterns*. New Haven: Yale University Press, 1975.

Langer, Ellen J. *Mindfulness*. Reading, MA: Wesley-Addison, 1989.

Lau, D. C. *The Analects*. New York: Penguin Books, 1979.

Legge, James. *Confucius: Confucian Analects, The Great Learning and the Doctrine of the Mean*. New York: Dover Publications Inc, 1971.

Leys, Simon (Pierre Ryckmans). *The Analects of Confucius*. New York: W. W. Norton & Company, 1997.

Liu, Xiusheng. *Mencius, Hume, and the Foundations of Ethics*. London: Ashgate, 2002.

Lopez, Barry. *Arctic Dreams. Imagination and Desire in a Northern Landscape*. New York: Scribner, 1986.

MacIntyre, Alasdair. *After Virtue: A Study in Moral Theory*. South Bend, IN: University of Notre Dame Press, 1981.

MacIntyre, Alasdair. *Dependent Rational Animals: Why Human Beings Need the Virtues*. Paul Carus Lectures 20. Chicago: Open Court, 1999.

Marinatos, Nanno. *Thucydides and Religion*. Anton Hein, 1981.

Martin, Robert Bernard. *Tennyson: The Unquiet Heart*. Oxford: Clarendon Press, 1980.

MacLeod, C. W. "Thucydides' Plataean Debate." *Greek, Roman and Byzantine Studies* 18 (1977), 227–46.

McDowell, John. "Two Sorts of Naturalism." In *Mind, Value, & Reality*. Cambridge, MA: Harvard University Press, 1998.

McPherran, Mark L. *The Religion of Socrates*. University Park: Pennsylvania State University Press, 1996.

Meineck, Peter, and Paul Woodruff. *Sophocles: Theban Plays*. Translated by Peter Meineck and Paul Woodruff, with an introduction by Paul Woodruff. Indianapolis: Hackett Publishing, 2003.

Meineck, Peter, and Paul Woodruff. *Sophocles: Four Tragedies*. Translated by Peter Meineck and Paul Woodruff, with an introduction by Paul Woodruff. Indianapolis: Hackett Publishing, 2007.

Morgan, Michael L. *Platonic Piety: Philosophy and Ritual in Fourth-Century Athens*. New Haven, CT: Yale University Press, 1990.

Nietzsche, Friedrich. *Beyond Good and Evil: Prelude to a Philosophy of the Future*. Edited by Rolf-Peter Horstmann and Judith Norman. Translated by Judith Norman. Cambridge: Cambridge University Press, 2002.

Nussbaum, Martha C. *The Fragility of Goodness: Luck and Ethics in Greek Tragedy and Philosophy*. Cambridge and New York: Cambridge University Press, 1986.

Nussbaum, Martha C. "Non-Relative Virtues: An Aristotelian Approach," pp. 32–53. In Peter A. French et al, eds., *Midwest Studies in Philosophy* XIII. South Bend, IN: University of Notre Dame Press, 1988.

Nussbaum, Martha C. "A Plea for Difficulty," pp. 105–114. In Susan Moller Okin et al., *Is Multiculturalism Bad for Women*. Princeton, NJ: Princeton University Press, 1999.

Nussbaum, Martha C. *Women and Human Development: The Capabilities Approach*. Cambridge and New York: Cambridge University Press, 2000.

Obbink, Dirk. *Philodemus: On Piety*. Oxford: Oxford University Press, 1996.

Okin, Susan Miller. *Is Multiculturalism Bad for Women*? Princeton, NJ: Princeton University Press, 1999.

Olson, James M. *Fair Play: The Moral Dilemmas of Spying*. Washington, DC: Potomac Books, 2006.

O'Neill, Onora. *Towards Justice and Virtue: A Constructive Account of Practical Reasoning*. Cambridge: Cambridge University Press, 1996.

Rud, A. G., and Jim Garrison. *Teaching with Reverence: Reviving an Ancient Virtue for Today's Schools*. New York: Palgrave Macmillan, 2012.

Parker, Robert. *Athenian Religion: A History*. New York: Oxford University Press, 1996.

Pincoffs, Edmund L. *Quandaries and Virtues: Against Reductivism in Ethics*. Lawrence, KS: University Press of Kansas, 1986.

Ricks, Christopher. *Tennyson*. 2nd ed. Berkeley: University of California Press, 1989.

Ross, Robert H. *Alfred, Lord Tennyson: In Memoriam. An Authoritative Text, Backgrounds and Sources of Criticism*. New York: Norton, 1963.

Schlesinger, James R. Chair. "Final Report of the Independent Panel to Review DoD Detention Operations." August 24, 2004. http://www.defense.gov/news/aug2004/d20040824finalreport.pdf

Schwartz, Benjamin I. *The World of Thought in Ancient China*. Cambridge, MA: Harvard University Press, 1985.

Seaford, Richard. *Ritual and Reciprocity*. Oxford: Oxford University Press, 1994.

Seaford, Richard. *Euripides' Bacchae*. Warminster: Aris and Phillips, 1996.

Segal, Charles. *Dionysiac Poetics*. Expanded edition. Princeton, NJ: Princeton University Press, 1997.

Sen, Amartya K. *Collective Choice and Social Welfare*. San Francisco: Holden-Day, Inc., 1970.

Shay, Jonathan. *Achilles in Vietnam: Combat Trauma and the Undoing of Character*. New York: Simon & Schuster, 1994.

Sherman, Nancy. *The Fabric of Character: Aristotle's Theory of Virtue*. Oxford: Clarendon Press, 1989.

Slingerland, Edward. *Confucius: Analects, with Selections from Traditional Commentaries*. Indianapolis: Hackett Publishing, 2003.

Smith, Nicholas D., and Paul B. Woodruff. *Reason and Religion in Socratic Philosophy*. Oxford: Oxford University Press, 2000.

Stafford, Kim, ed. *Every War Has Two Losers: William Stafford on Peace and War*. Minneapolis: Milkweed Editions, 2003.

Steinbeck, John. *Travels with Charley: In Search of America*. New York: Viking Press, 1962.

Thaler, Richard H., and Cass R. Sunstein. *Nudge: Improved Decisions About Health, Wealth, and Happiness*, Revised and Expanded Ed. New York: Penguin Books, 2009.

Thomas, Laurence. *Living Morally: A Psychology of Moral Character*. Philadelphia: Temple University Press, 1989.

Timberg, Robert. *The Nightingale's Song*. New York: Simon & Schuster, 1996.

Tu, Wei-ming. "*Li* as a Process of Humanization." *Philosophy East and West* XXII (1972): 187–201.

Tu, Wei-ming. *Confucian Thought: Selfhood as Creative Transformation*. Revised Ed. Albany, NY: State University of New York Press, 1985.

Vlastos, Gregory. *Socrates: Ironist and Moral Philosopher*. Ithaca, NY: Cornell University Press, 1991.

Voltaire. *Philosophical Dictionary*. Edited and translated by Theodore Besterman. London: Penguin, 1972.

Watson, Burton. *Hsun-tzu: Basic Writings*. New York: Columbia University Press, 1963.

Watson, Burton. *Selected Poems of Su Tung-p'o*. Port Townsend, WA: Copper Canyon Press, 1994.

Weick, Karl E., and Ted Putnam. "Organizing for Mindfulness: Eastern Wisdom and Western Knowledge." *Journal of Management Inquiry* 15 (2006), 275–87.

White, Steven A. *Sovereign Virtue: Aristotle on the Relation between Happiness and Prosperity*. Stanford, CA: Stanford University Press, 1992.

Woodruff, Paul. *Thucydides on Justice, Power, and Human Nature*. Indianapolis: Hackett Publishing, 1993.

Woodruff, Paul. *Euripides: Bacchae*. Indianapolis: Hackett Publishing, 1998.

Woodruff, Paul. "Rhetoric and Relativism." In *The Cambridge Companion to Early Greek Philosophy*, edited by A. A. Long, 290–310. Cambridge: Cambridge University Press, 1999.

Woodruff, Paul. "Natural Justice," in Victor Caston and Daniel W. Graham, eds. *Presocratic Philosophy; Essays in Honor of Alexander Mourelatos*. Aldershot: Ashgate, 2002, 195–204.

Woodruff, Paul. *The Ajax Dilemma: Justice, Fairness, and Rewards*. New York: Oxford University Press, 2011.

Woodruff, Paul. "Respect." *International Encyclopedia of Ethics*. Hoboken, NJ: Wiley-Blackwell: 2013.

Woodruff, Paul. "Theater as Sacrament." *Ramus, Critical Studies in Greek and Roman Literature* 42 (2013), 5–22.

Woodruff, Paul. "Euboulia as the Skill Protagoras Taught," pp. 179–193. In Johannes M. van Ophuijsen, Marlein van Raalte, and Peter Stork, eds. *Protagoras of Abdera: The Man, His Measure.* Leiden and Boston: Brill, 2013.

Yunis, Harvey. *A New Creed: Fundamental Religious Beliefs in the Athenian Polis and Euripidean Drama*. Gottingen: Vandenhoeck & Ruprecht, 1988.

Zimbardo, Philip. *The Lucifer Effect: Understanding How Good People Turn Evil.* New York: Random House, 2007.

Zimbardo, Philip. "You Can't Be a Sweet Cucumber in a Vinegar Barrel: A Talk with Philip Zimbardo." January 19, 2005. http://edge.org/3rd_culture/zimbardo05/zimbardo05_index.html

INDEX AND GLOSSARY OF PROPER NAMES

(Literary works are indexed under their authors' names. All notes are endnotes, identified by the page to which they refer.)